The Postwar Decline of American Newspapers, 1945–1965

The Postwar Decline of American Newspapers, 1945–1965

The History of American Journalism

DAVID R. DAVIES

The History of American Journalism Series, No. 6
James D. Startt and Wm. David Sloan, Series Editors

Westport, Connecticut
London

Library of Congress Cataloging-in-Publication Data

Davies, David R. (David Randall), 1957–
    The postwar decline of American newspapers, 1945-1965/
David R. Davies.
        p. cm. – (The history of American journalism, ISSN 1074–4193; no. 6)
    Includes bibliographical references and index.
    ISBN 0–313–30701–6 (alk. paper)
    1. Press–United States–History–20th century.
    2. Newspaper publishing–United States–History–20th century.
    3. Journalism–United States–History–20th century. I. Title.
    II. Series: History of American journalism; no. 6.
    PN4855.H57   1994
    [PN4867]
    071′.309045–dc22   2006015193

British Library Cataloguing in Publication Data is available.

Library of Congress Catalog Card Number: 2006015193
ISBN: 0–313–30701–6

First published in 2006

Praeger Publishers, 88 Post Road West, Westport, CT 06881
An imprint of Greenwood Publishing Group, Inc.
www.praeger.com

Printed in the United States of America

The paper used in this book complies with the
Permanent Paper Standard issued by the National
Information Standards Organization (Z39.48–1984).

10 9 8 7 6 5 4 3 2

Contents

Series Foreword

Since the renowned historian Allan Nevins issued his call for an improved journalism history in 1959, the field has experienced remarkable growth in terms of both quantity and quality. It can now be said with confidence that journalism history is a vital and vitalizing field full of scholarly activity and promise.

The new scholarship has widened the field's horizons and extended its depth. Today, especially with new bibliographic technologies at their disposal, journalism historians are able to explore literature pertinent to their studies to a greater extent than was previously possible. This expansion of literary sources has occurred in conjunction with other advances in the use of source materials. Today's historians incorporate primary and original records into their work more than was common when Nevins issued his call, and they also utilize sources produced by the electronic media. As the source foundation for journalism history has grown, so has its content also undergone a substantive expansion. Previously neglected or minimized subjects in the field now receive fairer and more concerted treatment. Contemporary journalism history, moreover, reflects more consciousness of culture than that written a generation ago.

Growth, however, has created problems. Abundance of sources, proliferation and diversity of writing, and the stimulation of new discoveries and interpretations combine to make scholarship in the field a formidable task. A broad study covering journalism history from its beginnings to the present, one combining the rich primary materials now available and the older and newer literature in the field, is needed.

The History of American Journalism series is designed to address this need. Each volume is written by an author or authors who are recognized scholars in the field. Each is intended to provide a coherent perspective on a major period, to facilitate further research in the field, and to engage general readers interested in the subject. A strong narrative and interpretive element is found in each volume, and each contains a bibliographical essay pointing readers to the most pertinent research sources and secondary literature.

The present volume, the sixth in the series, examines journalism in the two decades following World War II. During that short era, from 1945 to 1965, the press went through one of its most important periods. While it was confronting the challenge of a new mass medium (television), its relationship to the rest of American society changed drastically as it dealt with such matters as the Cold War, the Vietnam War, and the civil rights movement. As the other volumes in the series do, this volume focuses on the nature of journalism during the years surveyed, chronicles noteworthy figures, examines the relationship of journalism to society, and provides explanations for the main directions that journalism was taking.

Preface: The Decline of the American Newspaper

For America's newspapers in the twenty years after World War II, everything bad that could happen did. Television eclipsed print, readership stagnated, and newspaper critics found their voices. Worse still, traditional just-the-facts journalism proved ill-suited to explain the complex upheavals of postwar America. By 1965, the newspaper industry was reeling from these and other challenges, its influence on the wane and its business environment in flux. Daily newspapers, once the country's most dominant news medium, were in decline.

This book attempts to explain the industry's slow and steady weakening in the early postwar years. It describes how publishers and editors failed to cope with the numerous challenges facing their industry in the first two decades after World War II. Buoyed by profits during most of the early postwar years, publishers failed to act when business and societal pressures challenged newspapers to adapt. The challenges were daunting: the Cold War, the civil rights movement, and other postwar events transformed American society and newspapers' relationship to it. At the same time, daily journalism coped with advances in printing technology, competition from television, a professionalizing workforce, and increasing corporate ownership.

This plethora of challenges sent the daily newspaper industry on a decline that continues to this day. But the depth of turmoil was hidden behind profits and industry statistics. Many newspapers remained highly profitable in this period even as many others failed. Newspaper closings were often offset, in fact, by the founding of other newspapers as the locus of American newspaper publishing moved from the big cities to the suburbs. Throughout the period from 1945 to 1965, the total number of daily newspapers published in the United States held steady at about 1,750. And total daily newspaper circulation continued to rise, though it lagged far behind population growth in proportional terms. Such statistics gave a false sense of stability to the industry even as it was shaken to its very foundations.

The many challenges facing newspapers put pressure on them both as businesses and as journalistic institutions. Business pressures included steadily rising costs, which bedeviled newspapers throughout the postwar years and often thwarted publishers' efforts to adapt to a changing marketplace. In addition, two other trends, suburbanization and rapidly improving production techniques, took root in the 1950s and forced American daily newspapers to accommodate them. Suburbanization led to a booming suburban press and contributed to the multiplying woes of the metropolitan journals. The spread of offset printing in the 1950s offered newspapers an inexpensive alternative to entrenched letterpress printing methods, but too few newspapers took advantage of it.

Television's rapid rise posed a thorny challenge to daily newspapers. At first, publishers and editors saw little threat from the new electronic medium. Television coverage of news events, in fact, seemed to help rather than to hinder newspaper circulation. And the economic boom of the 1950s ensured increasing advertising revenues for all media, minimizing broadcasting's threat to newspaper income. But by the early 1960s, print journalists were increasingly viewing television as a rival both for advertising dollars and for readers' time.

While business concerns mounted, newspapers were coping with governmental and societal changes that put pressure upon the practice of print journalism. In the postwar years, the press faced criticism from both within and without that challenged journalists to cover a changing world more responsibly. As newspapers undertook numerous self-improvement efforts, several postwar events also forced a re-evaluation of journalistic methods. The civil rights movement proved difficult and divisive for journalists to cover. A rise in government secrecy paralleling the escalation of the Cold War led to increasing distrust of the government. In the 1950s, the rise of Senator Joseph R. McCarthy led newspapers to question their reliance upon traditional news values and objectivity. In the early 1960s, President John F. Kennedy's masterful use of television helped the public stature of this newspaper's rival. And his adept handling of the press during several foreign policy crises fostered deep resentment among journalists about his press policies.

In the 1960s, the trends that had converged upon the industry accelerated. Rising costs, new printing methods, suburbanization, and other factors all combined to create a crisis in metropolitan newspaper publishing. The longtime trend toward newspaper consolidations increased, and chain ownership grew. Suburban newspapers prospered. By 1965, the world that newspapers covered had changed drastically, and so had newspapers.

Of necessity, this book focuses only upon these most significant trends that changed daily newspapers from 1945 to 1965. It does not attempt an overview of *all* newspapers' history for this twenty-year period, an unmanageably broad topic that would fall short of this book's more specific goal. Nor does it delve in great detail into related media—television, magazines, and specialized newspapers. Instead, the focus here is limited to the trends that affected general-interest newspapers as an industry and journalists as a whole. While many of these trends have been studied individually, no other historical account has examined them collectively. While the trends chronicled here were not complete by 1965, they were in full swing. An industry in decline was being transformed, a metamorphosis that continues into the twenty-first century.

Chapter 1

Business Trends in the Postwar Press, 1945–1949

The end of World War II heralded both challenges and opportunities for the nation's newspapers. Like many of their fellow businessmen and women, publishers looked forward to a booming postwar economy unleashed from manpower shortages and government controls on raw materials. Yet publishers and editors would soon face problems peculiar to the newspaper business: the difficulty of explaining a complex postwar world to readers, a pronounced public criticism of the press, the expanding cost of doing business, and the prospect of a tough new competitor—television. These complex, persistent challenges, as it turned out, would confront newspapers for decades.

In the earliest postwar years, though, business challenges of reverting to a peacetime economy were paramount, and other problems seemed remote. Television was still too underdeveloped to be a serious competitor. Criticism of newspapers, on the rise through the 1930s, had abated during World War II as publishers and editors had thrown themselves into the war effort with gusto. Press criticism would certainly resurface and claim publishers' attention—the 1947 Hutchins Commission report would see to that—but concerns about newspaper content were subordinated in the early postwar years to practical problems of doing business.

While daily newspapers emerged from World War II on a solid financial footing, several postwar business trends troubled publishers. On the one hand, advertising revenues and newspaper circulation both improved significantly in the first years after the war. But the expense of putting out a daily newspaper also climbed dramatically, threatening profits and prompting the first tentative steps toward modernizing newspaper printing. This combination of steadily rising costs and impending technological change—some were calling it "a revolution" even then—tempered publishers' optimism in the profitable postwar years.

The times were indeed booming, a welcome turnaround from the crippling Great Depression and stagnant wartime years, and all media benefited. Both the radio and magazine industries enjoyed equally bright prospects in the first few postwar years. Radio's dominance as the preeminent national medium seemed unchallenged, and the development of television appeared likely to expand, not diminish, radio's influence. Similarly, the magazine industry remained profitable even as booming wartime circulation began to recede. "Ebbing sales give circulation veterans no alarm," *Time* magazine noted in 1946. "The country's 105,000 newsstands were crowded beyond reason anyway, and survival of the fittest might straighten things out by fall."[1]

As for daily newspapers, all indices of health were bright at war's end, including the most closely monitored indicator, circulation. "The outstanding thing which the war taught us about our newspaper business," declared the circulation manager of the *Pittsburgh Press*, "was that people need 'em and read 'em."[2] By the end of 1945, daily newspaper circulation had climbed to an all-time high of 48,384,188, a stunning increase of more than 2.5 million readers, or 5.3 percent, over 1944. The gain represented the largest numerical and percentage increase of any year since 1920. "The circulation figures tend to demonstrate the public must be satisfied only by the permanent newspaper record of the news," reflected *Editor & Publisher*, the industry's leading trade journal, in 1946.[3]

Significantly, newspapers continued to attract more readers in the years after the war, even without the pull of wartime headlines. Total circulation rose by 5.2 percent in 1946 and by about 1 percent in both 1947 and 1948. The steadily improving postwar figures, crowed *Editor & Publisher*, "set at rest once and for all the prognostication of some who said the 'fantastic' circulations of wartime would subside when battlefront news ceased and the boys came home." *Editor & Publisher*, like other trade journals, repeatedly equated rising circulations with increasing public approval of newspapers.[4] The year 1945 also marked a turning point in another yardstick of publishers' financial health: the number of daily journals. For the first time in decades, the number increased slightly, to 1,749, with ten new dailies offsetting eight closures during the year. The longtime trend of declining daily newspapers appeared to have reversed. The number increased to 1,763 in 1946, 1,769 in 1947, and 1,781 in 1948. "It is obvious that newspapers today are healthier than they have been for fifteen years," contended *Editor & Publisher* in a 1946 editorial. "They also have a brighter future than at any time in that period."[5]

Indeed, the bright future was reflected in all classifications of newspaper revenue: circulation, national advertising, and local advertising. The increased circulation brought in increased revenue; and circulation income, which for many years had covered only newspapers' expenses, even surpassed national advertising revenue for many newspapers. National advertising also continued to increase. It reached $216,000,000 in 1945, up by 7.4 percent over the previous year. Local advertising revenue also boomed.[6]

In all indices of growth, newspapers continued to perform well from 1946 to 1949 as compared to overall growth in the national economy. Total newspaper employment grew faster than total US employment. The number of pages printed in newspapers of more than 100,000 circulation increased by one-quarter. Advertising revenues and newsprint consumption grew faster than the gross national product. And circulation grew at about the same rate as the adult population.[7]

The growth in advertising was profound. Total newspaper advertising more than doubled from 1945 to 1949, from $921 million in 1945 to $1.91 billion in 1949. Newspapers' share of all advertising spent in all media jumped from 32 percent in 1945 to 37 percent in 1949. By contrast, radio and magazines' share of the advertising dollar dropped. And television, still in its infancy, attracted a mere 1.1 percent of all advertising in 1949.[8]

Circulation increases and rising advertising linage were particularly pronounced in the first two years after the war. The 100 largest daily newspapers enjoyed an average circulation increase of 5.3 percent between 1945 and 1946. Advertising linage for the 100 papers rose by a whopping 26.2 percent in the same period. Virtually all newspapers enjoyed a substantial boost in advertising revenues. The *New York Times* boosted its advertising linage by 46 percent from 1945 to 1946. In the same year, the *Chicago Tribune* increased its linage by 45 percent, the *Seattle* (WA) *Post-Intelligencer* by 53 percent, the *St. Paul* (MN) *Dispatch and Pioneer Press* by 54 percent, and the *Miami Herald* by 73 percent.[9] The boom in newspaper advertising resulted in healthy profits. Two medium-sized newspapers of 50,000 circulation, according to *Editor & Publisher* profiles of "typical" but unnamed newspapers in 1946 and 1947, expected after-tax net profits of 11 percent of revenue in 1946 and 16 percent in 1947, robust profit margins reflecting a robust industry.[10] Of the few newspapers that publicly released their profit and loss statements in these years, all reported healthy incomes. The parent company of the *Los Angeles Times* and the *Los Angeles Mirror* reported that the newspapers made a net profit of 11 percent in 1946 and 8 percent in 1947. The *Chicago Daily News* recorded net profits of 13 percent and the *Hartford* (CT) *Times* of 15 percent in 1947. The Federated Publications chain, owner of three medium-sized dailies in Michigan, reported a net profit of 20 percent in 1946 and 16 percent in 1947.[11] Journalism professor Raymond B. Nixon, reflecting the prevailing sentiment within the newspaper industry in the postwar era, declared in 1954 that since World War II the American newspaper industry had achieved "the highest degree of stability in its history." He cited rising circulation figures and advertising revenues and declining numbers of newspaper failures.[12]

The healthy financial picture and the end of wartime shortages led many newspapers to invest in improved facilities, either to expand their newspaper offices or modernize their presses, or both. During the war, virtually no new equipment had been manufactured, and only second-hand presses were available for expansion. Publishers had struggled just to keep their shopworn presses in operation. "It was really rough," recalled Carl Walters, managing editor of the *Tupelo* (MS) *Journal* during World War II. The *Journal*'s antiquated press was in terrible shape during the war, and new equipment could not be had at any price. A printer "kept the press going with baling wire and whatever," Walters said.[13] At the *Journal* as elsewhere, the end of the war unleashed expansion that had been postponed for years. In 1948 alone, the *New York Times* estimated that $50 million worth of expansion was underway in newspapers both large and small. From the *Washington Post* to the *St. Louis Post-Dispatch* to the *Portland* (OR) *Journal*, newspapers were expanding. A 1948 survey of American Newspaper Publishers Association (ANPA) member newspapers found that more than half projected constructing a new building or buying new presses and equipment within the next two years. Some were making room for new company-owned television stations.[14]

Neither the number of television stations nor television viewers increased appreciably. The infant television industry seemed to present little danger to the daily newspaper for the time being. "I do not believe that any mechanical device will put it out of business," wrote Lester Markel, the Sunday editor of the *New York Times*, in 1946. People want to spread the news out in front of them, not to hear it or see it, Markel claimed, expressing a common sentiment among his journalistic peers.[15] Frank E. Gannett, owner of a growing chain of northeastern dailies and weeklies, predicted in 1945 that television, like radio before it, would increase interest in the news and build newspaper circulation.[16]

To print journalists, television seemed more like a potential partner to newspapers than a threat. "By the 1940s, ANPA discussions reflected an attitude that broadcast news complemented and stimulated newspaper readership more than it competed with published news," wrote Professor Edwin Emery in the ANPA's official history.[17] At a 1946 national conference on television, former *New York World-Telegram* publisher Merlin Hall Aylesworth stressed not competition but close business ties between the two media. "It is impossible," he said, "for television to take the place of the newspapers any more than broadcasting did, but welded together, television will add to the newspaper's attractiveness and promote its drawing power." He found it difficult to imagine "an up-to-date newspaper without a television station as an affiliate in the future."[18]

Publishers dealt with the new medium by investing heavily in it, just as they had invested in AM radio that preceded it. They actively sought television station licenses as well as federal licenses for another new broadcasting medium, FM radio. The Federal Communications Commission reported in late 1945 that 40 percent of the pending applications for new television stations came from newspaper interests.[19]

Robert W. Brown, a reporter for the *Washington Daily News*, thought this period was the prime of American print journalism. "TV was not on the scene at that time," he recalled, "so it was sort of a heyday for newspapers. Everybody was reading newspapers to see what was going on."[20] In these last few years before television, daily newspapers ruled supreme as the nation's primary medium for news and advertising. J.E. Chappell, publisher of the *Birmingham* (AL) *News* and *Birmingham Age-Herald*, said that the thirty-five-day strike that had closed both his newspapers at war's end had proven newspapers' worth both to the public and to commerce. Advertisers had complained during the strike that business had suffered, and readers had remained hungry for news.[21]

But the postwar years brought newspapers uncertainty as well as prosperity. The industry, despite its financial health, faced both long-term and short-term problems. In the long term, newspapers faced spiraling production costs, especially in newsprint and labor. In the short term, they had to regain the manpower and material resources that all industries had lost to the war effort. "[D]uring the war," said *Oregon Journal* editor Donald J. Sterling in 1946, "we held the joint together with baling wire."[22]

For labor-intensive newspapers, the most important challenge was to rebuild staffs depleted by the wartime labor shortage. "Our first job is to get our staff back," declared Lee Wood, executive editor of the *New York World-Telegram*, at an editors' forum on postwar problems a month after V-J Day.[23] During the war, staff openings had been filled with older men and with women, the latter making their first inroads into newspapering in large numbers. The influx of women occurred in newspapers all over the nation, from small dailies to large metropolitan journals like the *Baltimore Sun* and the *New York Times*.[24] The Associated Press, which had only one woman reporter before Pearl Harbor, had sixty-five during the war. United Press employed 100 women, 20 percent of its wartime staff. According to one industry estimate, 8,000 reporters and editors had gone to war, most to be replaced by women. "Women have invaded such hitherto inviolate masculine precincts on newspapers as finance, politics, sports, and the police beat," the *Saturday Evening Post* reported in 1944. "Paper dolls are reading copy, working on the rewrite desk, taking pictures."[25]

The infusion of female workers was short-lived, however, since most were let go at war's end. At the *St. Petersburg* (FL) *Times*, for example, fourteen women reporters and typists were fired in one day. All had been hired with the understanding that their jobs would last only until the boys came home.[26] Women workers in newspapers were uncommon after the war, and those who became editors were even something of a novelty. For example, *Editor & Publisher* published a feature on Jerry Fox, the first woman city editor of the *Dayton* (OH) *Herald*, when she was promoted in August 1945. Agness Underwood's promotion to city editor at the *Los Angeles Herald & Express* in 1947 was unusual enough to warrant a spread in *Time* magazine.[27] While Fox, Underwood, and other women would make some inroads into the nation's newsrooms in the early postwar years, men dominated newsrooms well into the 1960s. The National Press Club in Washington did not admit women until 1955, when it permitted them to sit in the balcony.[28]

In the face of postwar labor shortages in the nation's newspapers, record enrollments at journalism and printing schools promised some relief. Educator Frank Luther Mott reported crowded classrooms at the University of Missouri, a leading journalism school. Returning veterans began to outnumber the women who had flooded to school during the war years.[29] Nationally, enrollments at journalism schools rose to pre-war levels by fall 1946, with many posting all-time highs. Returning veterans replaced women students at printing schools, which were also booming.[30]

If the returning veterans promised a resolution to the labor shortage in time, another war-related shortage—newsprint—was not so easily solved. Newsprint had been in short supply in wartime and had been rationed beginning in 1943. Federal Printing and Publishing General Limitation Order L-240 limited newspapers to using only as much newsprint per year as they had in 1941. The rationing limited the size of many newspapers, requiring editors to tightly edit articles for space and also limiting the amount of space sold for advertising. Smaller newspapers using fewer than twenty-five tons of newsprint per quarter were exempt under the controls, which lasted until the end of 1945.[31]

But the end of controls did not mean the end of shortages. Canadian newsprint mills were the chief suppliers for American newspapers, as domestic mills had long diverted production from newsprint into more profitable grades of paper. The lack of a domestic newsprint supply combined with burgeoning demand driven by postwar circulation increases steadily pushed up prices. The cost of newsprint jumped by 70 percent from 1945 to 1948, reaching $100 a ton in 1948.[32] A contributing factor to rising prices was the end of federal control of newsprint sales after the war. The ANPA, the Southern Newspaper Publishers Association (SNPA), and other newspaper groups had lobbied to end the price controls, believing the mills would meet the demand if the price were right.[33]

The postwar newsprint shortage especially hurt small newspapers. Accustomed to steady newsprint supplies during wartime rationing, they were now forced to rely upon the spot newsprint market, where prices skyrocketed during the shortage.[34] Among the small newspapers desperate for newsprint in 1946 was the tiny *Wenatchee* (WA) *World*, which nearly ran out of newsprint when the local mill stopped production while awaiting a new shipment of logs. Publisher Rufus Woods rallied thirty of his staffers, supplied them with axes and crosscut saws, and set them to work in a nearby forest. Their toil produced six carloads of logs for the local mill, resulting in forty tons of newsprint for the paper-starved daily.[35] Larger newspapers, unlike the *World*, benefited from long-term contracts with the mills, which usually ensured them a steady supply of paper. But periodic shortages of newsprint hurt even the largest dailies. The *Los Angeles Times* shrank one day in 1946 to eight pages because of the scarcity of newsprint. Newspapers in fifteen cities, including St. Louis, Dallas, and Houston, printed few or no advertisements during periods of scarcity the same year.[36]

Several congressional committees looked into the newsprint problem before the shortage began to ease in 1948 and 1949. A Senate small business committee held hearings on the problem in 1947 to determine its causes and effects. Witnesses testified that the shortage and high prices constituted the most pressing problems for the country's small- and medium-sized newspapers. The committee recommended that newspapers form co-operatives to finance paper mills in Alaska.[37] In late 1948, a House subcommittee found that the shortage was beginning to diminish because of higher imports from Europe, paper-sharing arrangements worked out among newspapers, greater production from the Canadian mills, and expanded mill capacity in the United States. The SNPA had coordinated the construction of a new mill in Childersburg, Alabama, after the war.[38] By 1949, the worst of the shortage was over, though demand still exceeded supply.

Newsprint prices were part of an upward spiral in overall production costs, which began to increase during the war, escalated immediately after it, and steadily continued to rise in the decades that followed. Labor costs also escalated. This was due partly to an overall increase in wages in the postwar era, when unions sought to hold on to wartime gains in fringe benefits and at the same time boost wages, which had held stable during the war. For newspapers, the overall trend was somewhat disguised, since the rising costs were occurring at a time of skyrocketing revenues. Still, of all the new revenue pouring into newspapers' coffers, wrote the historian of the SNPA, "very few pennies of the new income dollar remained in the till at the year's end."[39]

Publishers were concerned because the overall increase in costs permeated all areas of newspaper spending. *Editor & Publisher*, in a 1947 summary of publishing costs, noted that labor and material costs had increased across the board by 28 percent in the first six months of the year, as compared to the same period a year before. Newsprint, stereotyping, and composing costs took up most of the increase, with increased costs of 52 percent, 43 percent, and 36 percent, respectively.[40] Wage increases, of course, accounted for most of the spiraling expenses. Hourly wage rates in the newspaper printing trades increased 65 percent from 1945 to 1949, compared to an average increase of 40 percent in all manufacturing trades.[41]

"These costs are becoming unbearable and revenue is harder to obtain," Thomas F. Mowle, controller of the *Wall Street Journal*, told fellow newspaper finance officers in a 1948 speech. "We must prepare now, while we still have the time, to meet this situation." The rising costs, he observed, were a potential disaster for the newspaper industry.[42] Journalism researcher James E. Pollard, surveying daily newspapers' cost-and-revenue trends in 1949, noted that costs had increased steadily through the early 1940s but had accelerated at an even faster pace after World War II. Most worrisome about the trend, he noted, was that costs were continuing to increase while revenues were beginning to level off.[43]

Higher costs forced circulation rate increases, raising the cost of most daily newspapers from three cents—the dominant price at war's end—to five cents just one year later. The *New York Times* reported a rash of rate increases in 1946.[44] Most newspapers had little choice but to raise subscription and advertising rates. Production costs in the heavily unionized industry offered no room for cuts.

Unions, for their part, pushed for wage increases, leading to a spate of newspaper-related strikes in 1945, 1946, 1947, and 1948. The ANPA attributed the unusual jump in strikes to workers' eagerness to make up for wages held stagnant in wartime. Another factor, after 1947, was the International Typographical Union (ITU), the chief union for newspaper composing rooms, which adopted a no-contract policy after the adoption of the Labor-Management Relations Act of 1947, the so-called Taft-Hartley Law. The ITU had tried to circumvent Taft-Hartley's ban of closed union shops by requiring its locals to work under union "conditions of employment." The conditions were supposed to substitute for contracts with employers, but management balked.[45]

Strikes called by the ITU, coupled with walkouts by other craft unions, crippled scores of newspapers across the country throughout the late 1940s. The ITU struck seventy-eight newspapers between 1945 and 1947, more than the total of ITU strikes in the eight years from 1937 to 1944. A total of 17 newspapers were involved in strikes at the end of 1946, 38 at the end of 1947, and 50 at the end of 1948. The strikes hit cities both large and small. Some notable examples: in 1945, a Deliverer's Union strike impaired seventeen dailies in the New York City area for more than two weeks. St. Louis deliverers struck for three weeks. And composing room strikes shut down newspapers in Fort Wayne, Indiana; Reading, Pennsylvania; and Utica, New York. In 1946, strikes closed the newspapers in Seattle, Washington, for eight weeks and those in Cleveland for thirty-two days. In 1947, the newspapers in Colorado Springs, Colorado, and Kansas City were struck. And in 1948 alone, the ITU struck forty-four newspapers in twenty-seven cities.[46] The strikes began to taper off in late 1949, however, after an ANPA challenge of the ITU's no-contract policy wound its way through the National Labor Relations Board (NLRB), which decided against the ITU in October 1949. The NLRB's unanimous ruling found that the ITU's no-contract strategy was "a deliberate frustration of the bargaining process."[47] The ITU strikes were significant not just for the specific newspapers that were struck. While a minority of the nation's approximately 1,750 newspapers experienced work stoppages, publishers' innovations to keep their presses rolling had far-reaching implications for all newspapers. Their experiments with offset presses, photo-engraving, and other techniques marked the first large-scale efforts by the newspaper industry to update antiquated printing methods. These efforts prompted increased spending on printing research and foreshadowed a revolution in production methods that would transform the industry in decades to come.

Progress in printing, however tentative, was long overdue. "Newspapers have lagged far behind other media in technological advances," wrote *Chicago Daily News* publisher John S. Knight in 1947. "Basically, there have been no radical changes in the printing industry for generations."[48] Indeed, printing technology had progressed little from the 1880s, with the invention of the Linotype typesetting machine, until the 1940s. The Linotype had been improved somewhat over the years but nonetheless set type at a painfully slow rate of just twenty-two to thirty-three column inches an hour. As Jonathan Daniels of the *Raleigh News and Observer* complained in the early 1950s, "A few spiral gears have replaced tooth gears but otherwise there has been no basic change in the hot metal method of setting type in this century."[49]

The hot metal process was both labor intensive and expensive. Union Linotypers set copy into metal type on type-casting machines, complicated devices that required extensive training to use skillfully. Other union men took impressions of the pages of type to make curved metal plates to fit onto high-speed, union-operated metal presses.

Alternatives to hot type—offset printing and photo-engraving—had been used by job printers, magazines, and small weeklies for years, but the processes were much too slow to be of use to daily newspapers.[50] Still, at the close of the war, publishers began experimenting with the processes as a way to publish without printers. In San Antonio, where the newspapers suffered a seven-week strike in the summer and autumn of 1945, management had kept the newspaper open by printing each day's edition using the photo-engraving process, making page-sized photo-engravings that were then as plates for the printing press.[51] Similarly, in Jersey City, New Jersey, the *Jersey Journal* resumed publication after a two-month strike using photo-engraving. Copy was typed on fifteen electric typewriters with three interchangeable typefaces.[52]

The new technology was primitive but offered publishers a new weapon against the unions. Previously, highly skilled workers were virtually impossible to replace in strikes, which inevitably shut down newspapers or severely limited their ability to publish. The new technology changed all that. "A long-accepted belief that a daily newspaper had to suspend publication when ITU composing room workers struck is now a myth," the ANPA's special standing committee on labor relations declared in 1949, as the postwar surge in strikes was beginning to die down.[53]

The first large success with the new processes came in St. Petersburg, Florida, where innovative publisher Nelson Poynter was impressed with the new technologies not only for their strike-breaking potential but also for their potential long-term cost benefits. He bought an offset press and had his staff experiment with it. When St. Petersburg's printers went out on strike in November 1945, Poynter's staff at the *St. Petersburg Times* produced a sixteen-page newspaper using not offset but photo-engraving. In a front-page "Statement to Our Readers," Poynter apologized for the substandard quality of the poorly printed pages. "Don't shoot," he implored; "we're doing the best we can."[54] The experiment was successful enough to attract other publishers from around the country to observe Poynter's success against the unions, but it ended the following January when strike-breaking typesetters were hired to print the paper the old way, with hot type. Letterpress technology still offered a far superior product to photo-engraved newspapers.[55]

A larger-scale test of the new technology occurred in Chicago, where printers struck the *Tribune, Sun, Times,* and *Daily News* in November 1947 after the papers' management refused the ITU's demand to work without a contract. The newspapers hired typists to put out the newspaper using photo-engraving. By the end of the first week of the strike, the dailies were again printing papers their usual size, but the new process was not without its difficulties.[56] For one thing, photo-engraving was expensive, running about 30 percent higher than the cost of using typesetting machines. For another, it was slow. Deadlines had to be revised substantially in consideration of the new process. "Making a correction is such an involved process," one editor complained, "we don't do it unless it's libel."[57]

But the process was successful in several ways. Readers reacted positively to the larger typewritten typeface of photo-engraving. Advertisers were enthusiastic about its possibilities for creative ad layouts. And more importantly for publishers, the new process kept the Chicago newspapers printing throughout the strike, which lasted throughout 1948 and into much of 1949. By subverting the unions' ability to shut down the newspapers in a strike, photo-engraving gave publishers a powerful new weapon in collective bargaining. "If I were a member of the printers' union," declared executive editor Basil "Stuffy" Walters of the *Chicago Daily News* at the beginning of the strike, "I'd feel a bit scared."[58]

Publishers and editors talked up the potential of the new technology, which they believed could eventually lower costs for existing journals, encourage new newspapers, and improve printing quality. "Instead of [spending] $50,000 to $100,000 for Linotypes to start a small-town paper, I'll bet you could start one for $10,000" once photo-engraving was perfected, mused one Chicago editor. "And you could put out a damned good-looking paper."[59] Knight, the *Chicago Daily News* publisher, wrote that the strike was finally spurring newspapers to undertake innovations to produce both cheaper and more eye-pleasing newspapers.[60] Carl R. Kesler, an editor at the *Daily News* who saw the experimentation in Chicago firsthand, agreed. "The Chicago strike directly stimulated research in typesetting, photo-engraving, stereotyping and printing," he wrote after the strike ended.[61]

Another technological innovation, also in its early development after the war, was Teletypesetting. The system, begun mostly by smaller newspapers eager to cut costs, bypassed union Linotype operators by using low-skill typists to type copy into a machine that produced perforated paper tape. The tape was then fed into a machine attached to typesetting equipment. Teletypesetting was both cheap and fast, since low-wage stenographers could provide tape to keep typesetting machines operating steadily. "We use girl operators for the perforating equipment," one anonymous publisher told *Editor & Publisher* in 1946. "We try to get expert typists and find that in several months they make accurate and speedy Teletypesetter operators."[62] By contrast, high-wage union typesetters required a lengthy apprenticeship to become proficient.

"The typesetting machine run automatically will double the speed of the fastest operator," proclaimed Alexander H. Washburn, editor and publisher of the *Hope Star* in Arkansas. The *Star* and four other newspapers shared wire service reports over a special telegraph wire circuit used to transmit teletypesetter signals.[63] Teletypesetting equipment was also used with success at newspapers in Illinois, Texas, and elsewhere across the country. "We're more than satisfied," said W.W. Ward of the *Beaumont* (Texas) *Journal*. "Production has increased and costs are down."[64]

Publishers, eager to play their upper hand against the unions and demoralize the strikers, talked frequently of a printing "revolution." Donald L. Boyd, president of the Printing Industries of America, was one of those who believed that a revolution was underway. The revolution, he said in a 1948 speech, was not rooted in new technologies, many of which had been in use for years. Rather, what was revolutionary was the methods' rapid introduction and acceptance within the newspaper industry.[65] The new technologies indeed had far-reaching implications, but they fell far short of revolutionary in the late 1940s and early 1950s. Relatively few newspapers, after all, were using photo-engraving, and then only for the duration of strikes.

Revolution or not, the new methods awakened newspaper publishers to the necessity for research to assure continued printing progress. For the first time, newspaps put significant resources into developing new printing methods. In early 1947 ANPA hired a research director, C.M. Flint, and the next year established a research laboratory to develop new lower-cost, higher-quality processes and to train production employees in the new methods. A 25 percent dues increase provided a $140,000 budget for a lab in Easton, Pennsylvania.[66] Southern newspaper publishers passed a resolution in support of the ANPA's effort and reiterated the need "to achieve better, quicker, and more economical printing."[67]

Research and experimentation were reported across the country. New York suburban dailies and a chain of Florida weeklies were experimenting with ways to speed up photo-engraving. Large publishing firms like Time, Inc., and Curtis Publishing were working on similar developments. Gannett and the Eastman Company were cooperating on a project to improve engraving. Research was widespread but in its earliest stages. Mergenthaler Linotype Corporation, the largest manufacturer of typesetting equipment, in 1948 downplayed the recent advances. "None of the new machines," a company spokesman said, "measure up to the casting method of producing type."[68]

Indeed, the new methods were immature, but they represented a substantial change in direction for an industry whose production methods had changed little over decades. The "printing revolution" offered publishers their only hope for preventing rising costs from eroding record postwar revenues. Some optimistic publishers, like Gannett, even predicted that the wealth of research would eventually produce inventions as important as Gutenberg's. "Indeed, it is more important, for it will make possible the printing of books, magazines, and paper at such low cost that countless millions will be benefited," he proclaimed in 1947.[69]

Such optimism was typical of late 1940s publishers. Costs were up, but the industry was finally doing something about the problem. Research was underway to address rising costs, and at the same time revenues remained high enough to allow for comfortable profits. Uncertainty remained, however, whether newspapers would face continued dramatic cost increases and, if so, whether the "revolution" would reap benefits soon enough to stabilize the industry. Moreover, no one knew just how long the postwar boom would last. A Midwestern publisher who summarized the outlook for newspapers in his state in 1946 could have been speaking for newspaper publishers across the nation. "I expect the Iowa newspaper business to be very good for a time," he said; "just how long I don't know."[70]

Chapter 2

Improvement and Criticism, 1945–1949

"I have given you my opinion that newspapers today are in many ways stronger than they have ever been," reflected *Christian Science Monitor* editor Erwin D. Canham in 1946. But while newspapers were financially sound, "there are shakings and quiverings beneath the surface which should warn us that complacency is ruinous." Criticism of journalism was on the increase, Canham observed, and readers seemed more and more inclined to distrust the press.[1]

Canham, like many other editors, recognized that newspapers desperately needed to improve; the postwar world seemed to demand it. The rapid social change in the United States during and after World War II and the nation's emergence afterward as one of the world's premier powers both pointed to a need for improved newspaper content, more accountability to readers, and greater service to the nation and its voters.

Efforts to improve newspapers after the war blossomed both at individual newspapers and on a national scale through trade organizations, particularly the American Society of Newspaper Editors (ASNE), the Associated Press Managing Editors (APME), and the wire services. At the same time, newspapers were increasingly the targets of press critics, who charged that they were irresponsible, monopolistic, and out of touch with readers' concerns. This criticism came both from inside the industry and from outside it, from editors themselves, from government officials, from press critics, and from journalism schools. It reached a crescendo in the 1947 report of the Commission on Freedom of the Press and after Harry S. Truman's surprising victory in the 1948 presidential election.

The irony of it all, as Canham pointed out in 1948, was that the rise in newspaper criticism coincided with editors' and publishers' own increased efforts to improve the content of newspapers. The criticism seemed to reinforce the need for improvement, even if editors and publishers did not always agree with their critics. "There is not such a great gulf between the newspapers publishers and their critics as it might seem," Canham said in a speech before journalism educators. "The publishers are striving to remedy their product where the criticism applies even while the critics are hollering the loudest about it."[2]

The end of the war, and the complex world that emerged from it, pushed editors to improve their editorial product. A nation recovering from a world war and now coping with a booming postwar economy, returning veterans, and international tensions seemed to require a revision of the old tried-and-true formulas for news. Crime, sex, money, and politics still made headlines, of course, but now the sensational was crowded by labor, industrial, and science news emerging from a rapidly changing world. Editors and publishers believed that these newly prominent kinds of news, tied as they were to the nation's well-being, placed a greater responsibility on newspapers to better serve the public by presenting fuller, more understandable news accounts. "[N]ever has the news been so complex and the need of understanding it more urgent," observed Lester Markel, Sunday editor of the *New York Times*.[3]

Postwar problems seemed to pose great challenges to journalism. Getting the story right was more important than just for accuracy's sake; postwar peace now seemed in the balance. Moreover, the newly dominant categories of news—economic problems and world tensions, to name just two—were much more difficult to explain than the sensational news that had dominated so many prewar newspapers. In the postwar era, concluded *Toledo Blade* editor-in-chief Grove Patterson, "Ordinary, uninspired newspapers can no longer do what needs to be done in a confused world."[4]

Improvements to newspapers were overdue, believed many publishers. "Newsmen have known for a long time that their papers have fallen short of serving the public as they should, despite their commendable work," said John H. Biddle, publisher of the *Huntingdon* (PA) *Daily News* and president of the Pennsylvania Newspaper Publishers Association. Addressing fellow publishers in 1948, he said newspapers and their owners had far too long clung to "horse-and-buggy techniques" in both production and content. But after the war, "modern inventions and new responsibilities in the Atomic Age forced them to see the headline writing on the wall," he said. "It said in bold-face type: 'The Deadline for Improvement is Here.'"[5]

One improvement drive in newspapers was the effort to make newswriting easier to read. This trend had its roots in World War II, when the shortage of newsprint combined with a glut of news forced editors to shorten news articles. During and after the war, editors found that the shorter stories, born of necessity, were easier for readers to understand. Moreover, the continued newsprint shortages and postwar rise in advertising continued to crowd the "news hole," the portion of the newspaper devoted to editorial matter. The trend toward shorter writing appeared irreversible, agreed a panel of editors at the 1946 ASNE convention. "I, for one, would certainly never want the papers to go back to the size that they once were," declared George A. Cornish of the *New York Herald Tribune*, expressing a common sentiment among editors. "I think a tighter, better edited paper is, in the long run, a better one."[6]

Not only was newswriting shorter, but there was a concerted effort to make it more understandable. Readability experts such as Robert P. Gunning and Rudolph Flesch contracted with newspapers and wire services to help them improve their editorial product. The two experts emphasized, as Gunning once pointed out, what good city editors had been saying to their reporters for decades: "[W]rite simply and directly." Moreover, the readability studies were significant because the nation's leading newspapers and largest wire services used them, and the vast majority of newspapers received all their national and international news from the wire services.

The formulas devised by Flesch and Gunning gave editors, for the first time, an objective yardstick to measure readable prose.[7] Beginning in 1944, Gunning's company, Readable News Reports, worked with wire services and newspapers all over the country to make their prose more readable. A former reporter for the *Akron Beacon Journal*, Gunning had devised a formula for readability—his so-called Fog Index—that counted words in a prose passage and noted the frequency of multisyllable words. Through the late 1940s and into the 1950s, Gunning was hired by a wire service, the United Press, and by more than sixty newspapers to evaluate the readability of their prose, to offer suggestions, and to train writers in his techniques. The newspapers included the *Louisville Courier-Journal*, the *Washington Star*, and the *Wall Street Journal*.[8] "Write as you talk," he advised his clients. "Why should a Washington correspondent write 'bilateral concordance' when he means 'two-way pact?'"[9]

Gunning wrote in 1952 that as a result of readability studies at newspapers across the United States, "[t]he styles of the writers at these papers have altered markedly." In fifty newspapers he had advised, articles once written at the *Atlantic Monthly* level were now written, on average, as if for *Reader's Digest*.[10] "Good editors, since newspapers began, have used whatever means they could to influence writers of news to be simple and direct," Gunning wrote. "With the help of readability research they have made more rapid progress in recent years than they ever have before." Editors had become more interested in readability research, he observed, after surveys found that readers often ignored wordy, overly complex news articles in favor of comics and other features. The surveys were part of advertising research undertaken by the American Newspaper Publishers Association (ANPA).[11]

While Gunning worked with newspaper clients and the United Press, Flesch was working with the Associated Press (AP), which hired him as a consultant in 1948. "Too frequently it seems that we contrive the hardest way to say some of the simplest things," complained AP assistant general manager Alan J. Gould early in Flesch's study.[12] Flesch's readability formula took into account average word and sentence length and the human interest content of news stories. Flesch found that AP copy tended to be too long, with larger words often preferred over shorter ones.[13]

By the time Flesch had completed the first year of his two-year study of the AP, executive director Kent Cooper had hailed the effort as one of "the most intensive and fruitful endeavors ever undertaken by this association." The APME study committee spearheading the drive to improve writing concluded that the successful effort would serve both newspapers and democracy.[14] Almost every editor answering a 1948 APME poll said the readability project had made AP copy easier to read. Lee Hills of the *Miami Herald* believed the study was quickly showing results. "It's a great joy to read newspapers these days," he said in 1948.[15]

That is not to say that Gunning's and Flesch's ideas met no opposition, at least at first. Gould said that AP newsrooms were full of writers who had at first opposed Flesch's innovations because they seemed too restrictive, overplayed human interest, and oversimplified newswriting. But he said the readability principles had quickly gained acceptance. "It is no exaggeration to say," he concluded, "that the impact of Doctor Flesch's ideas on simpler, clearer ways of writing represents one of the most significant developments of our journalistic times."[16] Longtime journalism educator Roland E. Wolseley, who was teaching journalism at Northwestern University when Flesch published his first book, believed that Flesch's work had far-reaching consequences. "He and later scholars were good medicine for the media's language ills," he recalled.[17]

Another effort to improve newspaper content was interpretive reporting. At professional conferences and in trade journals, editors debated the merits of interpretive reporting for bringing the subtleties of a complex world into focus. By no means an innovation of the postwar years, it nonetheless took on increased importance as editors prepared to cover postwar events. For many editors, interpretation seemed to go hand-in-hand with clearer, simpler writing as a means to make a complex world understandable. "Interpretive reporting, couched in clear, concise writing, has become more and more important in these days of the war's aftermath and its problems," said Stanley P. Barnett of the *Cleveland Plain Dealer*, chairman of the APME's study committee in 1948.[18] The

AP's committee, the same one that had studied readability, said that interpretive material, especially more backgrounding of news articles, allowed a greater understanding of issues than simply a factual rendering of events. "What the reader wants in a news story," the committee report said, "is the essential facts plus sufficient explanatory matter to enable him to place the particular event in its true perspective and to evaluate its significance and importance."[19]

Not that editors agreed exactly what interpretive reporting was. Some believed it was an objective accounting of events with additional background. Others took interpretation as including "the writer's definition of what a given development or statement may mean," a subjective judgment of the writer, according to George E. Stansfield of the *Hartford Courant*. The debate was evident in a University of Oregon poll of fifty editors across the country in 1947. While most of the editors favored the use of some interpretive news articles, most also believed that such articles should be signed and that use of objective news articles should be preferred.[20]

A vocal exponent of interpretive reporting was James Reston, diplomatic correspondent of the *New York Times*, who admitted to being "nuts about the subject of explanatory reporting." He spoke often at editors' conferences and elsewhere on the technique, which he saw as necessary both for public understanding and for the survival of newspapers. Interpretation allowed newspapers to serve a need unfilled by any competitor, he said, either print or broadcast. "The future of newspapers depends on developing an adequate means of explaining what is going on in the world," he told an APME meeting in 1948.[21]

Driving much of the push for writing improvement, of course, was the continued competition from magazines and radio and the impending threat of television. Television posed no threat for the immediate future, of course, but it held great potential to compete for readers' time as an entertainment medium over the long term. Accordingly, editors such as Vincent S. Jones of Utica, New York, said newspapers should consider overhauling "the whole system of writing and presenting the news." Newspapers, he argued, remained mediocre despite recent improvements and should expand reader studies even as readership reached an all-time high.[22]

A significant advance in helping newspapers cope with emerging competition came with the founding of the American Press Institute (API). Organized in 1946 by Sevellon Brown of the *Providence* (RI) *Journal-Bulletin*, with the cooperation and financial contributions of thirty-seven publishers, the API was founded as a two-year experiment as a way to improve newspapers.[23] It marked the first time that editorial employees had undertaken an organized effort to share ideas for improvement of newspapers. Previously, any such efforts had been informal, usually limited to occasional shop-talk sessions at ASNE conventions or to after-hours bull sessions.[24]

Brown, the guiding force behind the API, envisioned it as a center at which journalists could discuss newspaper problems in seminars one to three weeks long. Seminars were to cater to all segments of newspaper content and were held at Columbia University in New York City. Better content, Brown believed, was crucial to newspapers' ability to fulfill their responsibilities to society. "Unless we improve our skills and techniques, we face a crisis of meaninglessness," he said at API's inaugural seminar. "Innumerable brief reports, presented without perspective or background, can only drive the reader into a mental fog—we must lift our sights."[25]

Brown said the API's founding was proof that journalists were becoming increasingly aware of their new obligations to society and to democracy. "Through clinical, self-driven study," he declared, "it is our high purpose to make ourselves and the newspapers we represent of greater service and effectiveness in performing the vital function of a free press in a democracy."[26] Dean Carl W. Ackerman of the Graduate School of Journalism at Columbia called the institute "one of the most challenging and unique educational projects in the entire history of Columbia University."[27]

The first API session began September 30, 1946, and lasted three weeks. Twenty-five managing editors, assistant managing editors, and news editors, each from a different newspaper, attended. A number of mid-sized papers, such as the *Sacramento Bee*, *Grand Rapids* (MI) *Press*, and *Salt Lake Telegram*, sent representatives. Most, however, were from larger papers such as the *Washington Post*, *Cleveland Plain Dealer*, *Philadelphia Evening Bulletin*, *New York Times*, and *Los Angeles Times*. "The critique session at the close of the first seminar resembled an old-fashioned religious experience meeting," wrote W.S. Kirkpatrick, managing editor of the *Atlanta Journal*, in a review for *Journalism Quarterly*. "Enthusiasm ran high."[28]

Editors were quick to credit the API with enriching journalism. In its first two years, the institute held twelve seminars for 275 participants from 113 newspapers. Grove Patterson of the *Toledo Blade* said that two years of successful seminars had had "a profound effect on the thinking and on the product of the editors, managing editors, city editors" and others who had attended. "Journalism needs new techniques, new spiritual conviction and new inspiration," he continued. "The American Press Institute is providing all this." It held six seminars a year for each of the following five years, and Patterson led the effort to endow the institute to provide it with permanent funding.[29]

Another self-improvement effort in newspapers was the development of a new accrediting process for journalism programs in the nation's colleges and universities. For many journalists, the accrediting program was a crucial first step toward the professionalization of journalism. Journalists could be professionals only if they had professional training, and accreditation was a way to ensure the quality of professional preparation. As *Quill* editor Carl R. Kesler put it in a 1946 editorial, "For the first time since colleges started teaching journalism as a profession, a measuring stick is being designed for such training."[30]

Accreditation had been discussed at professional meetings as far back as the late 1920s, but little had been done until the formation of the American Council of Education for Journalism (ACEJ) in 1938. Kenneth E. Olson, dean of the Medill School of Journalism at Northwestern University, lobbied newspaper organizations to take part in journalism education, and ACEJ was the result. It included deans of five journalism schools and representatives of each of the five major newspaper organizations—ASNE, the ANPA, the Southern Newspaper Publishers Association (SNPA), the National Editorial Association (NEA), and the Inland Daily Press Association.[31]

ACEJ research found that more than 520 colleges and universities, more than half of four-year institutions, offered some kind of journalism instruction, often just a course or two. That was too many programs with no assurance of any quality, many editors complained. Stephen C. Noland of the *Indianapolis News*, expressing a common sentiment, said the high numbers persuaded him that "something should be done about cleaning out some of the incompetent schools of journalism."[32] Dwight Marvin, who headed the ACEJ in the late 1940s, said doing so would benefit editors directly. "[I]f we could make the schools of journalism such that you men, you editors, knew that you could get from the schools of journalism men who knew something about journalism," he declared, "then you would have a source that was worth while. . . . But there ought to be some sort of school that you can trust. That is the idea."[33]

Accreditation efforts lagged during the war but picked up near its end. Marvin said the effort was pushed along by the 1944 decision in a newspaper labor dispute in Jackson, Tennessee, where a judge had ruled newspaper workers were not professionals. "When we realized that the Jackson judge thought we were tradesmen, immediately something had to be done," Marvin said.[34] In 1945, the American Association of Schools and Departments of Journalism (AASDJ) approved the formation of an accreditation committee under the ACEJ, which began work on standards.

A questionnaire was circulated to 120 colleges and universities with departments of journalism. Fewer than forty applied to be accredited, and a two-year process of visiting each school began in 1946. Two years later, the ACEJ released its list of the first thirty-four schools to be accredited in at least one sequence, or subject area. Of the thirty-four, thirty-one were accredited in news-editorial, thirteen in radio journalism, and nineteen in advertising. Other programs were accredited in agriculture journalism, photography, and magazines. Accredited schools were to be re-examined every five years.[35]

Norval Neil Luxon of Ohio State University, president of the AASDJ, believed the accreditation program would have numerous benefits. He said in 1948 that it would help professionals, students, and teachers recognize worthy schools, would strengthen the relationships between educators and professionals, and would stimulate improvements in journalism. The accreditation process set standards for schools in library holdings, teacher preparation, curriculum, and equipment.[36]

But while the progress in accreditation demonstrated a degree of consensus for improving journalism education, some editors remained unconvinced that any specialized professional training was necessary. They still believed that the best place to start in journalism was, in the words of Northwestern University professor Curtis D. MacDougall, as a copy boy in a newsroom, not in a classroom.[37] Some editors, such as V.M. Newton, Jr., of the *Tampa Morning Tribune*, believed that liberal arts training alone—without the technical training of journalism school—was preparation enough. "In the case of a journalism graduate it usually takes a good city editor from one to two years to knock out of him all the ridiculous theories taught in journalism schools," he remarked in 1948.[38]

A Bradley University survey conducted the same year found editors about evenly split on the value of specialized journalism training. Of sixty-eight editors who replied to a questionnaire about their employees' schooling, thirty-two said they preferred to hire journalism graduates over liberal arts graduates. Regardless, the fact was that college graduates in general were making inroads in the nation's newsrooms. The survey found that at some newspapers, including the *Philadelphia Inquirer* and the *Columbus* (OH) *Dispatch*, college graduates outnumbered non-graduates by three to one.[39]

Even as journalists tried to improve themselves and their newspapers through readability campaigns, API seminars, and better writing, criticism of the press seemed to rise on all fronts. It reinforced the need for improvement at the very time newspapers were already showing greater awareness of their shortcomings and undertaking efforts to overcome them. The public, it seemed, agreed with editors, reporters, and publishers that newspapers needed to improve. The irony was that while journalists were becoming quicker to criticize themselves and each other, they nonetheless remained sensitive to, and defensive about, outside criticism. "It is a fact that newspapers in general have become the national whipping boy," an *Editor & Publisher* editorial lamented in 1946.[40] This was a commonly expressed sentiment among journalists after the war, not only in the characteristically thin-skinned *Editor & Publisher* but also in other trade journals, in newspapers, and in magazines. By 1949, Edwin Emery, the historian of the ANPA, would write that postwar criticism was "[t]he biggest problem which confronted the daily newspapers of America."[41]

The criticism, as perceptively summarized by Emery, charged that newspapers did not fully serve the public interest, that most were owned by pro-business, pro-Republican interests, and that the continuing trend toward newspaper monopoly threatened the marketplace of ideas essential to the functioning of a democracy.[42] These concerns about press monopoly dominated the books and articles critical of the press that multiplied in the postwar period. This criticism was noteworthy not for its novelty—such concerns had been fodder of the critics for years—but for its increasing volume and frequency. Editors and publishers believed that newspapers were too frequently criticized.[43]

The Commission on the Freedom of the Press, which issued its report in 1947, was probably the best-known press critic. Founded by Henry Luce of Time Inc. and headed by University of Chicago president Robert M. Hutchins, the Commission of Hutchins and twelve other intellectuals took testimony and interviews from more than 275 journalists and others in the course of a four-year study. In its final report, the Commission called on the press to better meet its responsibilities to society and to democracy.[44] "Today our society needs, first, a truthful, comprehensive, and intelligent account of the day's events in a context which gives them meaning," the commissioners wrote, in what was the report's most-quoted phrase.[45] But many newspapers were falling far short of that goal because of shallowness, sensationalism, and dishonesty, the report said. Moreover, the entire newspaper industry was subject to a growing monopoly that threatened newspapers' ability to serve the public. The Commission suggested that a press council should be formed to comment on newspaper performance and warned that failure to address the press' problems might invite government regulation.[46]

Press response was sharply critical. Journalists accused the Commission of unfairly failing to include a journalist on the panel, of inviting government regulation, of unfairly lumping in radio and movies with the press, and of failing to conduct elaborate research. Louis M. Lyons, summarizing press reaction in an article for Atlantic Monthly, said that most newspapers either ignored the Commission's report, underplayed it, or misrepresented its findings.[47] Most newspapers, he said, ran brief wire stories on the report, played inside the newspaper. Time magazine hired a clipping service to survey editorial reaction to the report and found that only ninety-nine of 830 newspapers commented editorially on the Commission report. A third of those used the same editorial written by a syndicated columnist.[48]

"I believe the report to be wrongly conceived and badly executed," said Frank E. Gannett, president of Gannett Newspapers, in a remark typical of many publishers' reactions. "I think it is erroneous, inconsistent, ineffective, and dangerous."[49] The *Chicago Tribune*'s critical news account of the report was headlined, " 'A Free Press' (Hitler Style) Sought for U.S.; Totalitarians Tell How It Can Be Done."[50] An editorial in the *New York Herald Tribune* faulted the professorial language and impractical approach of the report but said it correctly pointed to a need for increased press responsibility. Less charitably, *Herald Tribune* book columnist Lewis Gannett said of the report, "[A] good $150-a-week newspaper man would have been ashamed to do as little work for a three-week assignment."[51]

The Hutchins Commission's criticisms of newspaper ownership and press practices, coupled with its call for journalists to exercise greater responsibility, epitomized much of the press criticism of its day. The report reinforced journalists' sense that public criticism of newspapers was increasing, not just from the Commission but from other sources. *Editor & Publisher International Yearbook* said that 1947, the year of the Hutchins report, subjected newspapers "to the most searching analysis and criticism in all their history."[52] Editors and publishers considered the Hutchins Commission report as one more critical voice in a stream of postwar press critics. At editors' and publishers' meetings and in the pages of trade journals throughout the late 1940s, the growing press criticism was a continual topic, and the Commission was only one critic, though a very important one.

Many critics, like the Commission, focused on concerns about press monopoly. The most prominent critic of this school was Morris L. Ernst, whose major critique of this trend appeared a year prior to the Commission's report. A labor lawyer, specializing in civil liberties cases, whose clients included the American Newspaper Guild, he was a persistent and fiery critic of growing concentration of ownership in the mass media. In articles and books, he decried the declining numbers of two-newspaper towns, newspaper control of radio stations, and concentration of ownership in the film and book publishing industries. He argued that freedom of the press meant freedom for citizens to have access to a variety of sources of information, not simply the freedom of newspapers to print without government control. "Only if they may hear a diversity of views," he said of newspaper readers and radio listeners, "have they that opportunity of choice which is the essence of freedom."[53] His arguments received wide currency in his book *The First Freedom*, published in 1946, which was widely reviewed in the popular and trade press.[54]

Ernst proposed changes in tax laws to discourage concentration, federal limits on chain ownership, government aid to small newspapers, and other measures. He believed that the declining number of newspapers was dangerous in and of itself but was careful to say he was not "charging the present dispensers of information with being low and destructive fellows."[55]

Defenders of newspapers agreed with Ernst's statistics but disputed their interpretation. Raymond B. Nixon of Emory University, whose studies of newspaper ownership patterns published in *Journalism Quarterly* provided Ernst and other critics with some of their supporting evidence, defended the industry in 1948 using arguments commonly touted among journalists: the economics of all large industries, including newspapers, made consolidations inevitable. Monopoly newspapers were most often found in towns that could support only one daily newspaper anyway, and sometimes they were of higher quality than newspapers subject to competitive pressures. "Monopoly" newspapers were in truth challenged in both advertising and newsgathering by magazines and by radio and television stations. And chain ownership, while regrettable, was declining slightly. Nixon argued that greater social responsibility among newspaper publishers, not competition, would improve newspapers.[56]

Congressional critics threatened to investigate monopolistic practices, but the hearings never materialized. In early 1947, at the close of his chairmanship of the US Senate Small Business Committee, Senator James E. Murray of Montana released a 71-page report, "The Small Newspaper: Democracy's Grass Roots," that criticized monopolistic tendencies in the newspaper and radio industries and called for government oversight. Murray, a Democrat, had planned hearings in 1947 on newspaper ownership trends and their effects on smaller publishers, but Republicans who took control of the Senate after the 1946 elections refocused the hearings upon newsprint shortages instead. *Editor & Publisher* dismissed Murray's report as a fruitless search for "bogeymen under the journalistic bed" that ignored the neutral economic forces behind newspaper consolidations.[57]

Still, the arguments took hold, and the degree of public distrust of the press was demonstrated in several forums. About 2,500 Akron, Ohio, residents attended a panel discussion on press monopoly and press freedom on October 17, 1946. The discussion, featuring Ernst, Erwin D. Canham, and *New Republic* editor Michael Straight, was broadcast nationally on the radio program *Town Meeting of the Air*. The discussion centered on monopoly ownership and advertiser influence of news coverage. When the audience was asked how many believed the American press was truly free, only a scattering of hands went up. The *Akron Beacon-Journal* was troubled at such a lack of faith in the press. "In the belief that an opinion held by more than 2,000 of our readers deserves consideration and respect, we're giving ourselves a going-over to see if we are exercising all the freedom which the Constitution gives us," *Beacon-Journal* editors said.[58] In 1948, the New York State Society of Newspaper Editors invited a clubwoman, a priest, and a businessman to its annual fall meeting to offer criticism. The clubwoman complained of one-sided columnists, sensationalism, and misrepresentation. The businessman faulted newspapers for publishing rumors, criticizing public officials, and overplaying murders and other sensational news. The assembled editors were stung by the criticism and did not take issue with it.[59]

Other media stepped up their criticism of newspapers. *Time* and *Newsweek* had each published weekly columns on the press, including regular exposés of press practices. To these columns were added, beginning in 1945, A.J. Liebling's "Wayward Press" columns in the *New Yorker*. "The Wayward Press" had been inaugurated by Robert Benchley in 1927 and published sporadically afterward. Liebling, a *New Yorker* veteran who had reported for New York City and Rhode Island newspapers, delighted in assailing journalists for their foibles. He focused most of his columns on the New York-area press and reserved his harshest words for owners. Publishers, Liebling once observed, "talk about their great public services while they treat a paper as if it were a drugstore."[60] His criticism, widely read and often quoted in *Editor & Publisher* and other trade journals of American journalism, made him the best-known press critic of his generation.

CBS launched its own program of press criticism, *CBS Views the Press*, in June 1947. The fifteen-minute program was broadcast every Saturday on WCBS, the CBS affiliate in New York, and was put together by veteran CBS correspondent Don Hollenbeck, himself a former newspaperman. He said some newspapers had been hostile to his program but that overall it had been received with "hopeful welcome tinged with cynicism." *Editor & Publisher* and other trade journals frequently reprinted Hollenbeck's critiques, and the program won a Peabody Award in 1948. It continued through the early 1950s.[61]

Another persistent, if less influential, critic of the postwar years was George Seldes, whose pro-labor publication *In Fact* was founded in 1940 and built up a weekly circulation of 200,000 before its demise in 1950. The eight-page newspaper, subtitled "An Antidote for Falsehood in the Daily Press," was helped along in subscription sales by the Congress of Industrial Organizations. Reporters from around the country, including Hollenbeck, supplied Seldes with information about overlooked news stories, pro-business bias, and other press misdeeds. Seldes' strong pro-labor views and vicious attacks on newspapers large and small kept him from enjoying the quasi-acceptance enjoyed by more mainstream critics such as Liebling, who was accorded a mostly positive press among rank-and-file newspaper reporters and even spoke to an ASNE meeting once. Seldes recalled that "in all the ten years *In Fact* was red-baited, libeled, branded 'red' and generally ostracized."[62]

A more significant contribution to criticism came with the founding of *Nieman Reports*, a quarterly journal published by the Nieman fellows of Harvard University beginning in March 1947, a month before the

Hutchins report was issued. The Nieman program, begun in the 1930s, brought a dozen journalists each year to Harvard for two semesters of study, and the founding of *Nieman Reports* provided a regular forum for press criticism from a variety of sources, though mostly from present and former Nieman fellows. Readers hailed *Nieman Reports* for filling a void in journalism, by providing at last a journal about newspapers and newspaper problems written by working journalists.[63]

Nieman fellows had also produced several notable works of press criticism in the late 1940s. The Nieman class of 1945–1946 published a book, *Your Newspaper: Blueprint for a Better Press*, in late 1947 that criticized newspapers for failing to serve readers by serving instead the class interests of their owners. The *New Republic* praised the book as "a work that deserves to stand with the valuable current investigations of the same subject by A.J. Liebling and Don Hollenbeck."[64] The 1949–1950 class of Nieman fellows published a special issue of *Nieman Reports* titled "Reading, Writing and Newspapers" criticizing the state of newswriting generally and applauding and encouraging efforts to improve readability, interpretation, and storytelling. Demand for reprints from newspapers and journalism schools required the printing of 7,000 additional copies, and newspaper executives across the country praised the issue.[65]

Nieman Reports, written as it was by experienced journalists still working in the profession, represented the extent to which criticism of newspapers came from inside, not just outside, the profession. Reporters and editors themselves, while often resentful of outside critics, nonetheless also viewed newspapers critically. This was evident at editors' meetings, where critics were found among both the editors and their guests.

The numerous critics included Ralph L. Crosman, director of the College of Journalism at the University of Colorado, who aired his views both at various editors' meetings and in the journalism department's publication, *Colorado Editor*. The vehemence of his criticism was surprising, given the traditional close ties between journalism schools and the profession. Crosman, foreshadowing criticism that would come from the Hutchins Commission the following year, issued a 10-count "indictment" of the press at the 1946 meeting of the Inland Daily Press Association in Chicago. He accused newspapers of failing to provide readers with adequate coverage of social, economic, and political conditions; of running biased and distorted news; of reflecting upper-class, Republican concerns; of guarding various sacred cows; and of overemphasizing trivial, inconsequential news. He said most rich publishers wanted to serve the public but had to be taught to do so. "I do know," he said, "that this businessman-publisher has got to be waked up, jolted alive, [and] retaught his duty to the people."[66]

Editors responded harshly yet took action. Frank Tripp of Gannett Newspapers compared Crosman to a quack selling a worthless universal remedy. "Crosman diagnoses all the ills of a far-flung, individualistic press [and] prescribes a cure-all," he said, "when all the average patient needs is an enema."[67] What the patient needed, Inland editors decided after conducting a national survey of readers, was better public relations to meet the growing tide of criticism. The Inland survey had found that most readers believed newspapers to be unfair and subject to pressure from advertisers and big business. A committee of Inland editors proposed and carried out two national advertising campaigns to educate the public about the role of the press in everyday life. The ads, using the slogan "Your right to know is the key to all your liberties," were published in newspapers across the country and were lauded in the trade press as an antidote to growing press criticism.[68]

Newspaper criticism abounded elsewhere. At the 1948 ASNE convention, Jenkin Lloyd Jones, editor of the *Tulsa Tribune*, delivered his "Afghanistanism" speech that became famous in newspaper circles. He decried the common practice among newspaper editorialists to comment extensively on non-local issues in faraway places, Afghanistan, say, while ignoring crucial issues at home.[69] The same year, at a southern editors' meeting, patrician *Arkansas Gazette* owner J.N. Heiskell persuaded the SNPA to pass a resolution lamenting the decline of southern editorial pages. Southern newspapers, he complained, were publishing far too much canned material and devoting inadequate time and resources to the editorial page.[70]

Such jousting between editors over journalistic issues was not uncommon in the late 1940s, and the disagreements were often vehement. Grove Patterson of the *Toledo Blade*, in a widely reported speech in 1947 at the American Press Institute (API), blasted biased news coverage. "Publishers who instruct or allow reporters to slant the news, in conformity with personal views and personal policy, are journalistic gangsters," Patterson said, without naming any names.[71] *New York Times* publisher Arthur Hays Sulzberger and John S. Knight, editor of newspapers in Akron, Detroit, and Miami, publicly debated the strengths and weaknesses of chain newspapers at a series of individual appearances and in trade journal articles. Sulzberger said national chains often failed to become involved in local issues. Knight responded that chain newspapers were often superior to locally owned journals.[72] A small-town publisher complained in the *ASNE Bulletin* that most small-city dailies were sloppily written and edited and lacked the initiative to adequately cover their communities.[73]

Events from 1945 to 1948 seemed to underscore the press criticism. Press coverage of the 1945 San Francisco conference to plan the United Nations and the 1946 Bikini Island atomic bomb tests prompted criticism of shallow newspaper coverage marked by sensationalism and speculative, contradictory news stories.[74] In reporting atomic bomb developments, most American newspapers are "unsurpassed for mediocrity," lamented Richard B. Gehman in the *Saturday Review of Literature* in 1948. "Today, with most American newspapers unsurpassed for mediocrity, one wonders if they could help making a mess of their coverage of Christ's arrival."[75] Later that year, the vast majority of press accounts predicted a comfortable win by New York Governor Thomas Dewey over President Truman in the presidential election, serving to underscore the perception that newspapers were out of touch with the public they served.

Such was the tenor of criticism within newspapers in the late 1940s. Journalists in the new Atomic Age could not help being aware of the press' shortcomings. Even as newspapers were undertaking wide-ranging efforts to improve, criticism continued, seemingly from all directions. The critics underscored the need for improvements, propelling efforts already underway. The self-examination would continue throughout the 1950s, as a heightening of Cold War tensions and the rapid growth of television brought new challenges for newspapers.

The criticism and the widespread efforts to improve the journalism profession, many editors believed, were slowly pushing print journalism to become more responsible. The critics were indeed harsh, but together with other forces they were pressuring newspapers to mature. "[A] world war—and the thought-provoking, soul-stretching years of this peace which is no peace—have given newspapers greater depth and a broader perspective," Oveta Culp Hobby, an executive of the *Houston Post* and SNPA president, said in 1950. "Journalism is maturing. The emphasis has shifted from scoop to scope."[76]

Chapter 3

Government, the Cold War, and Newspapers, 1950–1954

Newspapers' relationship with government and public officials seemed to crack in the early 1950s, challenging press practices on several fronts. National security concerns rooted in the Cold War accelerated a trend toward greater secrecy in government, igniting a "freedom of information" (FOI) movement in professional associations to fight the growing secrecy at both federal and local levels. At the same time, journalistic coverage of one of the most important news stories of the early 1950s—the rise of Senator Joseph R. McCarthy—prompted a reappraisal both of objectivity as a press standard and of newspapers' ability to meet that goal. Journalists' devotion to objectivity was shaken, not shattered, by these events, but their relationships with government officials suffered more substantially. Newspaper-government relations began what was to be a long, steady deterioration.

Through World War II, newspapers' relationship with government had been characterized more by trust than by disharmony. At home, press censorship was entirely voluntary and overseen by the Press Division of the Office of Censorship, itself staffed with journalists on leave from their jobs. In complying with government requests to withhold information, journalists prided themselves on their contributions to the war effort. As the *New York Times'* Raymond Daniell once put it, "There isn't any story in the world that is good enough to justify risking the life of a single American soldier."[1] Voluntary censorship worked, believed Theodore F. Koop, one of the self-described "blue pencil boys" in the Press Division, because editors were willing "to lean over backwards when security was involved."[2] Office of Censorship director

Byron Price, closing his bureau at war's end, told President Truman that the censorship program was "a heartening example of democracy at work."[3]

The experiences of the Associated Press' Edward Kennedy and the *New York Times'* William L. Laurence at the close of the war demonstrate the degree of newspaper-government cooperation. His fellow war correspondents were outraged when Kennedy, on May 7, 1945, filed an exclusive story from Paris announcing the end of the war in Europe. He had broken his promise to military authorities to withhold the information until a government-approved release time. More than fifty correspondents signed a letter describing his action as the "most disgraceful, deliberate, and unethical double cross in the history of journalism."[4] Laurence, by contrast, worked on a secret, four-month assignment for the government preparing articles about the invention and deployment of the atomic bomb. His articles were withheld until after the bombs were dropped in Japan, when his carefully censored articles were published in the *Times* and elsewhere. Laurence considered the opportunity to work in secret for the government as an honor for both him and his newspaper.[5]

Such press willingness to cooperate with the government—and press outrage at breaches of this relationship—did not preclude, of course, criticism of government officials, either before or after the war. But central to a newspaper's relationship with government officials was an understanding that the government's security aims, especially in wartime, deserved journalistic support. For their part, journalists expected easy access to newsmakers and to information. Such access was relatively easy even in wartime, but reporters and editors began to concern themselves with overcoming government obstacles to news as the United States emerged from World War II.[6]

At first, these obstacles were centered in the international arena. Journalists, through their trade associations, threw themselves into an effort to incorporate free press guarantees into postwar charters of the United Nations. The goal was to thwart the growth of totalitarianism by spreading democracy through an international free exchange of information, and the establishment of the United Nations seemed to provide an opportunity to lower the many barriers to a free press worldwide. Publishers wanted foreign correspondents to have easy access to news in foreign countries, unrestricted by any foreign censorship. "It is something of a shock," said International News Service general manager Seymour Berkson in 1946, "to realize that, of the fifty-four countries which are members of the United Nations, only a minority of those very countries have the same principles of freedom of information which we recognize and abide by in the United States."[7] The American Society of Newspaper Editors (ASNE), the Associated Press Managing Editors (APME), and Sigma Delta Chi (now the Society of Professional

Journalists) each organized FOI committees to deal with world press issues and to lobby the United Nations.

But journalists' efforts to further world freedom of information were frustrated from the beginning. In 1945, three editors representing ASNE toured the world to survey press freedoms and were disappointed at their findings. The three presented a 40,000-word report to President Harry S Truman, concluding that "facts are going to have as hard a time as ever getting around after the war."[8] Editors of ASNE also took part in U.N. freedom of information conferences, but the promising treaties and proposals that emerged from the sessions later stalled.[9] At an international conference on freedom of the press held in 1948 in Geneva, Switzerland, for example, fifty national governments approved drafts of treaties to protect the worldwide flow of news, but the treaties were whittled away later before the U.N. General Assembly. The Soviet Union was a particular opponent of the U.N. efforts, and the drive for world freedom of information withered as the Cold War accelerated.[10]

At the same time that international proposals for freedom of information faded, press barriers seemed to rise at home. "FOI's spiritual sire was a noble experiment called World Freedom of Information," recalled James S. Pope, executive editor of the Louisville, Kentucky, newspapers and an ASNE activist in FOI efforts, in 1958. "The leaders [of the FOI movement] were the first to see...that it was not possible to liberate information across the world until we had mastered the art in our own nation, our own states and cities."[11] In the early postwar years, government secrecy seemed to rise on all fronts. Journalists believed the federal government's increased emphasis on secrecy was rooted in the tense state of postwar international affairs, the increasing influence of the military in Washington, and the technological revolution in high-tech weaponry. Security measures had taken root in World War II only to expand in the postwar years as Cold War tensions escalated.[12] J. Russell Wiggins of the *Washington Post*, chairman of APME's freedom of information committee in the early 1950s, blamed several other factors as well. He believed that the overall growth of government had increased secretiveness, particularly as power had increased in the 1930s and 1940s in the executive branch, with its numerous administrative agencies and bureaucracies.[13]

In the late 1940s, the greatest domestic freedom of information questions concerned military security surrounding atomic secrets and the development of new weapons for the military. *New York Times* correspondent Hanson W. Baldwin complained to ASNE editors in 1948 of what he called a "velvet curtain." The curtain consisted, he said, of military restrictions that kept reporters from getting information, even information already known to the American public or to the Soviet Union. Military officials had tried to suppress, for example, news articles about the building of a new missile center in El Centro, California, and the development of new missiles. In one instance FBI agents had questioned the publishers of *Aviation Week* about its articles on the development of a supersonic plane, even though the plane was based on a Russian prototype.[14]

Baldwin was typical of journalists who believed that military withholding of information in peacetime was unnecessary and should be resisted. National security could be protected, he said, not by military censorship but by responsible journalists, just as in wartime. Newspapers could continue to guard national security, he believed, because responsible editors "will pause and ask before they publish technical stories dealing with military facts, 'Is it in the national interest to publish this?'"[15] The 1948 convention of ASNE editors adopted resolutions urging press-government cooperation in the publication of news about military weapons but opposing all censorship.[16]

But while journalists were inclined to cooperate with government officials in not divulging vital military information, they vehemently opposed any government secrecy in non-military matters. Such secrecy also showed a marked increased in the postwar years, journalists believed. "Most federal agencies are showing exceptional zeal in creating rules, regulations, directives, classifications and, policies which serve to hide, color or channel news," Pope said in 1951.[17]

An early and significant example of this phenomenon occurred in 1947, when the National Security Advisory Board released model security regulations to be used by federal agencies in their compliance with the president's federal loyalty program. The regulations, adopted first by the Veterans Administration, instructed officials to withhold any information that "would be prejudicial to the interests or prestige of the nation, any governmental activity or any individual, or would cause administration embarrassment or difficulty."[18]

Journalists reacted with outrage. The *Minneapolis Tribune* dismissed the order as an "unprecedented attempt to bottle up news and information at the source."[19] The ASNE board of directors urged repeal, saying the directive would "place even the ordinary affairs of federal civilian agencies beyond public scrutiny." Truman responded that he had not heard of the regulations and would not approve them as written.[20] The regulations were revised to eliminate official embarrassment as a cause for withholding information. But they did establish a uniform classification system for the military's security-related documents: "top secret," "secret," "confidential," and "restricted."

The ASNE World Freedom of Information Committee had expressed concerns about domestic secrecy from its founding in 1948. "It seems to me our responsibility lies in the domestic field as well as the international field," committee chairman Basil L. "Stuffy" Walters wrote to fellow committee members in 1948. "I have noted a growing tendency of some officials in some of the smallest governmental units, as well as the largest, to forget that they are servants of the people and to act instead as though the taxpayers were their servants." Walters, executive editor of Knight Newspapers, instructed three committee members to keep track of domestic secrecy problems and to help any editors around the country facing difficulty.[21] By 1950, with international freedom of information efforts stumbling and domestic secrecy on the rise, the committee dropped the "world" from its title to reflect its changing mission.[22]

Journalists grew steadily more alarmed about the domestic secrecy problems through 1950 and 1951. After Pope, the successor to Walters as ASNE's FOI chairman, enumerated secrecy difficulties at the 1950 ASNE meeting, he received 200 requests for copies of his talk from journalists around the country. "It was as if everybody suddenly had waked up to the dangers we had been far too busy to see," he said. Echoing other journalists, he maintained that the denial of information was an issue touching on the very essence of press freedom, since freedom of the press was worthless if public officials withheld journalists' source material.[23]

The litany of withheld information investigated by journalism groups in 1950 and 1951 alone was long indeed. The federal Board of Reserve was holding secret meetings. The Department of State was withholding a large volume of material from reporters. The U.S. military forbade photographers from taking pictures of airplane crashes on civilian property. At the local level, a school board in Torrington, Connecticut, closed its sessions and its minutes to the public. Pawtucket, Rhode Island, officials refused to release tax abatement records. The governor of Arizona was declining to release public reports.[24] "As FOI groped for a stance, a game plan," Pope later recalled of these early years, "the custodians of public business were romping over the field."[25]

Litigation by newspapers to force open records and meetings increased substantially. Harold Cross, the media lawyer ASNE had hired in 1951 to survey the growing secrecy and suggest how newspapers should respond, noted this trend in a report to the association during his first year on the job. "The last five years brought more newspaper lawsuits to open records than any previous twenty-five years," he said. For most of his thirty-five years in newspaper law, Cross said, he had encountered few cases involving access to information. "Now scarcely a week goes by without a new refusal," he said.[26] Cross' investigations of the state of freedom of information law at state and national levels eventually expanded into a book-length guide and casebook for editors. The work, *The Public's Right to Know*, was published in 1953. Cross was the FOI movement's most prominent spokesman and legal specialist until his death in 1959.[27]

While journalists on the FOI committees could often pry loose withheld information through protests, publicity, or lawsuits, they often encountered government arrogance that appalled them. When the U.S. Board of Parole flatly refused to supply records requested by the *Louisville Courier-Journal*, the ASNE committee intervened and the records were released, but under protest. "In the future," the Parole Board chairman haughtily explained, "desired information will be supplied if, *in our opinion*, such information would be compatible with the welfare of society."[28] When, in what Pope called "a particularly horrible crime," the Alcohol Tax Unit in Albany, New York, accused local bars of watering down their liquor, tax officials reached a settlement but refused to release details. Officials ultimately relented, and, to journalists' relief, the names of the offending bars were made public.[29]

For journalists, the stakes in fighting government secrecy were high, justifying the harsh rhetoric of an all-out war. Secretive government officials were "a well-entrenched enemy," declared Pope. "Certainly there is a vital connection," he said, "between growing scandals in government and the growing concealment of information."[30] Journalists cast government public relations officials as conniving bureaucrats, using press releases, government directives, secret meetings, and off-the-record conferences to further their bosses' public image. "I have never heard of a single government press agent who ever issued a news handout that was critical of his political boss," said V.M. Newton, Jr., of the *Tampa Tribune* in 1951.[31] The twin problems of public relations and concealed information, Washington reporter Clark Mollenhoff said in 1954, served to throttle democracy.[32]

The relationship between government and journalists was changing. Just as a government grown larger and more complex had forced changes in newswriting, it also forced changes in how reporters dealt with sources. David Lawrence, a newspaper columnist and publisher of *U.S. News & World Report*, said in 1950 that while the number of Washington correspondents had multiplied since he had first moved to Washington four decades earlier, the government had grown even faster, and it was much more difficult to cover capital news. Journalists now found themselves dealing more and more with intermediaries— public relations people—and thus more subject to manipulation. "This government of ours has grown so big," Lawrence said, "that it is easy for our newspapers to take the mimeographed handouts and give digests of them on their front pages, as we do every day." The result, he believed, was that much government propaganda was getting into the newspaper.[33]

This government public relations created resentment at the same time as it helped journalists cover a complex government. Some Washington correspondents said that government handouts had made reporters lazy—victims of "handoutitis"—and more reliant upon official government pronouncements for news.[34] Others complained that public relations offices created a "paper curtain" between reporters and sources, a familiar barrier newly ominous as secrecy increased.[35] Still, many journalists agreed that modern institutions had become so large and complex they would be impossible to cover without the help of public relations people. Philip W. Porter of the *Cleveland Plain Dealer* told an ASNE panel in 1951 that press agents are "in the same category as women—they are often puzzling and amazing, but we couldn't get along without them."[36]

Press agents were ubiquitous in both state and federal governments. A 1951 report by *Editor & Publisher* found 700 press agents in state government and 2,400 in the federal government, the latter considered a conservative estimate.[37] A 1949 federal study, more liberal in whom it counted as a public relations worker, put the number at 45,000, at an annual cost of $74.8 million.[38]

A low point of press-government relations in the early 1950s was the imposition by President Truman of a new executive order providing for a classification system of government information. The order, Executive Order 10290, was released September 24, 1951, for use by forty-five civilian government agencies to classify information into categories of top secret, secret, classified, and confidential, the same categories the military used.[39] Truman said many civilian departments needed the power to classify information because they, too, often handled sensitive government documents. Information must be protected, he said, that might otherwise be published by the news media and provide assistance to the Communist enemies in the Cold War. He cited a Central Intelligence Agency (CIA) report that found that "90 percent of all our top secret information had been published in either the daily newspapers or in the slick magazines."[40]

Truman's order met immediate criticism from journalists. His press conference of October 4, 1951, was devoted entirely to a defense of the order, and the White House issued a memorandum explaining that the directive did not amount to censorship.[41] The APME, which was holding its annual convention when the order was released, denounced it as "a dangerous instrument of news suppression." It said the order was unnecessarily vague and lacked an appeal process. Truman met with a delegation of APME editors to discuss their concerns on October 17, but neither side budged in its position.[42] *Editor & Publisher* editorialized that the security order amounted to "the most drastic peacetime censorship ever attempted in this country." Even in wartime, civilian agencies had not been given such power to suppress news, the magazine's editors warned.[43] The delegates to the Sigma Delta Chi convention in 1951 passed a resolution opposing the directive, saying it "duplicates in the name of national security the practices of totalitarian states."[44] A *New York Times* editorial said the order was unnecessarily vague and would invite abuse.[45]

Truman instituted an appeal process to address reporters' complaints, but the order remained unchanged until Eisenhower took office.[46] His attorney general, Herbert Brownell Jr., announced before APME editors in 1953 that the order was being revised to limit classification power to seventeen agencies. The "restricted" category was eliminated, leaving only "top secret," "secret," and "confidential," and authority to classify information was given only to the chief administrative officer of each agency. Brownell said Truman's order had "applied the military formula to a lot of things entirely outside the scope of national defense." The order had also led to overclassification, he said.[47]

Journalists were divided over the Eisenhower order. J. Russell Wiggins of the *Washington Post* said the revised order had remedied the short-comings in Truman's directive and was probably the best compromise newspaper editors could hope for in such insecure times.[48] Other editors said the order demonstrated that Eisenhower had accepted Truman's precedent to withhold government information. "It is not a 'milestone,'" *Indianapolis Star* editor Jameson G. Campaigne complained of the order. "It is a 'millstone' around the necks of the editors of the nation."[49]

The Truman and Eisenhower security orders had one advantage, that of contributing to a greater public awareness of the press' freedom of information campaign. "Millions have read and heard of freedom of information for the first time," James S. Pope said in 1952. The *Milwaukee Journal* had printed a fourteen-part series on news suppression by Wisconsin officials. Also in 1951–1952, the *Cleveland Plain Dealer, Detroit Free Press*, Associated Press (AP), and Scripps-Howard news service had each published articles or series on government withholding of information. The *Los Angeles News* had printed a yearlong series of reports on school boards that operated in secrecy.[50]

Paradoxically, the Korean Conflict, which lasted from June 1950 to July 1953, created minimal freedom of information concerns under either Truman or Eisenhower. It would prove, however, to be the last war in which print reporters had primacy over their media rivals. As David Halberstam has observed, neither television nor radio covered Korea. "The best reporting in Korea," he wrote in *The Fifties*, "was done by daily journalists, who caught its remarkable drama, heroism, and pathos for a nation that largely didn't care and was not at all sure it wanted to pay attention to such grim news."[51]

When Communist North Korean forces crossed the 38th Parallel June 25, 1950, they met little resistance from the undermanned Republic of Korea Army. At South Korea's request, President Harry Truman imme-diately authorized additional U.S. forces to the region, supplementing the small group of American advisers already on the peninsula. The United Nations authorized a multinational force, led by the United States, to repel the invasion. General Douglas MacArthur was named commanding general, though Truman relieved him of duty in 1951 for ignoring White House directives.[52]

Reporters who poured into South Korea found a bloody war of attrition, with battle lines stabilized at the 38th Parallel by 1951. About 36,500 American troops, as well as eleven journalists, died in the two years it took to negotiate peace. "It was not like other wars," one journalist recalled. "In other wars you had a pretty good idea of where the enemy was and where you were. In Korea you didn't."[53]

Officially at least, the government didn't censor the press. "General MacArthur does not desire to invoke censorship," a Department of Defense spokesman declared in the opening weeks of the war. "He prefers that the press establish a voluntary code that will insure the security of operations and the safety of personnel." The Department advised reporters against naming specific units, giving details of troop movements, or providing other details of value to the enemy.[54]

But the lack of clear guidelines caused occasional conflict. Since officials controlled information at the source, reporters complained they had no clear idea of what could be reported. The military provided far less information than correspondents wanted, and facilities for the press to send their stories back home were meager, particularly at first. For a short time, reporters had the use of just one telephone, and even then their calls were subject to interruption by Army officials, who had top priority.[55]

Early on, Col. Marion P. Echols, one of MacArthur's public information officers, was harshly critical of coverage, and official discontent with war coverage would continue. He said there had been "inaccurate and irresponsible reporting" and chided reporters for "lack of decency, honesty and regard for procedure."[56] Later the Army warned reporters against criticizing United Nations commanders or American soldiers. Commanders had authority to retaliate against reporters who broke their rules, and several reporters were briefly barred from the front. [57]

A more significant challenge to journalists in the early 1950s was posed by the anti-Communist accusations of the junior US senator from Wisconsin, Joseph R. McCarthy. His political rise, like the growth of government secrecy, was tied to an increasing Cold War emphasis on national security. McCarthy prompted newspapers to change their practices even as most journalists shared his distrust of communism and the Soviet Union.

Indeed, the nation's newspapers, both before and after World War II, reflected the anti-Communist consensus that dominated the United States. Central to this view were a virulent hatred of communism, faith in the superiority of capitalism over other political systems, and a deep distrust of the Soviet Union and its satellites. Such a worldview had its roots in the anticommunism that followed World War I, deepening first in the world crises of the 1930s and 1940s and then in the Cold War years. Anticommunism was particularly receptive to publishers of most daily newspapers, pro-business by disposition and distrustful of any threat to laissez-faire capitalism, including many of the reforms of the New Deal.

The newspaper challenges of covering the political developments of the 1950s and 1960s, then, can only be understood against the backdrop of Cold War events. Journalists did not respond to McCarthyism (or indeed to other Cold War developments to be described in subsequent chapters) in a vacuum. Postwar developments made communism and the Soviet Union very considerable threats to US security. After a few short years as a U.S. ally, the Soviet Union moved quickly to bring eastern Europe under its control in the late 1940s. It cut off ground transportation into Berlin, necessitating the Berlin Airlift of 1948–1949. And in 1949 the Soviet Union shocked Americans by exploding its own atom bomb, fueling suspicions that Soviet spies had stolen American secrets. No less surprising was the Communists' rise to power in China following a lengthy civil war, leading to questions of who in the US government might be to blame. When the Korean War broke out, World War III seemed imminent.[58]

That daily newspapers reflected the anticommunism of their day is not surprising. By and large, daily newspapers were, after all, politically conservative institutions whose editorial pages reflected the pro-business sentiments of their publishers. *Editor & Publisher* magazine's survey of presidential endorsements shows that only once in the twenty years following World War II, in 1964, did more newspapers endorse the Democratic presidential candidate rather than the Republican one. In particular, the Hearst chain, as well as virulently conservative newspapers such as Robert R. McCormick's *Chicago Tribune*, were staunchly anti-Communist and anti-New Deal, with their columnists often equating one with the other.[59]

McCarthy would prove a formidable challenge to the nation's editors throughout the early 1950s, from his infamous speech in Wheeling, West Virginia, on February 9, 1950, to his censure by his fellow US senators in 1954. Jack Anderson and Ronald W. May, two critics of McCarthy and his anti-Communist crusade, summarized in a 1952 book the essential dilemma that the senator's charges posed to newspapers. They imagined the editor of an afternoon newspaper, worried in the last few minutes before deadline about what to place on page one. Then, the latest charge leveled by McCarthy arrives on the wire. At last, the editor had his lead page one story.

There, in a nutshell, you have 99 percent of the reason for Joe McCarthy's success. You can discount his personal ambition: that may have started the McCarthy flywheel, but it was the press that kept the wheel turning.... Any way you slice it, it adds up to the same thing: if Joe McCarthy is a political monster, then the press has been his Dr. Frankenstein.[60]

Anderson and May's view of McCarthy as "a political monster" was by no means unanimous among journalists. But the two expressed a common sentiment in the nation's newsrooms: that McCarthy's newfound political power owed much to the publicity the nation's newspapers lavished upon him. There was little doubt, *Washington Post* editorial writer Alan Barth said at the height of McCarthy's power, that most newspapers' unquestioning coverage "serves Senator McCarthy's partisan political purposes much more than it serves the purposes of the press, the interest of truth."[61] McCarthy's masterful ability to stay in the nation's headlines delighted his allies and confounded his enemies and reflected his skill at manipulating the news media. Journalists, increasingly aware of the difficulty of proving many of McCarthy's charges of Communist infiltration in the State Department, the Army, and the press, soon felt trapped by the journalistic conventions that required them to report every charge, no matter how outrageous.[62]

McCarthy had indeed manipulated the news media skillfully. Particularly in the beginning of his climb to national prominence, reporters were willing to cooperate because he was news. "McCarthy was a dream story," remembered Willard Edwards, who covered the senator in Washington for the *Chicago Tribune*. "I wasn't off page one for four years."[63] McCarthy, gregarious and cooperative, was helpful to reporters, often providing tips to those in need of a story. Sometimes, he even telephoned government officials to fish for information while reporters listened in on the extension.[64]

Significantly, McCarthy knew newspapers' and wire services' deadlines and timed his public releases for maximum exposure. Often he would call a morning press conference only to announce the scheduling of an afternoon press conference, reaping double the publicity in the process. "If, as is often the case, he has nothing of news value to announce, he has at least profited by the afternoon headlines," observed correspondent Richard H. Rovere of the *New Yorker* in 1950.[65] *Milwaukee Journal* editor Wallace Lomoe complained that McCarthy was "a sideshow barker" in dealing with the press. "He can get three stories instead of one. First he drops a hint. Then he gives out a name. Third, he gives out his version of what the name said or did. And the press carries all three."[66]

McCarthy's technique of leveling charge and counter-charge left reporters little time to confirm his allegations. "He has always kept one sensation ahead of his trackers," wrote *Christian Science Monitor* correspondent Richard L. Strout a few months after McCarthy's speech at Wheeling. "He has blanketed replies with fresh attacks." The freshly leveled charge, as Strout put it, "always has the head start" and overshadows any repudiation of earlier attacks.[67]

Journalistic conventions of newsworthiness and objectivity also helped McCarthy. His statements were automatically considered news because of his status as a US senator, and convention required journalists to report them objectively no matter how preposterous his charges might seem to them. "My own impression is that he was a demagogue, but what could I do?" recalled Bob Baskin of the *Dallas Morning News*. "I had to report— and quote—McCarthy. That's all I could do. How do you say in the middle of your story 'This is a lie'? The press is supposedly neutral. You write what the man says."[68]

The McCarthy story both shook journalists' faith in objectivity and pointed to a need for better reporting. But what were newspapers to do about McCarthy, then? How were they supposed to present "the whole truth"? Some journalists believed that nothing at all should be done, that McCarthy's status as a US senator made him a bona fide newsmaker whose views should be published, and objectively reported at that, without elaboration. Other journalists faced a dilemma in reporting McCarthy—how to cover him adequately without promoting him personally or trampling on the rights of those he accused. Editors and publishers across the country pursued different ways of solving this dilemma.

A very few newspapers simply withheld news dealing with charges of communism. The *Claremont* (N.H.) *Daily Eagle*, for example, announced in its columns in 1951 that it was not releasing a list of prominent Americans named by the House Un-American Activities Committee as having been involved in a Communist peace initiative. The newspaper declared that it was withholding the accusations because of the committee's record for making unsubstantiated charges.[69] For the same reason, it had refused to print any news about McCarthy for eight or ten months in 1950, finally relenting out of concerns that readers were being denied the news. "It wasn't fair to them," recalled *Daily Eagle* publisher Melvin Wax. "A newspaper can't put its head in the sand."[70]

At the *Christian Science Monitor*, editors tried to avoid overplaying McCarthy's charges. In 1953, the board of directors of the *Christian Science Monitor*, published in Boston and circulated nationally, expressed concern to the newspaper's editors that McCarthy was using the press solely to obtain publicity for running for office. Accordingly, the board proposed that the *Monitor* "desist from lending itself to such a purpose by omitting [McCarthy's] name from headlines and from copy where the name of [his] committee can be substituted." The board also proposed that the newspaper minimize its use of the word "McCarthyism" on the grounds that Mary Baker Eddy, the founder both of Christian Science and of the *Monitor*, would not have approved. The board's suggestions were carried out. *Monitor* editors, who had been considering such actions on their own, agreed that "McCarthyism" was a dubious term and should be avoided, except in quotations. Editors also consented to exercise caution in using McCarthy's name in headlines and in placing stories about him on the front page. "In addition we should avoid build-ups for Senator McCarthy," *Monitor* editor Erwin D. Canham directed his top editors in a memorandum. "Without deviating from absolutely objective news standards, let us do what we can to avoid excessive promotion— either positive or negative—for the junior senator from Wisconsin."[71]

Despite their concerns about his tactics, even publishers of liberal newspapers wanted to treat McCarthy fairly. Underplaying his charges, publishers feared, might help the enemy, the Communists. Joseph Pulitzer II, the publisher of the *St. Louis Post-Dispatch*, told his editors in 1953 that although he despised McCarthy and his methods, many *Post-Dispatch* readers believed deeply in the senator's anti-Communist crusade. Accordingly, the newspaper's McCarthy coverage, Pulitzer said, should be fair and generous to McCarthy while supplying readers the facts they needed to judge him.[72] The publisher had a continuous disagreement with his editorial page editor, Irving Dilliard, over Dilliard's persistent criticism of McCarthy's abuses of civil liberties. Pulitzer did not want criticism of McCarthy to undermine the newspaper's anti-Communist stance.[73]

Most often, newspapers solved their dilemma by turning to greater use of interpretive writing. At the nation's most influential journalistic institutions—the large metropolitan dailies and the AP—the McCarthy phenomenon accelerated the trend toward interpretation that was already underway in the postwar years. The McCarthy story seemed to embody the kind of complex news story that needed to be explained to readers. Among the dailies, the trend toward interpretation was seen primarily in larger newspapers that had their own Washington correspondents and at journals that tended to be skeptical of McCarthy's charges. The trend was widely noted at editors' meetings and at press association meetings, and while many editors agreed that more interpretation was necessary, they interpreted that necessity and carried it out in different ways.

At the *Denver Post*, a memorandum instructed the staff to take special care in reporting "loose charges, irresponsible utterances and character assassination by spokesmen, official or otherwise," noted the *Post*'s managing editor, Ed Dooley, in 1953. The memo, written by editor-publisher

E. Palmer Hoyt, told reporters and editors to evaluate the source of the charges and to consider withholding the story until proof and the victim's response could be obtained. Reporters should ask themselves whether they knew the charges to be false, and then to explain any reasonable doubt in their articles. The memo represented an expanded effort "to try and get all the facts," Dooley said.[74] Editors were also told to take special care that headlines were not biased. One historian of the *Post* said the McCarthy period was "[p]erhaps the finest hour for Hoyt's *Post* in the eyes of professional journalists."[75]

The foremost advocate of interpretation was the *New York Times*. Publisher Arthur Hays Sulzberger believed that interpretive analyses were necessary to understand a complex world. But he believed that interpretive pieces should be separated from news articles, which should be objective. "Despite everything I have said about the need for interpretation of the news, it does not take the place of the factual news report," he told journalism educators in 1952. "It is supplementary and, essential as it is, it is dangerous if not watched and done correctly within rigid limits. The balance between interpretation and opinion is delicate and it must be preserved."[76]

Many reporters and editors had concrete suggestions as to how to better report McCarthy using interpretive methods. Dozier C. Cade, a former reporter for the *Atlanta Journal* and a teacher at Northwestern University, suggested in 1952 that newspapers should play down unsubstantiated accusations and expose untruths in such stories by investigating them before publication. Without such innovations, he said, the McCarthy "witch-hunters" would continue to stifle self-expression. "The press should lead the fight for a free country and a free world," he said.[77] Melvin Mencher, a reporter at the *Albuquerque Journal*, suggested in *Nieman Reports* in 1953 that newspapers should require McCarthy to submit advance copies of his speeches with supporting documents to allow reporters time to check them for accuracy. Newspapers should also put victims' responses to the charges in the lead paragraph of their news articles, Mencher said. The next demagogue to follow McCarthy would have equal opportunity to take advantage of the press without such changes, Mencher said.[78]

Nieman Reports was a leader in urging the expansion of interpretive reporting, encouraging the trend by often printing articles about the subject. Louis M. Lyons, curator of the Nieman Foundation and a veteran reporter for newspapers in Boston and elsewhere, applauded the trend. He opposed McCarthy's methods and believed reporters had an obligation to set the record straight concerning his allegations. "Who but a newspaperman can show you the record?" Lyons told a Newspaper Guild audience in 1953. "If a politician distorts it, the newspaperman needs to straighten it out for the reader."[79]

Lyons, a perceptive observer of newspapers and reporting practices who was active in the Nieman program through the early 1960s, believed McCarthy's rise led to the rapid spread of interpretive reporting. The McCarthy era, he said in 1971, was a "dim period" for the press, when objective reporting was proven to be shallow reporting. He credited some newspapers in particular with investigating McCarthy's charges, notably the *Washington Post, New York Times, Baltimore Sun,* and *Milwaukee Journal.* Most newspapers in the McCarthy era, he recalled, relied heavily upon the wire services for their news about McCarthy and his charges. Few fought him.[80]

The wire services, and the AP in particular, were a battleground for editors as they wrestled with the McCarthy story. The wire services were especially vulnerable to the senator's methods in two ways. First, their intense competition pushed reporters to get newsworthy copy onto the wires quickly, often without a response to McCarthy's charges. Second, wire services faced intense pressure to file inoffensive, straightforward copy that would please a variety of newspapers with disparate political views. Disputes about McCarthy within the AP from 1950 to 1953 illustrate both the concerns that he raised among journalists and the trend toward interpretation to which those concerns contributed.

In 1950, William T. Evjue, editor and publisher of the *Madison* (WI) *Capital-Times,* an anti-McCarthy newspaper, complained in a letter to the AP that the wire service was exhibiting right-wing bias by playing up McCarthy's stories unquestioningly.[81] He had complained, to cite one example, that the AP had distributed a picture of McCarthy on the front steps of the U.S. Capitol posing with a broom sent to him by constituents for use in sweeping the government clean of Communist influence. The caption on the photograph accepted McCarthy's assumption, Evjue said, that there indeed was Communist infiltration into the government.[82]

Other editors complained, however, that the AP was anti-McCarthy. In 1950 Charles A. Hazen, editor of the *Shreveport* (LA) *Times,* filed a sixty-six-page report with the Associated Press management alleging fifty-eight instances of left-wing bias within the wire service, with most of the complaints involving McCarthy. With Hazen's charges, the AP now stood accused of bias by both sides in the volatile debate. "Thus we have one sincere editor accusing the AP of being flagrantly anti-McCarthy and another sincere editor accusing the AP of being flagrantly pro-McCarthy," V.M. Newton, Jr., of the *Tampa Tribune* summarized the situation before the APME in 1950. Still other editors had taken a different position, he said. Many had complained that the AP "is too timid, frightened at the very thought of being accused of partiality, and utterly bound by a too rigid adherence to the principle of objectivity."[83]

Newton was chairman of the APME Domestic News Committee, which investigated both Evjue's and Hazen's charges and found no willful bias on the part of the wire service. He said that he believed the AP's coverage of McCarthy sometimes showed incompetence—occasional carelessness and incomplete reporting—but not bias. Hazen's accusations of left-wing bias were especially disturbing, Newton said, because they pointed to "a general lack of initiative, due mainly to a rigid adherence to a too narrow and frustrating definition of objectivity, which shackles enterprise and leaves many questions unanswered and truth unsought."[84]

In both 1950 and 1952, the AP's Washington News Committee recommended that the wire service use more background articles to get at the truth involving McCarthy. The executive editor of AP, Alan Gould, reiterated in 1952 that AP reporters had latitude to interpret the news, meaning that they were allowed to appraise the cause and effect of news developments and to state as facts—without attribution—what they knew to be true from their own experience and observations. He said that interpretive writing was encouraged "assuming that certain safeguards are established to preserve the fundamental objectivity of the AP news report."[85]

Many, but not all, AP editors were convinced of the need for interpretation. Charles H. Hamilton of the *Richmond News Leader* complained that in its zeal to interpret the news the AP was introducing opinion into the news columns. "I firmly believe there is no place for 'think pieces' on the AP wire," he said. "A fact needs no defense." Warden Woolard of the *Los Angeles Examiner* decried "so-called interpretive writing" and proposed a resolution in 1952 requiring that any complaints about abuses of the practice come before the entire membership for action. The resolution died, ending the debate over interpretation within the wire service.[86]

The McCarthy story both encouraged the trend toward interpretation and contributed to the growing breach between press and government. McCarthy was a constant critic of journalists, heaping abuse on what he called "the left-wing press." He "concentrated his attacks upon those newspapers he knew were opposing him," concluded Edwin R. Bayley, who covered the senator as a reporter for the *Milwaukee Journal* and who later wrote a book about McCarthy's press relations.[87] In particular, McCarthy carried on running feuds with the *Milwaukee Journal* and the *Madison* (WI) *Capital-Times*, the largest papers that opposed him in his home state. The *Journal*, lukewarm for McCarthy in his 1946 Senate race, grew steadily more critical in his first term and later exposed his lies about his military record. McCarthy had falsely claimed to have suffered war wounds and had exaggerated his battle experience. In response, he frequently ridiculed the newspaper and even urged an advertiser boycott of it.[88] He also urged a boycott against the *Capital-Times*, whose editor was one of McCarthy's harshest critics and which had unearthed his failure to pay taxes on stock income.[89] McCarthy's antinewspaper campaign also included the *Washington Post, Portland Oregonian,* and *Christian Science*

Monitor, all of which were critical of him, as well as individual reporters and newspaper columnists who attacked him.[90]

McCarthy's feud with the *New York Post* and its editor, James Wechsler, seemed to enlarge the crack in the press-government relationship most substantially. As part of his Senate investigation into alleged Communist influences in books in U.S. State Department libraries, McCarthy called Wechsler before his committee on April 24 and May 5, 1953. The pretext was Wechsler's background, particularly his membership as a youth in the Young Communist League and whether books he had written that were now in Department libraries manifested Communist influences. Wechsler agreed to answer McCarthy's questions, saying that he feared that McCarthy would distort his stand if he refused. McCarthy asked about the *Post*'s editorial policies and the background of its editorial employees, including the editor's. Wechsler told McCarthy's committee that he had left the Young Communist League in 1937 and had since been an ardent anti-Communist, which was true. He said he believed his appearance before the committee was intended solely to intimidate editors who had criticized McCarthy. "I regard this inquiry as a clear invasion of what used to be considered the newspaper's right to act and function independently," he told the committee. "I am hopeful that there will be voices raised by newspapers throughout the country in protest against this inquiry."[91]

Indeed, a number of newspapers and journalists criticized McCarthy after Wechsler's appearance. Criticism was most often found in newspapers that had opposed McCarthy. "In fact, in my view, far and away the most serious danger to American newspapers today lies in the success of such strong-arm politicians as McCarthy," said John B. Oakes, *New York Times* editorial writer.[92] The *Washington Post* decried McCarthy's "star chamber" treatment of Wechsler and said that while he was not intimidated by it, others might be.[93] The *New York Times* editorialized that McCarthy's obvious purpose was to intimidate the *New York Post* and that the committee's effort "gets very close to an infringement of one of America's basic freedoms."[94]

An ASNE committee, at Wechsler's request, investigated McCarthy's hearing on the *Post* to determine if it amounted to an infringement of the press. A majority of the divided committee found that it did not.[95] The committee, and a panel of newspaper editors who appeared on the television show *Meet the Press* in May 1953, believed that no press rights were violated since Wechsler's newspaper remained free to print the news afterward. *New York Times* political columnist Arthur Krock said he agreed with the panel of editors, who were "unanimously bearish on any contention that these actions infringed on the freedom of the press." He said that Wechsler's repeated statements that he refused to be intimidated weakened his arguments that free press rights were violated.[96]

It was television, not newspapers, that finally did in McCarthy. His popularity plummeted after his televised hearings into alleged Communist infiltration into the military in 1954. Beginning in 1953, Edward R. Murrow had used his CBS television documentary *See It Now* to question McCarthy's methods. Murrow believed he had waited far too long to publicly question the senator, but the program was nonetheless the most widely publicized media criticism of the senator. "I ain't exactly a pioneer in this thing, you know," Murrow told a colleague.[97] The U.S. Senate censured McCarthy in 1954, and he died a broken man three years later.

The McCarthy years accelerated trends already well underway by the early 1950s. Press-government relations had begun to deteriorate in the late 1940s as increasing government secrecy in the Cold War required journalists to lobby for non-military public information that previously had been accessible to them. Truman and Eisenhower's security orders widened the breach between press and government. This fissure was evident but not great, as journalists remained respectful of government's security interests in military information. Indeed, journalists often worried that they were too respectful of government. The press-government breach would not reach great proportions until the early 1960s.

The trend toward interpretation demonstrated the changing press-government relationship. Government was now so complex that objective journalism could no longer explain it. McCarthy's mastery of the press illustrated both the greater need for interpretation and newspapers' difficulty in coming to terms with meeting this increased need. Events later in the 1950s would further challenge newspapers to change their methods of gathering and presenting the news.

Chapter 4

The Press and Television, 1948–1960

Television grew rapidly in the early and middle 1950s, presenting newspapers with a new competitor both for advertising revenue and for consumers' time. While the continued prosperity of newspapers seemed to minimize the threat of the new medium at first, publishers and editors took greater notice of television's competition for advertising and newsgathering as the 1950s wore on. Television's potency as a rival became clearer just as publishers were growing increasingly concerned with steadily rising costs and narrowing profit margins. By decade's end, television's vast audiences had forced newspapers to adjust to a new media marketplace.

While television would ultimately be one of the greatest competitors to newspapers in the years following World War II, print journalists were slow to come to terms with it, particularly in the early postwar years when television seemed to affect newspapers only minimally. Especially in the late 1940s, television posed little threat to newspapers. Publishers and editors were confident that they could come to terms with television just as they had with radio in previous decades. "Fifty-four million buyers of newspapers prove every day that newspapers are indispensable to the people," boasted Frank Tripp, publisher of the Elmira, New York, newspapers and general manager of the Gannett newspaper chain, in a 1948 column. "In the face of every development which bade fair to harm them, newspapers have risen to an all-time high in readership, and continue to climb." Television would prove a greater threat to magazines and to radio than to newspapers, he predicted.[1]

With newspapers enjoying a postwar boom, the few television stations on the air seemed more a curiosity than a competitor in the late 1940s. The prosperous newspaper business, predicted *New York Daily News* executive editor Richard W. Clarke in 1947, could easily meet any news-gathering challenge from television. Print journalism, after all, seemed "far more fascinating, far more varied, and offers far greater possibility of financial reward" than ever. But Clarke added that newspaper companies were nonetheless wise to hedge their bets and buy into their competitor. Newspapers owned six of the fifteen television stations broadcasting in 1947.[2]

The earliest television attempts at presenting the news certainly provided little cause for alarm among print journalists. In the 1940s and 1950s, television stations and networks put little effort into covering day-to-day, routine news. Television news was in its infancy. "Pictorial news is great when it is great," said TV news director Paul W. White of San Diego, California, in 1953. "But more frequently it ranges from the dull to the mediocre—and even more frequently it's painfully slow and inadequate." Television, he said, turned in only a "lackluster performance" in explaining the day's in-depth news.[3] Critics dismissed early television news, as Sig Mickelson of CBS News put it in 1957, as "a hybrid monstrosity derived from newspapers, radio news, and news-reels, which inherited none of the merits of its ancestors."[4]

Network newscasts began in 1948, when NBC launched *The Camel Newsreel Theatre*, hosted by John Cameron Swayze. The weekday program lasted just ten minutes at first but was expanded to fifteen minutes soon after its debut. Later in 1948 CBS launched *The CBS-TV News*, a fifteen-minute program anchored by Douglas Edwards. ABC and DuMont also began news broadcasts in the late 1940s. The networks employed correspondents and film crews in a few major cities but other-wise depended upon stringers and newsreel companies for film. The bulky cameras used in newsreels proved ill-suited to newsgathering, a difficulty that lingered until the late 1950s when stations began using portable 16-mm film. Videotape machines were finally developed in 1956, allowing tape-delay of national newscasts. As its pioneers halt-ingly adapted radio and newsreel techniques and technology, television news reporting developed slowly.[5]

The documentary series *See It Now* was one of the rare programs that emphasized original reporting. Its producers, Edward R. Murrow and Fred W. Friendly, brought the skills they had honed in radio to the new form of journalism, though at first they contracted with news-reel companies for film. *See It Now*, launched in 1951, covered a wide range of subjects. Crews traveled to Korea in 1952 to show viewers how American soldiers were celebrating Christmas. It profiled Tennessee Senator Estes Kefauver. And beginning in 1953, *See It Now* examined

Senator Joseph R. McCarthy and his methods of investigating alleged Communist influences in the government and armed forces.[6]

Through the 1940s and 1950s, the networks concentrated their news coverage not on newscasts but on special events, a strength of the young medium. Print journalists ridiculed some of these early, crude efforts, as when memorial services commemorating Abraham Lincoln's birthday were telecast February 12, 1946. The television industry had hyped the event because it was to be broadcast over a network of several stations, but it lacked editing and appeared unprofessional, as when "some dumb cluck" walked in front of the camera, complained *Editor & Publisher* reviewer Jerry Walker. Television had wasted a day's effort on an event that would have rated only a picture and a caption in the newspaper. "The big show fell flat," Walker concluded.[7]

In 1948, the major networks televised both the Democratic and Republican presidential conventions on the few stations on the air. Both political parties had chosen Philadelphia as their convention site out of consideration for network television's technical requirements, and the conventions were broadcast to fourteen stations in thirteen eastern states. The convention attracted an audience of 10 million, a sizable achievement given the technical limitations of the networks and the youth of television.[8] Newspaper correspondents at the convention regarded the TV cameras as an amusing but harmless nuisance. The earliest live broadcasts, critics noted, did not seem particularly informative. But the bulky equipment and bright lights of the television crews had threatened to turn convention press conferences into "Hollywood side shows," lamented *Chicago Sun-Times* columnist Robert E. Kennedy after the Democratic National Convention. "The correspondents are being used for props and for free, too," he said. "But at the same time the gimmick is so new that they go along against their better judgment."[9]

But the "gimmick" of television had a vastly expanding audience in the early and middle 1950s. From 1952, the year the Federal Communications Commission resumed issuing television broadcast licenses following a four-year freeze, through 1957, the number of television stations jumped from 108 stations to 544.[10] By 1957, stations were operating in 317 US cities, and sales of television sets skyrocketed throughout the decade. In 1954, 1955, and 1956, more than seven million sets were manufactured each year in the United States alone.[11] In 1957, 78 percent of all American homes included a television set. Television viewing increased throughout the 1950s, reaching five and a half hours a day in the average home by the end of the decade.[12] As television viewing grew, so did television advertising receipts. The medium that had taken in only $57.8 million in advertising revenues nationwide in 1949 grew by 1962 to take in $1.74 billion.[13] Between 1949 and 1955, television's advertising volume increased an average of

61.5 percent a year, leveling off to a 6.3 percent annual increase between 1956 and 1962.[14]

Newspapers, by contrast, were having a prosperous but not spectacular decade. The number of daily newspapers held steady while circulation continued to hit new highs through much of the 1950s, reaching a high of 58,881,746 by 1960. However, yearly circulation increases were usually quite small—from one to two percent—and total circulation of all news-papers actually declined in the years 1952 and 1958, reflecting dips in the national economy.[15] Total daily newspaper advertising revenue was very healthy, climbing to $3.23 billion in 1956, dwarfing the $1.2 billion spent on television the same year.[16] Television had indeed cut deeply into news-papers' national advertising revenues, but newspapers' commanding lead in overall receipts seemed to diminish the upstart's potential advertising threat, particularly in the first half of the 1950s. Television had also bene-fited newspapers in two ways—directly through advertisements for TV programs and TV sets, and indirectly through newspaper ownership of TV stations. By 1958, newspapers would own one-fourth of all commercial television stations.[17]

Television's on-the-spot coverage of special events came into its own in the 1950s and demonstrated television's power to a degree that gave many print journalists pause. Even before the Kefauver hearings or the national tour of General Douglas MacArthur on his return from Korea—both televised in 1951 to rapt national audiences—print journalists had marveled at television's unique power to transfix audiences. When three-year-old Kathy Fiscus fell into a well in Southern California in April 1949, Los Angeles television station KTLA kept reporters on the scene for twenty-eight hours as rescuers tried to save her. The story, transmitted to television stations in the Far West in a primitive network hookup and later picked up by stations nationwide, impressed newspaper reporters with its drawing power. "I haven't seen anything like this since the end of World War II," observed a telephone operator for the *Salt Lake City Tribune*. "Even tiny children, almost too young to talk, are calling for news about Kathy."[18] Los Angeles newspaperman Will Fowler remembered the story years later as a turning point for television news. "This was the first time that the cathode ray tube had out-and-out scooped the newspapers," he said. "There was no argument, not even a rebuttal."[19]

The US Senate hearings conducted in 1951 by Senator Estes Kefauver's Crime Investigating Committee provided a similar demonstration of tele-vision's prowess. At times the hearings into the problem of organized crime captured 100 percent of the television viewing audience.[20] The hearings transformed television overnight "from everybody's whipping boy" to a public benefactor, wrote the editors of *Broadcasting* magazine after the hearings. "Its camera eye opened the public's."[21] Print journalists took notice. The melodramatic hearings had brought the shadowy world of organized crime to life. "The last week has demonstrated with awesome vividness what television can do to enlighten, to educate and to drive home a lesson," wrote *New York Times* television critic Jack Gould.[22] John W. Bloomer, managing editor of the *Columbus* (GA) *Ledger*, said the hearings "got a reaction that stunned even the most enthusiastic of the television drum beaters. TV suddenly came of age as a medium for dissemination of news."[23]

Similarly, the triumphant return of General Douglas MacArthur to the United States after his firing by President Truman attracted a large television audience. An estimated 44 million people watched some part of his four-day tour.[24] "We'll follow MacArthur from the time he arrives until he's down to his shorts in his hotel room," one television executive said, and the TV crews did almost that.[25] Cameras followed MacArthur's arrival in Hawaii, his stop in San Francisco, his triumphant Manhattan ticker tape parade, and his address to Congress. *Time* magazine opined that "the MacArthur show was TV's biggest and best job to date."[26]

But MacArthur's congressional speech also demonstrated a benefit to newspapers of television's live coverage of special events: such events seemed to increase, not decrease, newspaper circulation. The *Atlanta Constitution*'s Ralph McGill, in Washington for the American Society of Newspaper Editors (ASNE) convention, conducted a spot check of area newspapers after the address and found that street sales were up for every newspaper.[27] Televised news events seemed to increase readers' curiosity about those events, pushing them to buy the newspaper to read about what they had just seen. "Sensational news over radio and TV brings a flood of inquiries into our office," reported Ralph Anderson of the *Eau Claire* (WI) *Leader* at an editors' meeting in 1953.[28] Likewise, newspapers across the country consistently reported a boost in sales after televised special events. The *New York Daily News*, for example, sold 100,000 more copies than usual the day after the televised coronation of Britain's Queen Elizabeth II in 1953. "It was nothing short of sensational," the *Daily News* reported.[29] Print journalists took such news as proof that television and newspapers were not direct competitors. "They are two media of information, just as bourbon and water are two liquids," noted *Fort Worth Star-Telegram* editor Phil North in 1951, "and as many editors know so well, neither will replace the other but they are fine together."[30]

"I do not believe," wrote *New York Times* publisher Arthur Hays Sulzberger in 1951, "that television has decreased our circulation at all. If anything, it has stimulated it." He said that serious newspapers like the *Times*, which emphasized news rather than entertainment, had the least to fear from television. The *Times*' executive editor, Turner Catledge, agreed. "We do not regard TV as a direct competitor of the type of newspaper we publish," he wrote a colleague in 1951. But both Sulzberger and

Catledge agreed that television might threaten those journals that relied upon entertainment and features to attract readers. Their audience would be lost to their electronic rival, a far more effective and compelling entertainment medium.[31]

Other publishers and editors took comfort in surveys and studies showing that newspapers suffered far less from television's rapid rise than did other media. "As for the reading of newspapers and magazines, the impact of the television medium apparently is so negligible as to be significant only to a statistician," wrote Gould of the *New York Times* in 1949.[32] NBC interviewed 7,500 people in Fort Wayne, Indiana, and found that radio listening had fallen by 50 percent and magazine reading by 40 percent six months after the introduction of television in the early 1950s. But newspaper reading had declined far less, by only 18 percent, from thirty-nine to thirty-two minutes a day.[33] Other studies showed even less impact on newspaper reading time. Media researcher Leo Bogart concluded in 1958 that newspaper reading was protected from substantial encroachment by its importance as a local medium that readers habitually turned to.[34]

An editors' panel at the 1951 ASNE convention assessed "The Challenge of Radio and Television to Newspapers." Most panelists agreed that coverage of Kefauver and MacArthur had demonstrated television's power but doubted that newspapers' circulation and news dominance were threatened. "As a competitor in news, apart from Kefauver, apart from these special events...I don't think television is nearly as serious a threat as radio was," *New York Herald Tribune* television columnist John Crosby said. Other editors, however, were troubled, saying television should be considered a direct competitor and treated accordingly. "Yes, the battle is on, whether we like to admit it or not," said L.L. Winship of the *Boston Globe*. "It is a battle over the time it takes to watch television and the time it takes to read a newspaper. It's a battle for the revenue we need to keep our newspapers free and prosperous."[35]

As television's audience and influence increased throughout the 1950s, so did print journalists' respect for their competitor; newspapers would clearly have to adapt. Television's increasing influence was evident in the medium's coverage of the 1952 and 1956 national political conventions, which TV cameras dominated. The audiences for the televised events were far larger than in 1948, and the massive crews the networks used to staff the conventions seemed for the first time to intrude on turf previously reserved for delegates and for print and radio reporters. More than 60 million people watched the 1952 Republican National Convention, the largest audience for a live television event to that date. The major broadcast networks—ABC, CBS, NBC, and DuMont—sent crews of 300 broadcasters and technicians to the International Amphitheater in Chicago, selected as the convention site because it was the only hall in town big enough for the television equipment and cables. *Newsweek* magazine dubbed it the "television convention."[36]

After covering the convention, some reporters were despondent at television's advantage over the printed word. *New Orleans Item* correspondent Thomas Sancton reported that print reporters "have come up against a machine that scoops them automatically, and can never itself be scooped." Newspaper reporters might still be needed to provide depth reporting and background, of course, but they seemed downright irrelevant at national events television covered live. "I had one brief memorable insight into the impact of TV on the news business," Sancton recalled of covering the convention. "Standing in a massed group of reporters at an Eisenhower press conference, two TV receiving sets carried his image as he spoke—and also, in the background, our notebooks and moving pencils as we wrote."[37] The *Manchester Guardian*'s correspondent, Alistair Cooke, was equally impressed. "An honest reporter can only admit that the incomparable mobility of the television camera has beaten him to an impotent standstill," he said.[38]

Gould, the *New York Times'* television critic, wrote after the Republican convention that it had marked the maturation of television as a news medium. He found that television coverage had provided viewers with insight into the workings of democracy in a personal, immediate way. Television had complemented, but not replaced, the in-depth coverage of newspapers. "Millions had the best seats in the house for a show that lived up to its advance billing," Gould said.[39] Television's performance in the 1956 conventions was equally impressive. More than 100 million people saw some part of the conventions, prompting broadcasters to claim that the public had now become accustomed to a new kind of pictorial journalism.[40]

At the conventions as elsewhere, print journalists resented the intrusion of TV cameras into news events and were dismayed at television's rapid acceptance by newsmakers. The technical requirements and glamour of television gave TV correspondents the upper hand with some sources, particularly politicians. Much to print journalists' dismay, public men and women soon learned to like the new electronic medium for the control it gave them over their public utterances. McGill of the *Atlanta Constitution* complained at the 1956 Democratic National Convention that only the most famous newspaper writers could get any interviews because the politicians had much rather be on television. As one CBS producer put it, "The smart politicians just automatically seem to give us priority."[41] Walter Trohan, a veteran reporter for the *Chicago Tribune*, also noticed this phenomenon, which he said made it harder and harder for print reporters to do their jobs. "Reporters find their sources preferring to spill their secrets or make their observations over the airwaves," Trohan recalled years later.[42]

Television's growing importance to public affairs was beyond doubt, and its rising influence seemed to come at the expense of the print medium. President Dwight D. Eisenhower noted in 1955 that television was becoming more important than newspapers in fostering understanding of public issues. Broadcasting, he said, engaged and involved viewers to a degree that cold print never could. "In many ways therefore the effect of your industry in swaying public opinion, and I think, particularly about burning questions of the moment, may be even greater than the press, although I am sure my friends here of the press will have plenty to criticize in that statement," he said.[43]

Eisenhower had recognized this increasing importance of television in 1953, when he suggested allowing television and newsreel cameras into his presidential press conferences. Print reporters were aghast. *Editor & Publisher* was speaking for many newspaper journalists when it editorialized against the proposal. Its editors said that "to inject television with all its equipment and other handicaps into present White House press conferences would disrupt and alter the institution as we know it."[44] Over the objections of grumbling print reporters, filming was allowed beginning January 19, 1955. Eisenhower's press secretary, James Hagerty, defended the new practice and playfully reminded the print journalists that "we are in the twentieth century—the second part." The cameras did not prove to be disruptive, however, and about two-thirds of the first conference was later shown on film or on television, after the White House approved the content.[45]

To newspaper reporters, television seemed in the 1950s to have taken over the press conference, a venerable institution whose very name reflected the domination of print. Broadcasting first intruded on the press conference in the national political conventions in 1952. "The press conference is an instrument vital to democratic processes and it is being overwhelmed by paraphernalia," complained *New York Times* correspondent James Reston after the Republican National Convention in 1952. Reporters claimed that showoff television correspondents accompanied by bulky cameras had wrecked convention press conferences. The chaos often eliminated the opportunity for important follow-up questions, and the partisan audiences who invariably followed the television cameras violated decorum. Print reporters were now actors in a TV show, with TV reporters asking most of the questions. "It is difficult to pursue your question when someone is insisting on a phony entertainment angle," lamented William S. White of the *New York Times*. A group of print reporters proposed press conference ground rules to permit follow-up questions and forbid partisan audiences, but the proposals went nowhere.[46]

Broadcast coverage of press conferences remained a sore point for newspaper reporters throughout the 1950s. They resented the fact that

their questions at news conferences elicited news that benefited the
television crews, whose reports were then broadcast before the newspapers went to press. To newspaper reporters at least, broadcast journalists
contributed nothing to news conferences except bright lights, softball
questions, and frequent delays. "I look upon them as parasites," one
New Orleans editor said of television reporters in 1957.[47] For a time in
1957, reporters from three of the four Los Angeles newspapers refused to
attend any press conference at which television news crews were present.
They wanted the broadcasters relegated to separate sessions. "They
should handle their own news instead of cashing in on our brains and
experience," said the *Los Angeles Times'* city editor, Bud Lewis.[48] The
impractical proposal for holding separate news conferences never caught
on, however.

As television audiences increased through the 1950s, newspaper
editors and publishers were forced to adjust editorial content to take
television audiences into account. Editors found that television viewing
was changing the expectations that readers brought to their newspapers.
Particularly, they expected newspapers to flesh out the sketchy accounts
seen on television and to cater to interests that television had created. For
example, since readers had seen many sporting events for themselves on
television, sports writers began to write fewer play-by-play accounts in
favor of feature and interpretive articles. Sports editors also began to
increase coverage of sports that were given wider popularity by television, such as boxing and wrestling. *Chicago Herald-American* sports editor
Leo Fischer declared in 1951 that sports fans would buy only the newspaper "that complements what they see on their TV screen."[49] Other
editors agreed. A 1955 survey of 272 editors at Associated Press (AP)
newspapers in forty-six states found that television had created more
"casual" sports readers who were demanding to read more about
what they had already seen. Editors surveyed said they believed that
better, simpler writing and more human interest features were needed
to appeal to this expanding readership.[50]

At the *New York Times*, the nation's leading daily newspaper, editors
were mindful of television coverage in crafting their own coverage of an
event. Robert E. Garst, the *Times'* assistant managing editor, noted in 1956
that the newspaper's reporters regularly monitored television coverage of
a news event to determine what they had missed. "We merely try to give
the reader all the answers to incidents he might have seen on TV," Garst
said.[51] Turner Catledge, the *Times* executive editor, said in 1956 that television had altered both sports and political coverage at the newspaper.
In both areas *Times* reporters were attempting to provide ample details
about what viewers had seen and to supply information about interests
that broadcasting had created. TV broadcasts, he said, had also accelerated an effort at the *Times* to shorten and simplify news articles. "In short,

our view is that TV has opened up new vistas of interest, new areas for coverage, and has suggested methods by which newspapers can actually meet its thrust," he said.[52]

Readers' new ability to witness news firsthand on television had led some to be more critical of what they read in the newspaper. Harry C. Withers of the *Dallas News* complained in 1954 that some readers who had watched the Army-McCarthy hearings on television believed the *News'* coverage was slanted because it omitted some portions of the hearings.[53] The *Washington Star's* Herbert F. Corn noticed the same phenomenon. "The TV viewer assumed a more important role," he said. "He combed the newspaper for that particular portion of the hearing that he had witnessed and we became accountable for the largest array of amateur reporters ever assembled—the entire television audience."[54]

Television also exerted conflicting pressures on editors as to what kinds of news they should publish. On the one hand, television, by pre-empting newspapers' ability to get breaking news first, seemed to encourage the trend toward interpretive reporting, newspapers' apparent strength against their electronic competitor. On the other hand, the entertainment fare that dominated television's schedule threatened to encourage newspapers to print more features to meet the competition. Many editors viewed these conflicting pressures with dismay. *New York Times* Sunday editor Lester Markel, no stranger to overstatement, likened the editors' consternation to an episode of delirium tremens. "American journalism is suffering a severe case of D-T-V's," he declared in 1954. "Some of the shaking and quivering is justified, but there is no excuse whatsoever for the atomic ague now in process." Markel, long an advocate of interpretive articles, said the press could best compete by emphasizing the delivery of detailed news with ample perspective and background.[55]

The immediacy of television, and the promise of color television in years to come, had other effects on newspapers. They began to print more color. While the use of color in newspapers dated to the late nineteenth century, technical improvements after World War II had made it far more practical. "Newspaper color has captured the imagination of both advertisers and newspapers," declared Robert U. Brown of *Editor & Publisher* magazine in 1958. Spurred by demands of national advertisers, by the late 1950s half of all newspapers were printing some spot color, and one-quarter were printing full color, with color most often used in advertising.[56] Forty to fifty newspapers were running news photographs in full color by 1958.[57]

Television also forced newspapers to deliver afternoon editions to readers' homes earlier in the day, before families began their evening television viewing. Delivery changes were necessary because reader surveys, such as those conducted by the American Press Institute (API), found that afternoon newspapers were especially hurt by the rise in television viewing. "So the big battle between television and the newspaper is for the reader's time," said API's Benjamin H. Reese in 1954. George Wise of the *Bloomington* (IN) *Herald-Telephone* believed that many afternoon newspapers were losing that battle. "We have found that with television to turn to," he said in 1954, "people just don't spend as much time with their newspapers."[58] W.C. Todd of the *Gary* (IN) *Post-Tribune* surveyed forty newspapers in 1955 about the effects of television and found that many were changing their deadlines. "With television making its big play between 6:30 and 9:30 p.m.," he said, "it becomes a necessity to get the evening papers in the readers' hands as early as possible."[59]

While some print journalists resented broadcasting's rapid rise, broadcasters also resented criticism from newspapers. *Variety* rounded up broadcasters' complaints in a front-page article in 1955 headlined "Do Newspapers Hate TV?" Television executives said newspapers needed to re-evaluate broadcasting and give it a "better shake" in the news columns. "Too many dailies," *Variety* argued, "are still being ostriches and refuse to face the fact that television today, both as entertainment and in the area of public enlightenment, has achieved a full-blown status."[60] In 1958, NBC president Robert W. Sarnoff decried "print hostility" to television. He said newspapers tended to treat television harshly, both in news coverage and in criticism, because of television's increasing competition with print.[61] Taking note of Sarnoff's criticism, *Editor & Publisher* editor Robert U. Brown declared in 1958 that the newspaper-television honeymoon was finally over.[62]

In the middle and late 1950s, after a decade of watching television grow in influence and advertising, newspaper publishers and editors were much more wary of television. While confident of newspapers' continued dominance in advertising and news, they were now taking television much more seriously as a competitor. Increasing newspaper animosity toward television had been evident for some time. In the mid-1950s some newspapers had refused to print guides to television programming unless stations paid for them as advertising. Newspapers in Nashville, Oklahoma City, and Chico, California, were among those that discontinued free programming guides in 1953 and 1954. The trend was encouraged editorially by *Editor & Publisher*, which argued that newspapers should not give free publicity to a competitor.[63] A television industry survey in 1954 found that stations had to buy the program guides in one-half of the communities surveyed.[64] But the practice faded by the late 1950s as television gained even wider audiences and as many editors came to believe that television, competitor or not, was important to readers. "About twenty years ago we took the same attitude toward radio and started to boycott it," recalled Sam Day of the *New York Journal-American* in 1954. "It got along very well without us."[65]

Publishers—and indeed all media—particularly worried about the growing loss of national advertising to television. Each medium was forced to adjust. Hardest hit was radio, which entered a six-year slump in 1948, the first year of the television explosion. Industry profits plummeted as listeners, advertisers, and the national networks turned their attention to television. Radio revenues dropped from $137.5 million in 1948 to $76 million in 1954. By late in the decade, however, radio's fortunes were reversing, with stations rebuilding programming schedules around music and talk. Typical was KLIF in Dallas, whose formula of Top 40 songs, local news, and heavily publicized promotions set a standard for other stations attempting to reinvent themselves to reconnect with audiences.[66]

Magazines also suffered as a result of the television boom. Since the late nineteenth century, the high-cost, low-profit magazine industry had relied heavily upon national advertising revenues. The introduction of television coincided with rising production costs to devastate the largest general-interest weeklies and monthlies. Profits shrank even as circulations remained high. The Magazine Publishers Association reported that after-tax profits for thirty-five leading magazines plummeted from 8.3 percent in 1946 to 1.4 percent in 1961 before rebounding to 4.1 percent by 1964. Citing soaring production costs and the loss of national advertising, *Collier's* closed down in 1956, one of dozens of national magazines to cease publication in the postwar era.[67]

From the 1950s onward, the magazine industry shifted its emphasis to regional or specialized publications. The highly successful *Sports Illustrated*, introduced in 1954, was a forerunner of this trend. The large newsweeklies—*Time, Newsweek,* and *U.S. News & World Report*—also prospered. *Time's* circulation, for example, reached 2 million in 1956 and increased by more than 100,000 a year through 1964, when it hit 3 million. *Newsweek's* and *U.S. News'* circulation also increased. Time Inc.'s historian determined that the circulation increases reflected "an apparent rekindling of American interest in public affairs, dating," in the *Time* circulation department's view, "from about the time of Kennedy's inauguration."[68]

Even though newspapers remained the leading advertising medium, their share of total advertising revenue continued to drop through the 1950s due to competition from television, radio, and other media. From 45.1 percent of total advertising revenues in 1935, newspapers had dropped to 31 percent of total advertising by 1962, with much of the difference due to national advertising lost to television.[69] While newspapers' local advertising revenues nearly doubled from 1950 to 1960, reaching $2.9 billion, national advertising revenues increased only by half, to $778 million.[70] National advertisers, such as the Detroit automakers, found it much more convenient to place advertisements on national radio and television networks rather than to "deal direct with a lot of pesky hometown newspapers," observed advertising executive Gene Alleman in 1957. Many newspapers lost some of their national automotive advertising beginning in 1956 when Detroit manufacturers began placing ads themselves rather than farming out national advertising budgets to local dealers.[71]

The decline in national advertising revenues particularly hurt very small publications. The experience of publisher O.G. McDavid was typical. He bought a small weekly, the *Wilk-Amite Record* in Gloster, Mississippi, after World War II. "I paid for the newspaper in three years, and I thought that there was never any end to the money that was coming," he recalled years later. But in the mid-1950s he lost the local auto dealer advertising to television and faced a new competitor when a radio station signed on in town. "I was having to work harder and harder to obtain the volume," McDavid said. He sold the paper and moved to Houston.[72]

Television's rapid rise in the 1950s was matched by continued rising costs in the newspaper business. Rising costs had forced some papers to close and others to merge. *Editor & Publisher's* yearly summary of newspaper costs showed that increases in expenses had outpaced increases in revenue in all but two years, 1955 and 1959, in the fifteen years following World War II. Rising newsprint and labor costs explained the majority of cost increases, which steadily eroded newspapers' profit margins and made television seem all the more threatening.[73]

Newspapers responded to the changing advertising market in myriad ways. In 1956, the American Newspaper Publishers Association's Bureau of Advertising launched a campaign to woo back national advertisers lost to television.[74] Many newspapers increased their advertising and promotion budgets to sell themselves better to their communities and advertisers. "Daily newspapers of the country today are spending more money on sales and promotion than in their entire history," declared C.B. Lafromboise, manager of the Washington Newspaper Publishers Association, in 1955.[75] The National Editorial Association (NEA), the trade association of more than 5,000 weekly and small daily newspapers, founded the Weekly Newspaper Representatives, an organization to solicit national advertising on behalf of member newspapers, as a way to regain national accounts lost to the competition.[76]

"Our road ahead won't be easy," said Richard Lloyd Jones, publisher of the *Tulsa Tribune*, in a 1954 speech that summarized newspapers' battle against television and rising costs. "It's going to take real planning, budgeting, and the best of judgment and initiative." He said television was a thorny problem for newspapers, a heavily unionized and static industry selling a product both expensive to produce and difficult to distribute. He noted that 500 employees, 18,000 tons of newsprint, and a fleet of delivery trucks were required to deliver the *Tribune* each day. "At the same time, in television, we see a literal newcomer deliver a picture with voice accompaniment to the same area, with thirty-three employees." Television and rising costs, Jones accurately predicted, would bedevil newspapers for years to come.[77]

Chapter 5

Newspapers and the Civil Rights Movement, 1954–1957

In the early postwar years newspapers struggled with a challenging, continuing news story—black Americans' civil rights struggle in the years before and after the US Supreme Court's decision in *Brown v Board of Education* in 1954. The civil rights story revealed newspapers' profound difficulty in covering social upheaval. Reporters and editors were as slow to come to terms with the civil rights story as they had been with television. The complicated story of long-term societal change would eventually strain relations between northern and southern editors, exacerbate journalists' questions about objectivity, and sharpen newspapers' competition with television news. Moreover, newspapers' treatment of black Americans highlighted their resistance to change. Desegregation would indeed prove a difficult story to tell.

The civil rights story forced mainstream white newspapers to deal with a subject they had long ignored—black Americans. *Brown v Board of Education* finally brought blacks into the pages of the nation's white-owned press. Before *Brown*, blacks seldom merited a mention in most newspapers unless a member of the race had suffered an unusual death or had violated the law. The newspapers that did publish black news took care to publish it in a segregated news section. But in the early postwar years, newspapers' treatment of black Americans had shown some improvement.

Just after World War II, some journals began to drop longstanding policies of identifying blacks by race in news articles. Black leaders had long pushed for this change, arguing that it stigmatized their race and was unfair. Whites, after all, were never singled out and identified as "white" in news copy, but blacks were.[1] The *New York Times* announced in an editorial published August 11, 1946, that it was dropping racial designations. "This may seem like a small thing," the editorialist wrote. "The Negroes don't think so." The new policy, radical enough to merit coverage by *Time* magazine, was to use racial designations only when they served a newsworthy purpose.[2]

At most newspapers, however, black news never made it into the newspaper at all. Ben Bradlee, later the *Washington Post*'s managing editor, had just begun work at the newspaper in 1948 when he volunteered to cover a crime he had heard about on the police radio. "Naw," the night city editor told Bradlee, "that's black." At the *Post* as at other newspapers, Bradlee recalled, "Incidents were routinely not covered because they involved blacks."[3] At the *New Orleans Times-Picayune*, where Ira B. Harkey, Jr., worked before and after World War II, photographers had standing instructions to shoot pictures of whites only. Blacks in crowd photographs were cut or airbrushed out.[4]

Harkey, like a few other liberal and moderate southern editors, challenged some of the prevailing newspaper practices regarding race during his ownership of the *Pascagoula* (MS) *Chronicle*. His egalitarian ideals held that blacks and whites should be treated equitably, and he applied that philosophy to his newspaper. After he bought the *Chronicle*, it began covering more news of the black community and dropped the practice of separating black from white news. Harkey gradually began to give the courtesy title "Mrs." to some prominent black women, and, without telling even his staff, he dropped the Negro tag in virtually all news articles. The policy went unnoticed by the public until a local father was charged with beating his four-year-old stepson in 1950, and the wire services picked up Harkey's stories about the crime. Sympathetic letters flooded the local police and the victim's home until an Associated Press (AP) photographer obtained a picture of the boy, who was black. The show of sympathy halted immediately, and some readers were chagrined. "If you have to write about niggers," one reader told Harkey, "call 'em niggers right up at the top so I don't waste my time reading about 'em." Throughout the 1950s, Harkey unsuccessfully urged his colleagues in the Mississippi press to drop racial tags.[5]

Many southern newspapers did print black news but relegated it to special sections or pages separated from white news. Some produced "colored editions" delivered only to black neighborhoods. The *St. Petersburg Times*, for example, started its "Negro makeover" page in 1939, remaking one newspaper page a week of black news in editions distributed only in black neighborhoods. The special page, not uncommon in the South, was printed daily beginning in 1948.[6] The *Montgomery Advertiser* and the *Alabama Journal* each published separate editions for blacks for more than thirty years, finally discontinuing them in the 1960s because of the extra cost of producing them.[7]

An important factor in coverage of racial news was the racial makeup of the staffs of daily newspapers. Most had virtually all-white staffs. Blacks were rare in both newsrooms and in journalism organizations, though black reporters made a few important inroads into print journalism in the early postwar years. The Nieman program at Harvard University, one of the journalism profession's most prestigious fellowships, selected its first black Nieman fellow, Fletcher Martin of the weekly *Louisville* (KY) *Defender*, in 1946. The following year the US Senate press gallery admitted its first black reporter, Louis R. Lautier of the *Atlanta World*, then the nation's only black daily. The Standing Committee of Correspondents had denied Lautier admittance because he also worked for a black press association, and committee rules required reporters to work exclusively for a daily newspaper. The Senate Rules Committee overruled the correspondents and admitted Lautier anyway. However, the American Society of Newspaper Editors (ASNE)—the nation's most influential organization of newspaper editors—remained all-white well into the 1950s. Society officials said the scarcity of black daily newspapers had limited blacks' opportunity for membership. ASNE members reported in 1955 that no black journalist had ever even applied for admission. A.M. Piper of the *Council Bluffs* (IA) *Nonpareil*, an ASNE veteran, said he'd never seen a black editor at the society's annual convention.[8]

But black reporters found jobs at a few newspapers in the 1950s. The *Milwaukee Journal* hired its first black reporter, Bob Teague, a former star halfback at the University of Wisconsin, to cover sports beginning in 1950. But its city desk did not hire a black worker until 1963.[9] Unusual among southern dailies, the *St. Petersburg Times* hired a full-time black reporter, Calvin Adams, in 1951 and even took the dramatic step of integrating both the drinking fountains and the restrooms in the *Times* newsroom.[10] The *Detroit Free Press* hired Collins George, formerly of the black weekly the *Pittsburgh Courier*, as the newspaper's first black reporter in 1955.[11] Fletcher Martin, the first black Nieman fellow, began work at the *Chicago Sun-Times* in the early 1950s after being turned down by the *Louisville Courier-Journal*, whose city editor had told him that the all-white staff would never tolerate a black reporter.[12] By the mid-1950s, black journalists were working at the *Denver Post, Fort Wayne* (IN) *News-Sentinel, Toledo Blade, Minneapolis Tribune, St. Louis Post-Dispatch, Portland Oregonian*, three newspapers in Chicago, two newspapers in New York, and two of Cleveland's three dailies. But in all, just twenty-one black reporters were at work on white-owned daily newspapers in 1955, according to a study by researchers at Lincoln University in Jefferson City, Missouri. The pioneering black journalists were concentrated at newspapers in the Northeast and Midwest. It would be years before blacks would enter newsrooms in significant numbers.[13]

Despite their thin ranks, black reporters attracted notice for their pioneering coverage of desegregation. Carl T. Rowan of the *Minneapolis Tribune*, for example, won wide praise for a three-week series of articles he wrote about the South in 1951. Ted Poston of the *New York Post*, George Brown of the *Denver Post*, and William Brower of the *Toledo Blade* also did ground-breaking work in the South.[14] But the strain of covering segregation took a heavy toll on some of these journalists, such as Simeon Booker, hired in 1952 by the *Washington Post* as the first black reporter at a capital city daily. "After a year and a half I had to give up," he recalled. "Trying to cover news in a city where even animal cemeteries were segregated overwhelmed me." He quit the *Post* in 1953 and went to work for *Jet*.[15]

The Supreme Court's *Brown v Board of Education* forced newspapers to give blacks more attention on the news pages. The *Brown* case, a consolidation of school desegregation lawsuits in Kansas, South Carolina, Virginia, and Delaware, struck down segregation in public schools as a violation of the equal protection clause of the Fourteenth Amendment. The original *Brown* decision, combined with the court's follow-up decree a year later, transformed school desegregation into what one veteran editor described in 1955 as "the biggest regional story of the century."[16]

A few of the nation's leading newspapers responded admirably to the challenge of covering desegregation, devoting considerable resources to the story. The *New York Times* covered *Brown* in detail from the beginning, publishing ten pages of background and interpretive material on the day of the decision. In 1955, executive editor Turner Catledge dispatched a team of ten reporters on a five-week survey of desegregation efforts in seventeen Deep South and border states and the District of Columbia. The *Times* both undertook extensive efforts to explain the *Brown* decision and supported it editorially.[17]

The *Times* had first assigned a correspondent to cover the South in 1947, when Catledge, a Mississippi native, had tapped Virginia-born John N. Popham to report on the tremendous social change brewing in the region. On his rounds he met with black leaders, college professors, and moderate southern editors.[18] His reputation for hard work and fairness was legendary among newspaper reporters. After his hiring, he set up shop in the Hotel Patten, near the office of the *Chattanooga Times*, also owned by the Sulzberger family. He bought a Dodge coupe, paid for with deductions against his *Times* paycheck, and began a long series of travels across the South, putting 40,000 to 50,000 miles a year on his car. "By now," he wrote Catledge after years of travel, "every hotel clerk in the South knows me personally." His reporting won him both praise and awards. In 1953 he was named the South's most outstanding journalist by Sigma Delta Chi, now the Society of Professional Journalists. Colleagues admired his writing's emphasis on the complicated background of southern racial strife.[19] Popham worked at the *New York Times* until 1958, when he left to become executive editor of the *Chattanooga Times*. His replacement was Claude F. Sitton, a *New York Times* copy reader and former wire service reporter whose reputation on the civil rights beat in the 1960s would rival Popham's.[20]

Just as the *Times'* coverage was a model for newspapers around the country, so too was the reporting of the *Southern School News*, the monthly newspaper of the Southern Education Reporting Service (SERS) in Nashville. A group of southern newspaper editors founded SERS in 1954 "to tell the story," as the *News* once put it, "factually and objectively, of what happens in education as a result of the Supreme Court ruling that segregation in public schools is unconstitutional." Correspondents from southern and border states provided reports to the *News*, which quickly developed a monthly circulation of 30,000 among educators, journalists, public officials, and libraries. The newspaper included detailed monthly reports on desegregation issues in Alabama, Arkansas, Delaware, Florida, Georgia, Kentucky, Louisiana, Maryland, Mississippi, Missouri, North Carolina, Oklahoma, South Carolina, Tennessee, Texas, Virginia, West Virginia, and the District of Columbia. Its correspondents were reporters from the larger dailies in each state. The *News* and SERS provided journalists across the nation with a clearinghouse for unbiased accounts of desegregation-related developments, serving as both a resource and a model. In addition, scores of journalists, both print and broadcast, used the service's extensive library.[21]

But while the *New York Times* and the SERS led the way in desegregation coverage, the vast majority of daily newspapers were lacking both in editorial leadership and in quality of news coverage. Editors in both the South and North reflected white bias in racial matters. "Most of the press, no less than most of the politicians, responded miserably," recalled Mississippi editor Hodding Carter II of the years following *Brown*.[22] J. Oliver Emmerich, veteran editor of the *McComb* (MS) *Enterprise-Journal*, recalled that it was difficult for most editors to see southern treatment of blacks as wrong. "The prejudices were recognized as traditions and not as prejudices," he said.[23]

To their credit, at least, newspapers both North and South spoke out against violence. The unanimity of southern press sentiment was demonstrated in a pamphlet titled "The South Speaks Out," a compilation of southern editorial sentiment published in 1958 by national religious groups. The purpose of the publication was to demonstrate that most southerners—and virtually all southern newspapers—opposed violence whatever their reaction to *Brown*. The pamphlet reprinted editorials from across the South opposing race-related violence.[24]

But beyond an opposition to violence, southern newspapers offered little support for the law of the land, in sharp contrast to the enthusiastic support offered by northern dailies, the black weeklies, and the nation's one black daily, the *Atlanta World*. Of the thirty largest dailies in the South and border states, the SERS concluded in 1957, all were hostile to *Brown* except for a dozen in the border states of Arkansas, Georgia, North Carolina, and Tennessee. "Once away from the border states," the SERS found, "no single large newspaper has emerged as enthusiastically integrationist." However, a few large and influential newspapers, such as the *St. Louis Post-Dispatch* and the *Louisville Courier-Journal*, had urged compliance with *Brown*. Others, such as the *Nashville Tennessean*, had favored gradual integration.[25]

Reed Sarratt, a southern editor and astute student of the press who had worked for the SERS, believed that in covering desegregation, public opinion molded newspaper opinion, not vice versa. In the 1950s, he recalled, "most editors were looking over their shoulders to see who was following them." Thus, opposition to *Brown* tended to be most heated in the newspapers of Deep South, staunchly segregationist states. As Sarratt summarized southern newspapers' editorial stance by region,

> The general pattern is clear. In the border area, where the Supreme Court decision was widely accepted, the major newspapers supported the ruling and urged compliance. Around the outer fringe of the eleven southern states, public reaction was to recognize the authority of the Court but to hold compliance to a minimum; this was the position taken by most newspapers in these states. In the Deep South the controlling whites denounced the decision and resolutely resisted compliance; the majority of newspapers were in tune with this point of view.[26]

The South had some, but not many, moderate or liberal newspaper editors. Harry S. Ashmore, editor of the *Charlotte* (NC) *News* in the late 1940s and the *Arkansas Gazette* in the 1950s, two moderate newspapers, recalled that there were fewer than a dozen southern newspapers that were liberal in racial matters.[27] The few outspoken editors who favored upholding the law were vilified in the South but honored by their peers in journalism. In the ten years after 1954, six of the Pulitzer Prizes in editorial writing went to southern editors who took a stand for moderation during desegregation crises in their communities. They were Buford Boone of the *Tuscaloosa* (AL) *News* in 1957; Harry S. Ashmore of the *Arkansas Gazette* in 1958; Ralph McGill of the *Atlanta Constitution* in 1959; Lenoir Chambers of the *Norfolk Virginian-Pilot* in 1960; Ira B. Harkey, Jr., of the *Pascagoula Chronicle* in 1963; and Hazel Brannon Smith of the *Lexington* (MS) *Advertiser* in 1964. These and other editors—such as Mississippi's Carter—often provided the only voices of moderation during the backlash of massive resistance following *Brown*.[28]

The vast majority of the southern press, however, opposed *Brown*. South Carolina and Virginia newspapers were typical. Andrew McDowd Secrest, editor of the weekly *Cheraw* (SC) *Chronicle* in the 1950s, believed that editorially the South Carolina press was ineffectual in racial matters. "The press as a whole was at best irrelevant in the struggle for equal rights in South Carolina and, at worst, an exacerbating, agitating element in the situation," recalled Secrest, who subscribed to or exchanged papers with all of the state's major weeklies and dailies in the 1950s and 1960s. "Its repeated calls for 'law and order' were usually overshadowed by the more insistent theme of resistance to so-called Negro 'agitation' and federal intervention with the 'sovereign rights' of the states. The treatment by the leading newspapers of racial issues and related problems amounted to a combination in restraint of trade in new ideas." Secrest believed that persistent press opposition to *Brown* discouraged racial moderates from speaking out.[29]

In Virginia, as in South Carolina, most newspapers—like the state's political leadership—bitterly opposed desegregation. James J. Kilpatrick, editor of the *Richmond News Leader*, the state's most influential daily, launched a campaign in 1955 favoring "interposition," a long-discredited legal doctrine that held that a state could reject Supreme Court rulings that trampled upon its rights. "Once state policy pointed toward resistance," longtime Virginia newspaperman Benjamin Muse observed, "nearly all of the press had fallen into line with it."[30] The one exception was the *Norfolk Virginian-Pilot*, whose editor, Lenoir Chambers, while not an integrationist, opposed massive resistance. He believed that Virginia newspapers were decades behind the times in using illogical and emotional arguments against school desegregation.[31]

As for reporting of the civil rights movement, journalists agreed that the desegregation story after *Brown* was difficult and that the press had a spotty record of covering it. Coverage generally concentrated on crises of desegregation as opposed to explanations of social change, said Carl E. Lindstrom, longtime editor of the *Hartford Times*, in 1960. "The desegregation story is as thorny a challenge as the American press has ever faced," he observed.[32] C.A. McKnight, the first executive director of SERS, told the 1955 ASNE convention that newspapers had given the desegregation story considerably less coverage than it had deserved in the first year after *Brown*. In the fifty southern dailies clipped by SERS, desegregation had received minimal attention. This McKnight attributed to inexperienced and inexpert reporters, editors' fear of offending readers, and a general lack of initiative at newspapers. He said he knew of only three full-time education reporters in the entire country: Popham, Max Gilstrap of the *Christian Science Monitor*, and Ed Lahey of the Knight newspapers.[33]

Newspapers not only gave too little coverage to the desegregation story, McKnight observed, but what little coverage there was tended to be "unbalanced and frequently distorted." Articles about racial issues often lacked context and emphasized conflict rather than progress, even though many of the earliest desegregation efforts in the border states had been successful. "It is my impression that many of our regional newspapers are still looking at the desegregation issue as something apart from the context of a rapidly changing region," McKnight said. The story, he said, deserved better. The "handling of the race problem in the United States is one of the biggest and one of the most important stories of our lifetime," he said. "Is it asking too much to suggest that there is a field for original, enterprising reporting in the months and years after the forthcoming [Supreme] Court decrees in the school desegregation cases?"[34] He told a North Carolina press group in 1955 that newspapers too often concentrated on legal and philosophical questions surrounding school desegregation while ignoring the practical administrative problems it posed.[35]

The volume of desegregation-related articles in southern newspapers picked up substantially, the SERS reported, after the Supreme Court's 1955 decision ordering desegregation to proceed.[36] A 1960 Southern Regional Council study of five large southern dailies found that their handling of racial stories was remarkably similar. Their news stories showed little bias or distortion, but newspapers usually relied upon the wire services rather than their own reporters to cover desegregation news. Southern newspapers were ignoring the opportunity to cover and interpret a story in their own backyards, leaving readers with event-centered wire service accounts that offered little interpretation of complicated events. Still, the Council's study concluded,

> Southern newspapers generally are doing a conscientious, thorough, and predominantly fair job of reporting racial news. They are conforming more closely to the accepted standards of good journalism than the atmosphere of the times or the charges of their critics would indicate.[37]

Other studies found that in reporting the bare facts of desegregation, southern papers were often fair and balanced but displayed little reportorial initiative or editorial daring.[38]

The desegregation story was difficult because it was a complex story of societal change, a long-term process hard to chronicle for event-oriented daily newspapers. As a result, they tended to play up day-to-day desegregation difficulties while overlooking, as McKnight had pointed out, the longer-term successes of desegregation elsewhere. Sam Ragan of the *Raleigh* (NC) *News & Observer* complained in 1957, for example, that the Associated Press had overlooked "something of a social revolution" when three schools in his state had integrated successfully. Peace and progress, he noted, seldom attracted as much journalistic notice as disorder or bloodshed.[39]

As desegregation efforts increased in the late 1950s, northern newspapers turned greater attention to the South, prompting an influx of reporters from northern news organizations into the region. "There are as many Yankee reporters dropping off planes and trains as there were carpetbaggers in the 1860s," complained the segregationist Thomas R. Waring, editor of the *Charleston* (SC) *News and Courier*, in 1956. The South's leading moderate, Ralph McGill of the *Atlanta Constitution*, said of the mass of incoming journalists, "It's been like waves beating on a stern and rockbound shore."[40] Sixty reporters were on hand at the University of Alabama riots in 1956. Seventy-five had flocked in 1955 to the Sumner, Mississippi, trial of the men accused of killing fourteen-year-old Emmett Till.[41]

The Till trial had been a turning point in increasing coverage of racial friction in the South. The murder, as journalist David Halberstam has observed, was "the first great media event of the civil rights movement."[42] Reporters, photographers, television cameramen, radio announcers, and newspaper columnists from across the country crowded into tiny Sumner for the trial of Roy Bryant and J.W. Milam, half-brothers accused of killing Till. The Chicago youth had been visiting relatives in Money, Mississippi, when he had either whistled at or spoken suggestively to a white woman in a grocery. White men kidnapped Till from his uncle's home, and his body—tied to a cotton-gin fan and shot in the head—was found several days later in the Tallahatchie River. The crush of outside press for the trial of Bryant and Milam prompted the judge, Curtis Swango, to enlist the *New York Times'* John Popham to coordinate press security.[43] Popham complied, stunned at press attention given to a racial story in the region he for years had covered alone. "Never in our region," marveled the *Mississippi Sun* during the Till trial, "has so much out-of-state interest been taken in a case involving white and negro."[44]

Reporters took over Sumner's only hotel, the Delta Inn, to cover the trial. Popham oversaw press accommodations, obtaining housing for the black reporters in Mound Bayou, an all-black community, and also riding herd on the northern reporters to ensure they complied with southern customs, racial and otherwise. He once chastised the *New York Post's* Murray Kempton, for example, for wearing British walking shorts at dinner.[45] At the trial, reporters sat at segregated tables. Sheriff H.C. Strider had laid down the law to the visiting black journalists. Any mixing between black and white reporters, he warned, would result in ejection from the courtroom. *Jet* reporter Simeon Booker believed the sheriff's treatment of black reporters was in retaliation for their perceived mistreatment of the South in the news columns.[46] "[T]he Till case was unbelievable," recalled James Hicks of the National Negro Press Association. "I mean, I just didn't get the sense of being in a courtroom." Dan Wakefield of the *Nation* admitted, "I am not ashamed to confess that I was afraid."[47] At the trial's end, the all-white jury acquitted Milam and Bryant.

If the Till trial was the first great media event of the civil rights movement, the largest was the integration of Central High School in Little Rock, Arkansas, in 1957. The court-ordered admission of nine blacks to Central was opposed by Arkansas Governor Orval Faubus, who called out the Arkansas National Guard, ostensibly to preserve order at the school. His actions eventually prompted President Dwight D. Eisenhower to nationalize the Arkansas Guard and to enforce integration with federal troops. Only five out-of-town reporters were in Little Rock when Faubus called out the Guard. Four weeks later there were 225. Little Rock was "transformed into a kind of giant press room," said NBC reporter John Chancellor.[48]

In covering the Central crisis, reporters faced anger from both Faubus and the mobs that gathered in front of the school. Faubus was irritated at the prointegration *Arkansas Gazette* and believed that its editors were indoctrinating visiting newsmen with prejudice against him. The mobs equated the out-of-town reporters with the enforcement of integration. At various times, members of the mob taunted journalists, called them "nigger lovers," jostled them, and rocked telephone booths when reporters tried to make calls. In all, six white and four black reporters were beaten while covering the Central crisis.[49]

Scripps-Howard reporter Dickson Preston said that while most reporters had acted with restraint at Little Rock, some "extremists" had acted irresponsibly. On occasion television camera crews had incited crowds to demonstrate for the cameras. And some reporters, such as the *New York Times'* Benjamin Fine, had appeared openly sympathetic to the nine black students and had angered crowds with pointed questions. "Fine asked the kind of questions that would get anybody's hackles up," Preston said. "He symbolized to southerners the kind of 'Yankee reporting' they dislike."[50] In fact, Fine was sympathetic to integration and had often tangled with crowds. "They hurled insulting remarks and told me to go back North where I came from," he reported after one encounter with a mob.[51] A National Guard officer led him away and warned him and other reporters that they would be arrested if they incited violence. Fine's emotional involvement in the desegregation story prompted *Times* editors to remove him as the newspaper's education editor in late 1957.[52]

At a panel discussion in late 1957 on the press coverage at Central, reporters agreed that journalists had improperly made news by staging pictures and by getting attacked by the mob. Even worse, many reporters—not just Fine—had taken sides. "The northern newspaper reporter has been definitely tied in with the machinery of enforcing integration," concluded Bob Allison of CBS News.[53] Accordingly, he and other northern reporters now felt unsafe in the South, whereas, before Central, reporters had mingled safely in crowds. "Today I feel I am up against a hard wall," Allison said. "Apparently now there is a solidified conviction in the South that the reporter from the North is going to do everything wrong."[54]

Southern editors resented the northern press' support of southern integration and press coverage devoted to it. Moreover, the southerners believed that the nation's press exaggerated racial upheaval in their region, while northern upheaval received little notice.[55] "[W]e have rarely seen the heat that is now being generated," Editor and Publisher's Robert U. Brown observed in 1955, "between editors of two sections of the country over the desegregation issue."[56] Tempers flared at the 1956 ASNE meeting when southern editors took the floor to complain about northern reporters during a panel discussion on the difficulties of covering integration. "[D]own in our part of the country we wish you northerners would ease up just a little bit on the pressure," admonished the Texarkana (TX) Gazette's J.Q. Mahaffey. He charged that northern editors habitually ignored or downplayed their own racial disturbances and disputes, a charge that prompted a spirited denial from a contingent of Chicago journalists. Then Harry M. Ayers of the Anniston (AL) Star took the floor to defend segregation and to lament the alleged inferiority of blacks, but he was cut off as he was about to undertake a forceful denunciation of racial intermarriage. "The consuming desire of every Negro is to possess a white woman," Ayers declared in what turned out to be his closing remark, which prompted, observers said, a collective shudder from the assembled editors. The day's discussion concluded with editors agreeing that newspapers were adequately covering breaking developments about integration but failing to explain much beyond that.[57]

The most outspoken southern critics of race coverage were Thomas Waring, of the Charleston News and Courier, and Grover C. Hall, Jr., of the Montgomery Advertiser. Waring declared in speeches and articles that the northern press was printing propaganda, writing in Harper's in 1956 that "the metropolitan press without exception has abandoned fair and objective reporting of the race story."[58] Hall, a moderate in racial matters, was nonetheless so offended at a New York Post reporter's coverage of race relations in Montgomery that he challenged Post editor James Wechsler in 1956 to provide him with a guided tour of New York for a profile of that city's race relations. Wechsler declined.[59]

In Mississippi, state officials were so convinced of the bias of northern accounts that they invited a group of twenty New England editors to Mississippi in 1956 to view the state's race relations firsthand. The weeklong visit was arranged and partially financed by the Mississippi State Sovereignty Commission, the agency formed to fight desegregation efforts.[60] Commission representatives believed they had gotten their money's worth for the $2,000 cost of the trip, which resulted in considerable, if not always favorable, publicity for segregation positions in newspapers that otherwise would have been difficult to crack.[61]

The segregation story proved especially vexing for the wire services, which served both northern and southern newspapers, whose editors were always scanning the wires for evidence of bias. Editors in both the North and the South wanted the wire services to cover racial problems outside their region, on the assumption that racial problems in the other fellow's territory were being downplayed. So many southern editors complained that the wire services were overplaying southern racial problems that both the United Press and AP assigned reporters on several occasions to cover race problems outside the South. At the urging of southern editors, the United Press agreed in 1958 to send a Georgia-born correspondent to assess school segregation problems in the North. The correspondent, Al Kuettner, wrote a series titled "A Southerner Looks at New York Schools," which highlighted racial friction in response to school integration.[62] Similarly, the Associated Press in 1956 had assigned a staffer to survey northern racial difficulties. His eighteen-hundred-word piece was widely used by member newspapers. The piece was part of a conscious attempt by the wire service to cover the explosive topic of desegregation as neutrally as possible.[63]

The civil rights story, beginning especially with Central High, also marked the coming of age of the newsgathering capabilities of television news reporters. Television covered the crisis extensively, sometimes with live broadcasts and with dramatic pictures of high impact. "The thing about Little Rock is that it was where television reporting came to influence, if not to maturity," recalled Harry Reasoner, who covered Central as a young reporter for CBS News. "You could not hide from news as delineated by TV."[64] Even to some of the print reporters, such as Wallace Westfeldt of the *Nashville Tennessean*, it seemed that television might have outperformed print for the first time.[65] The civil rights movement was, as former *New York Times* television critic Peter J. Boyer once observed,

> the first running story of national importance that television fully covered. . . . Television brought home to the nation the civil rights struggle in vivid images that were difficult to ignore, and for television, it was a story that finally proved the value of TV news *gathering* as opposed to mere news dissemination.[66]

But both television and print reporters fell short at Central, as they had in other civil rights news stories of the 1950s. "The cowboy reporters rode in to the scent of blood," *Arkansas Gazette* editor Harry Ashmore recalled in a 1958 speech. They had failed to consider the broader picture of social change in Little Rock and in the South, he said. Reporters had been too concerned with "the sound and the fury on the surface." They had ignored the failure of national leadership before the crisis and its contribution to the rise of extremists afterward. "I think we have got to get over the notion that objectivity means giving a villain equal space with a saint—and above all of paying the greatest attention to those who shout the loudest," Ashmore said. "We've got to learn that a set of indisputable facts do not necessarily add up to truth."[67]

Increasing reporting of civil rights news into the 1960s had a profound effect on black newspapers. As the mainstream white press, both print and broadcast, increased reporting of black-related news, readership of black publications declined. "The Negro press may well become a major casualty of the revolution it helped create," declared *Newsweek* magazine in 1963. By the early 1960s, only a few black newspapers made money consistently, and previously dominant black newspapers like the *Pittsburgh Courier* lost much of their circulation.

Black reporters and black advertising shifted to white media. "Very few bright young Negroes even think of joining Negro papers," commented the *New York Post*'s Ted Poston, who formerly reported for black papers, in 1963. "The goal is to get on the white paper because of better pay and better standards of journalism."[68] George Barbour, who started his career with the *Courier*, left the black press for a higher-paying job in broadcasting. "The reason why I didn't stay with the black newspapers, the black press, and I loved it—it was a freedom that a reporter dreams of—is because of the money, the financial situation."[69]

Roy Wilkins, executive secretary of the National Association for the Advancement of Colored People, gloomily predicted in 1963 that the changing nature of the black press would hasten its decline. "I can't escape the belief that the Negro press, by and large, up to the present day performed a great function and now, in an increasingly unsegregated world, it finds itself faced with the problem of reexamining its functions," Wilkins said in *Newsweek*. "Negro papers came into being as crusaders. And the minute they stop being crusaders and become chroniclers, they're done."[70]

By 1971, the black press had declined to an extent that a reviewer for *Journalism Quarterly* felt compelled to reassure readers—"Yes, Virginia, there is a black press," he wrote. The *Columbia Journalism Review* forecast in 1970 that "the end of the national black paper is clearly in sight." Indeed, the once-dominant *Courier* saw its national circulation slip below 50,000, a far cry from the quarter-million circulation it held in World War II. The *Chicago Defender* had just as precipitous a decline, to below 40,000 in 1969.[71] Falling readership, as well as declining numbers of black newspapers, was typical across the country.

An advertisement placed by civil rights activists was the impetus for the most significant libel case in the twentieth century, *New York Times v Sullivan*, decided in 1964. L.B. Sullivan was a city commissioner in Montgomery, Alabama, who sued the *Times* claiming a fundaising advertisement inaccurately accused the Montgomery police of misdeeds against civil rights demonstrators. Though he was not named in the advertisement, Sullivan won $500,000 in damages in Alabama courts, claiming it had damaged his reputation.[72]

In a unanimous decision, the Supreme Court ruled in the *Times'* favor. Citing the social benefits of rigorous debate of important issues, the court ruled that public officials suing media organizations must prove that a falsehood was printed or broadcast with "actual malice," that is, "with knowledge that it was false or with reckless disregard of whether it was false or not."[73] The decision made it extremely difficult for public officials to sue and win. "The effects of *New York Times v Sullivan* are apparent to this day," the *Columbia Journalism Review* concluded in 2001. "[O]nly eleven trials against the media on libel, privacy, and related claims were held in the year 2000 . . . reflecting a downward trend that's been going on for decades."[74]

Facing the challenges of both television and of covering rapid social change, newspapers had struggled to adapt. Both challenges increased in the 1950s, and both pointed out the slowness with which newspapers and print journalists responded to change. By decade's end, with the civil rights movement picking up momentum and television growing in influence, newspapers had begun to adjust or at least had recognized their deficiencies. But the process of change was slow, as contrasted with the rapid shift of the media environment. While the rise of television and a shifting social landscape were newspapers' biggest challenges in the mid-1950s, other trends were simultaneously shaping the newspapers in ways that were becoming increasingly clear by decade's end. Observing the wide range of emerging problems, Barry Bingham of the Louisville *Courier-Journal* observed in 1959 that newspapers were in crisis. "I think journalism is in the grip of a process that is painful to every human being: the necessity to change," he said.[75]

Chapter 6

The Seeds of Long-term Change, 1950–1963

Long overdue progress in printing technology made a little headway throughout the 1950s, enough to make it evident by decade's end that profound change was on the horizon. The coming technological revolution was one of several long-term trends that had become clearer to publishers by the late 1950s. These trends were slowly changing the newspaper industry on numerous fronts—especially in how newspapers were produced and where readers lived. Their effects were all the more significant for their interaction with other developments in newspapers' eventful decade, specifically the rapid rise of television and escalating costs. All of these changes, as they matured in the 1960s and 1970s, would transform newspapers both in how they were produced and in the readership they served. Publishers and editors had begun to recognize the significance of these trends by the late 1950s and had also begun—albeit slowly—to adapt.

The first and most significant trend in the 1950s, one that drove many of the decade's developments in printing technology, was escalating costs. Throughout the 1950s, except for two years—1955 and 1959—the average yearly cost of publishing a newspaper had continued to climb faster than did revenues.[1] By the end of the 1950s, a decade of ever-rising advertising sales was finally coming to an end. *Editor & Publisher*'s annual survey of costs in 1957, for example, found that nearly half of all newspapers in all circulation classes had suffered a *decline* in local revenues from the previous year. Three-quarters had experienced a loss in national advertising revenue. Expenses for the average daily had increased by 3.59 percent from 1956 to 1957, offset by a paltry 1.51 percent increase in revenues, due almost entirely to rising circulation rates.[2] In 1958, an anonymous 50,000-circulation daily newspaper surveyed by *Editor & Publisher* reported its lowest profit—4.44 percent of total revenue—of any year since the end of World War II.[3]

Rising costs had been a concern throughout the decade. "The day of easy money is gone," declared American Newspaper Publishers Association President Richard W. Slocum of the *Philadelphia Bulletin* in a 1954 speech to fellow publishers. "Some newspapers have shrunk, and more have died than we like to talk about. More will shrink and die if we do not meet our present-day problems." The rising costs, he said, were dominated by increases in labor rates and newsprint prices, which had continued their upward spiral begun immediately after the war.[4] Between 1948 and 1959, hourly earnings of production workers increased from $1.98 to $2.98, and newsprint prices rose by half from $88.50 to $135 a ton.[5] The newsprint prices—depressed by slack demand in previous decades but inflated in the booming postwar years—were particularly burdensome because newspapers were printing larger daily editions filled with advertising in the 1950s.[6]

Through the 1950s, publishers took a number of measures to solve the cost problem. Many newspapers trimmed the size of their pages by an inch or more. By doing so, the *New York Herald Tribune* saved an estimated $400,000 a year in newsprint. In Chicago, the tabloid *Sun-Times* added a sixth column to accommodate more news on less paper. Some broadsheet dailies switched from eight columns to nine for the same reason.[7] Significantly, newspapers also ran proportionately more advertising to maintain profits as costs rose. In 1941, according to *Media Records* statistics compiled from newspapers in 118 cities, the average evening newspaper had contained 43.3 percent advertising. By 1952, that figure had reached 60.3 percent. Newspapers were getting bigger—an average of thirty-two broadsheet pages in evening newspapers in 1952—but the percentage of advertising was growing at the expense of editorial content.[8] The proportion of advertising to editorial matter would hold at 60 percent to 40 percent throughout the 1950s.

But publishers were left with relatively few options for raising revenue. On the one hand, television competition inhibited newspapers from raising advertising rates or subscription prices too substantially. Raising revenue through increased circulation, on the other hand, was both difficult and costly. Unlike other businesses with a product to sell, newspapers could not easily make more money simply by manufacturing and selling more of their product. Selling more copies required expenses in promotion, newsprint, and wages. Facing so many difficulties in raising revenues in a decade of rising costs, many publishers looked to a more fundamental change—making newspapers cheaper to produce.

Newspapers had flirted with the new production methods in the late 1940s, when a wave of postwar strikes prompted some to make printing innovations. In Chicago, St. Petersburg, and other cities, publishers had used photo-engraving to compose pages in the absence of striking printers. While such methods had quickly introduced many publishers to the potential benefits of printing innovations, few stuck with the new methods once the strikes ended. Traditional letterpress printing remained quicker and more attractive than photo-engraving. But publishers' experiences with the new methods had, at least, foreshadowed the printing revolution to come and had prompted initial forays into research, such as the American Newspaper Publishers Association (ANPA) research program begun in 1947.[9]

The short-lived experiments in the 1940s had also convinced many publishers that technical improvements in production were long overdue. The newspaper industry, as always, was slow to change, and innovation was coming far too slowly. "The press has done less to improve and modernize its product through research and consultation than any industry I know of," complained James S. Pope, managing editor of the *Louisville Courier-Journal*, in 1947.[10] In 1948, Northwestern University's Charles V. Kinter agreed. "The cost problem has become so critical," he said, "it now seems clear that intensive research designed to reduce costs should have been initiated long ago." The lush sellers' market of the 1940s had made it easier to offset rising costs through increases in advertising and subscription rates than to undertake research that might have resulted in cheaper printing, he wrote.[11]

Production methods had been static for half a century. Letterpress technology had changed little for decades. The most recent far-reaching innovation had been the Linotype machine, invented in the 1880s. Newspaper production with hot metal—despite some fine-tuning over the years—remained a multiple-step, labor-intensive, high-cost process. As Georgia newspaperman Millard B. Grimes once described the state of newspaper technology in this period,

> A pencil, a pad and a manual typewriter were the only tools of the reporter and the copy editors. Men with ink-stained muscles put metal type into page forms and passed them on to other muscled men called stereotypers who made heavy lead plates of the pages which were then placed on the press by more muscled men.[12]

"Our own trade is very much out of gear with the trend of the times," complained *Editor & Publisher*'s Robert U. Brown in 1955. He said that newspapers, unlike other industries, had failed to show any substantial gains in productivity in the last generation. Production methods were being improved by degrees, but few radical advances were on the drawing boards. Other industries, meanwhile, had boosted productivity by 150 percent in recent years.[13] In 1959, an *Editor & Publisher* editorial blamed newspapers' mechanical backwardness on the paltry sum that publishers spent on research. "What other $4.5 billion industry besides newspapers do you know that spends less than one-hundredth of one percent of its gross revenue on research to find new and cheaper methods of production?" asked the magazine's editors. Outside of research at ANPA's institute and at a few scattered newspapers, the bulk of pioneering work had been left to equipment manufacturers. "The combined impact of these research efforts has hardly been sufficient to provide completely new production techniques so badly needed by newspapers," the editors wrote.[14]

But this growing realization that newspapers were lagging behind in updating technology, combined with the pressures of steadily rising costs throughout the 1950s, led to increasing experimentation with printing innovations. The three most significant areas of development were offset printing, photocomposition, and the Teletypesetter. A refinement of a technique developed years earlier, Teletypesetting (TTS) made the most advances during the decade. But the slower-moving developments in offset printing and photocomposition promised, even in the 1950s, far greater benefits for the long term. This was primarily because both, to a greater extent than TTS, promised fundamental changes in how newspapers were produced.

In the earliest postwar years, offset printing had seemed to offer the best hope for cheaper printing. For one thing, offset was an old technology in wide use in print shops.[15] Though it was primarily used for job printing, not for newspaper work, publishers recognized offset's potential, over time, for ready applicability to newspapers. The process seemed the brightest prospect for lowering production costs as early as the 1940s. "Innovations in printing are due in the postwar period, but the new processes will not engulf your composing room," Harry Loose of American Type Founders warned Iowa publishers in 1946. He predicted that publishers should expect orderly development, not radical change, but he said publishers should "keep both eyes on offset."[16]

Offset printing differs substantially from traditional letterpress printing. In letterpress, to put it simply, raised images in metal are inked and pressed against a blank page to leave an image. In newspaper production, letterpress printing is labor intensive because it requires Linotype operators to convert editorial and advertising into hot type, engravers to transform photographs and artwork into metal plates, stereotypers to convert the page forms into curved metal plates for the presses, and pressmen to operate the printing presses. In offset printing, a branch of lithography, printed matter—whether artwork or typewritten—is "pasted up" on a page and then photographed to make a sensitized metal plate, which is then inked and pressed, or offset, to paper. Offset printing requires less labor because it eliminates some of the multiple steps of hot type.

The earliest leader in offset printing among daily newspapers was the *Opelousas* (LA) *Daily World*, which had first converted to offset in 1939. Its publisher, John R. Thistlethwaite, was offset printing's most widely known advocate through the 1950s. So many publishers sought him out for advice that he developed a folder of materials to mail out to them. He said that offset technology was far superior to letterpress. "We find offset much more flexible in every respect," he said in a 1956 letter to *National Publisher* magazine. Offset's ability to reproduce anything pasted up on a page, he said, cleared the way for the *Daily World* to subscribe to filler services that supplied proofs to be pasted directly on the page, thus allowing production workers "to slap out pages like mad." Much advertising also arrived in proof form.[17] Moreover, offset required few technical skills, unlike letterpress methods. Workers could be quickly trained to make plates for the offset presses and to paste up pages. Thistlethwaite bragged that his wife could paste up an entire newspaper page in two minutes.[18]

The economics of offset printing limited its use to weeklies and small dailies at first. To small-town publishers, offset was attractive because of the rising costs of some elements of the letterpress process. Smaller newspapers printing by letterpress could not afford their own departments for engraving photographs, illustrations, and artwork, requiring them to send such work to engraving shops, an expensive and time-consuming process. For these newspapers, the flexibility of offset printing provided a way to avoid such headaches. At the *Montezuma* (IA) *Republican*, for example, publisher Dave Sutherland switched from letterpress to offset in July 1956 and immediately saved $100 a month in engraving costs. After a few rocky months while Sutherland's printers learned the new offset process, the *Republican* had both speeded up production time and increased its profits. Moreover, its use of photographs skyrocketed because of the affordability of offset. More than 150 publishers from ten states visited the *Republican*'s printing plant to see its printing operation.[19] At the *Republican* and elsewhere, offset indeed had a few mechanical limitations. The printing plates, for example, could only be used for limited press runs and were time-consuming and expensive to make. But such problems were manageable for weeklies and small dailies, with fewer editions, more flexible deadlines, and smaller press runs than large dailies.[20]

Success stories of publishers' experiences with offset filled the trade press in the middle and late 1950s. In Missouri, the *Salisbury Press-Spectator* switched from letterpress to offset in 1959 because the new method allowed for more varied makeup and for quicker and better production of pictures. The overall printing quality of newspapers improved with the new method, which proved to be cheaper, too. One part-time and two full-time printers were replaced by one full-time printer and two part-time female workers, all trained by the manufacturer of the newspaper's offset press. The newspaper's switch to offset cost about $10,000 plus the cost of the press. Jack Fidler, the publisher, said after the switchover, "We wouldn't change back to the old method for anything."[21]

Scattered small dailies began switching to offset in the mid-1950s. In Georgia, weekly newspaper publisher Charles L. Hardy, Sr., visited the Opelousas production plant and was so impressed with its potential he founded a daily newspaper in 1955, the *Gainesville Morning News*, printed by offset. "As far as we know," the *Morning News* proclaimed in an editorial in its debut issue, "there is nothing we cannot do with this photographic method of production."[22] Competition and a shortage of capital forced Hardy to close the paper after eight months, but he was nonetheless convinced of offset's potential. "This pioneering in a new field of printing," he wrote in a farewell column in July 1956, "has been most fascinating, and it holds tremendous potentialities two to five years from now." Offset was held back, he wrote, only by technical limitations that could have been easily solved with adequate research.[23]

Even with its technical limitations, offset had established a firm foothold in the nation's newspapers by the end of the 1950s. By 1960, fifty of Georgia's 189 weeklies were printed by the process.[24] Nationally, offset printing grew rapidly enough in the late 1950s to prompt the National Editorial Association (NEA), the national organization of weekly and small daily newspapers, to organize an offset printing committee so that offset newspaper publishers could swap information. In late 1957, *National Publisher*, the NEA monthly magazine, counted 150 newspapers published by offset, the vast majority of them weeklies.[25] Offset began to grow substantially, however, in the early and mid-1960s as technical limitations were worked out. A 1960 survey by *American Press* magazine found that more than 100 dailies and 750 weeklies were considering switching to offset.[26] By 1963, about 650 newspapers—forty of them dailies—had made the switch.[27] By 1967, about 170 small dailies and 1,500 weeklies were printed on offset presses.[28] The increasing number of newspapers switching to offset prompted the University of Missouri to inaugurate a training program in the process in January 1964.[29]

By 1960, Prescott Low, publisher of the daily *Quincy* (MA) *Patriot-Ledger*, was predicting that offset printing was on the verge of a period of major growth. "There are only one or two problems left standing in the way of even the largest daily going to offset," he said. "It is expected that these outstanding problems will be overcome in the next five to seven years."[30] "What is happening," wrote journalism professor John Tebbel in 1961, "is a quiet revolution in the composing room which may well have far-reaching and not wholly predictable consequences for the communications industry."[31] Allan Woods, longtime production manager of *Newsday* in suburban New York City, wrote in 1963 that offset printing was the most dramatic development in newspaper publishing since the nineteenth century.[32]

But, as Woods pointed out, it was the pairing of offset with another development of the 1950s that had such far-reaching implications for newspapers. Offset combined with photocomposition—that is, the process of electronically setting type directly onto paper or metal without using line-casting machines—to give newspapers a way to completely bypass the hot-metal typesetting system. Photocomposition advanced slowly in the 1950s, as publishers learned how it could be paired with offset to print newspapers much more economically. With photocomposition (also called "cold type") and offset, Woods said, "Theoretically, it would be possible to set, compose, and make up complete pages of type without recourse to the use of any hot metal slugs or the time-consuming composition of the traditional methods."[33]

Photocomposition machines were first introduced in the mid-1950s. The Intertype Corporation's Fotosetter machine was marketed beginning in 1954. The Photon Corporation's Photon and the Mergenthaler Linotype Company's Linofilm were each introduced for field testing the same year. "The long-awaited 'revolution in printing' appears to be drawing closer," said *Editor & Publisher* in announcing the manufacture of the new machines.[34] The process spread relatively slowly, however. Only twenty to thirty newspapers were using photocomposition machines four years after their introduction.[35] By 1958, manufacturers had spent $8 million to develop cold type, but Martin M. Reed, the president of Mergenthaler, said the technology needed even more engineering work to make it feasible. "Photocomposition has passed its fledgling stage," he said. "Right now it needs to be shoved out of the nest and made to prove itself."[36]

Even in its early development, however, photocomposition showed promise. Most of the newspapers using the technology found that it was best suited to set display advertising, which usually required long deadlines and complicated makeup. Most journals used the photocomposition machines to print ads onto paper or film, which was then used, depending upon the newspaper's presses, to make an offset plate or a photo-engraving for letterpress. Among the newspapers using the photocomposition process in the 1950s were the *Louisville Courier-Journal*, *Milwaukee Journal*, and *Washington Post*, as well as smaller papers such as the *South Bend* (IN) *Tribune* and *Quincy* (MA) *Patriot-Ledger*.[37]

At the *South Bend Tribune*, managers marveled at the speed and cost-savings of photocomposition. Beginning in late 1958, the *Tribune* began setting all of its display advertising using four Photon machines that were used in place of six hot metal machines. Because the cold type process is less cumbersome than hot metal, with Photon the *Tribune* was able to set ads into type much more quickly without increased cost. The cold-type process allowed the *Tribune* to hold its overall engraving and composing costs steady even as its ad lineage rose. "We decided to change completely to [the] cold-type method because we believed it would be best in the long run," explained Roy N. Walden, the newspaper's chief accountant, in 1959. "Results so far confirm our judgment."[38]

The speed, flexibility, and quality of cold type impressed the *Spokane* (WA) *Spokesman-Review and Chronicle*. "The savings in time required for make-up between the so-called hot metal and Photon plate metal can be fantastic," said Frederick H. Trantow, the journal's chief accountant, in 1960. For example, a food advertisement that required an hour and a half of composition time using hot metal could be set with a Photon machine in five minutes. A two-page supermarket advertisement that required seven hours to compose in hot metal could be assembled in only forty-five minutes with Photon. Some of the newspaper's advertisers so appreciated the quality of ads set in cold type that they began to insist on Photon composition.[39]

While changes in printing processes were slowly gaining momentum in the 1950s and early 1960s, another technological development—Teletypesetting (TTS)—exploded in the same period. Teletypesetting was a process by which typesetting machines could be operated by remote control without Linotype operators. In the 1940s publishers had used TTS to thwart printers' strikes by using low-skill typists to type newspaper copy into special typewriters that produced perforated tape, which was then fed into a device that operated a Linotype machine. Beginning in the early 1950s, newspapers began to receive wire reports on TTS tape. TTS was actually a very old process—chain newspapers first used it in the 1930s—but the process grew most rapidly in the 1950s as a cost-cutting measure. Its adoption was boosted both by the manufacture of new TTS-capable linecasting machines and by concern over rising costs in the early 1950s. TTS saved newspapers money because it gave editors a way to get copy set into type without using their own Linotype operators.

Publishers welcomed the rapid growth of TTS with enthusiasm. "Transmission of press association news reports by Teletypesetter," said Claude S. Ramsey of the *Asheville* (NC) *Citizen and Times* at the Associated Press Managing Editors' meeting in 1952, "is perhaps the greatest development in the newspaper business in the last fifteen or twenty years." J. Curtis Lyons of the *Petersburg* (VA) *Progress* told the Associated Press Managing Editors (APME) colleagues that TTS had become "the salvation of the small newspapers."[40] It saved newspapers both time and money: the rapid transmission of news over TTS lines meant that wire copy was set into type quickly and with lower labor costs. It also speeded up production because TTS-operated linecasting machines could run full-time without the occasional interruptions required by human operators. Linecasting machines could set from seven to twelve lines of type a minute when driven by TTS tape, while manually operated linecasting machines averaged just three to four lines a minute.[41]

The savings in costs were well worth the changes that newspapers had to make to adjust to the new system. Newspapers began to receive two sets of wire copy—one set in TTS tape and one typewritten copy transmitted over the traditional teletype. Some newspapers set all of their copy using the TTS tape and then edited the copy from proofs. Others monitored the wire copy closely and then decided what TTS tape would be set in type. The new system eliminated the need for Linotype operators to set wire copy, which low-skill tape operators could now handle. The Fort Wayne, Indiana, newspapers, for example, switched entirely to TTS wire copy in 1952 and reassigned all of their printers to setting advertising copy or to working on various jobs on the pressroom floor.[42]

The first wire service TTS circuit was established in North Carolina in April 1951. In the next year and a half TTS circuits spread to virtually every state. By late 1952, the Associated Press (AP) was using TTS to transmit day and night state wire reports, day and night national news, market reports, and sports scores. A 1952 AP survey of 198 newspapers in twenty-two states found that the process had substantially speeded up production in three-quarters of the newspapers. TTS delivered wire reports quickly, thus allowing editors to include more state and national news and lessening the need for filler.[43] "Best of all," an APME committee wrote of TTS in 1952, "it is coming at a time when newspapers are under the terrible compulsion of finding less costly methods of producing their issues."[44] At first, TTS was used primarily at smaller newspapers. A 1952 ANPA survey found that 76 percent of all newspapers using Teletypesetters were under 50,000 circulation. The new method caused some grumbling from the typesetters' union, which responded by seeking to control it. As newspaper union contracts were renegotiated, the International Typographical Union (ITU) usually won control over the process.[45]

But if TTS offered newspapers tremendous advantages, it also posed some difficulties as the process became more widespread in the 1950s. Before TTS, the major wire services—AP, United Press, and International News Service—each had similar styles that governed capitalization, spelling, punctuation, abbreviation, and the like. Newspapers receiving wire service reports usually edited wire copy to conform with their own local style. After the spread of TTS, however, many editors began dropping their own local style in favor of wire service style because editing copy from TTS tape was time-consuming and troublesome. Editors also pushed for improved wire service style books that would clear up any ambiguities. In July 1953, the largest wire service, the Associated Press, issued a 100-page, 12,000-word style book that replaced an older, much smaller, and less comprehensive guide.[46] "TTS brought about the new style book," C.P. (Gus) Winkler, the AP's TTS supervisor, who worked more than six months with an APME committee to compile the guide, said when it was unveiled. "Style whims for local conditions will prevail in some cases but basically the styles established in the composing rooms will prevail." The new book governed all AP copy in both state AP circuits and the national wires. *Editor & Publisher* reported that the new rules and regulations "are expected to become gospel law in hundreds of composing rooms and on copy desks everywhere."[47]

But while the new consistency in style required less editing of TTS-supplied copy, it also had another effect: it made articles more likely to be similar in newspapers across the country. Basil L. Walters, executive editor of Knight Newspapers, saw dangers in TTS even before the new AP style book was released. TTS threatened to be "a Frankenstein monster" to editors, he warned. He believed that the standardization of copy that would result would make newspapers resemble each other more and more, a considerable handicap in an era of increasing competition.[48] *Editor & Publisher*'s editors said Walters' timely warning should serve notice on editors that they "must never completely delegate or abrogate their duty to edit their own papers."[49] Still, TTS so diminished the need for local editing that many editors believed by the late 1950s that good copyediting was a thing of the past. As *Hartford* (CT) *Times* copyeditor George K. Moriarty complained in 1957, "Copy editing was becoming a lost art when technology in the form of TTS came along and firmly closed the book."[50]

Carl Lindstrom, longtime editor of *American Editor* and a former editor of the *Hartford Times*, wrote in 1960 that TTS had contributed to a sameness in American newspapers at the worst possible time—as they were facing new competition from television. "This is practical, efficient, and in fairly general operation," he summarized the situation in his 1960 book about American newspapers.

> The result calls, however, for serious attention because it also stereotypes the language of every line of telegraph news in the country, telling every story in identical words—including typographical errors.... It is a valuable agent in cutting costs and labor, but it should not be used and its effects should be carefully weighed.[51]

TTS bred not only sameness but also encouraged many papers to print more wire news at the expense of local content. An Indiana University researcher found in 1954 that of twenty-six United Press newspapers that used TTS, all expanded wire news after its introduction. "Through use of TTS," one editor said, "we have almost doubled our wire coverage while holding the line on local."[52] University of Wisconsin researcher Scott M. Cutlip studied four non-metropolitan newspapers in 1954 and found that all used more wire news and less local after getting TTS. "If this trend becomes a widespread fact, it has serious implications for newspapers as they buck increased competition," he concluded.[53] *Editor & Publisher's* Robert U. Brown said the study was evidence that some editors were taking too much advantage of the "wonderful invention" of TTS. "[I]t seems to us," he declared, "that many small newspapers have gone too far in relying on TTS to reduce costs not only in the composing room but in the news room."[54] In the late 1950s, the use of TTS spread from smaller papers to larger, metropolitan journals. By 1960, one-half of AP's 1,778 newspapers took some form of TTS service. The same year, about 600 United Press International (UPI) clients received wire reports by TTS. UPI was the combined news service formed in 1958 by the merger of United Press and International News Service.[55]

Though TTS was spreading fast and printing technology was finally beginning to advance by the end of the 1950s, newspapers still seemed behind the times to many publishers. Photocomposition and offset showed promise for the future but offered the vast majority of newspaper publishers little immediate relief from steadily rising costs. Letterpress technology was far too entrenched. Many publishers had invested heavily in new presses after World War II and were in no hurry to switch to new processes not yet in wide use. Many editors believed that the changes in printing technology were significant but were coming far too slowly to help newspapers in their cost squeeze. "Editors know, as well as publishers, that the often-predicted revolution has not taken place," *American Editor* magazine said in a 1960 editorial.[56] Indeed, offset presses constituted only a minute part of the $100 million that newspapers invested in capital expenditures in the late 1950s and early 1960s.[57]

Many publishers blamed unions for impeding change. Indiana University journalism teacher Poynter McEvoy, reflecting sentiments often expressed by publishers, wrote in 1960 that union work policies had long kept productivity low despite technological improvements. He called for management to fight unions head-on by breaking up traditional composing room functions and by eliminating make-work rules that cost publishers time and money.[58] But even as publishers criticized unions for opposing change, they usually admitted that management had been equally slow to modernize. "I do not exonerate management of responsibility," declared *Chicago Sun-Times* executive editor Milburn P. Akers in 1958. "As a whole, management has not risen to the crisis any better than the unions."[59]

The slow pace of updating printing technology was a frequent subject of discussion in trade journals. "The effort to solve the problem of costs through these various methods is still in the early stages of an industry which has stood on dead center for two generations," wrote Allan Woods of *Newsday* in 1963. He said the nation's largest newspapers had made the fewest gains in productivity in recent years.[60] *Washington Post* editor J. Russell Wiggins was particularly pessimistic about newspapers' prospects. "Problems darken the horizons of the American press," he wrote in 1959. Recent progress aside, he said, newspapers for decades had progressed far too slowly in both content and production. Productivity remained static or had declined while workers' strikes and wages increased. "Fifty years filled with revolutionary developments in the printing trades have really changed newspapers but very little," Wiggins said. "It grows harder and costlier to get and print the news for citizens who have less and less time to read it. What a challenging situation this is!"[61]

The challenge entailed far more than just impending technological change. In addition, a second, and equally important, trend was building throughout the 1950s that profoundly affected newspapers. America's population, beginning at the end of World War II, began to shift from urban areas to the suburbs. Numerous factors fueled the shift, including a shortage of housing and the slow decay of many central cities, improvements in transportation, and a burgeoning middle class. Newspapers' fortunes shifted along with the population. Metropolitan papers found that the core of their central city readership had left for the suburbs, where they were served by a newly energized suburban press of weeklies and small- and medium-sized dailies. The shift in population left newspapers in both metropolitan and suburban areas struggling to meet the challenges of a changing readership.[62]

Nationwide demographic trends were evident in circulation figures from newspapers in the nation's ten major metropolitan areas—Boston, Chicago, Detroit, Los Angeles, New York, Philadelphia, Pittsburgh, St. Louis, San Francisco, and Washington. Between 1945 and 1962, according to a study prepared for the ANPA in 1963, circulation of suburban weeklies and community dailies (which covered their circulation area and carried little or no state and national news) grew thirty times as fast as did that of the metropolitan dailies. In the seventeen-year period, weeklies grew by 94 percent, community dailies by 81 percent, and metropolitan dailies by just 3 percent. The largest percentage circulation gains in community dailies were in Washington, with 174 percent; Los Angeles, 163 percent; San Francisco, 152 percent; and Detroit, 115 percent. In New York, circulation of community dailies grew by 75 percent while large metropolitan dailies had grown by just 1 percent. In 1945, the big metropolitan newspapers in the ten most populous areas had captured two-thirds of all newspaper circulation. By 1962, their share had fallen to just half.[63]

Newspapers in large cities were gaining only slightly or even losing circulation as many readers moved to the suburbs. Population in the ten metropolitan areas climbed by 45.2 percent in the seventeen-year period, the majority of it in the suburbs, and newspaper circulation reflected the population movement. As a result, community dailies grew by nearly twice the rate of population growth while metropolitan papers experienced little or no growth.[64]

The shift in readership was clear by the mid-1950s. *Business Week* magazine perceptively described the trend in February 1955. "In the big-city downtown areas, more papers, struggling against higher costs, are combining their mechanical operations, merging, or being bought up by chains," it noted. But in the suburbs,

> more small-town papers are coming to life to take care of the population boom and the move to the suburbs. They may be new papers started from scratch, weeklies turned into dailies, or just old papers with a new zest for living. As some metropolitan areas began to have trouble with downtown decay, suburbia grew since the war into an unwieldy place, shouting for some form of community expression.[65]

Both weeklies and small dailies benefited from the rush to the suburbs. The biggest beneficiary, of course, was *Newsday*, the tabloid daily founded on Long Island in 1940 by Alicia Patterson, a relative of the McCormick-Patterson publishing dynasty of Chicago and Washington. *Newsday*'s circulation skyrocketed after World War II, reaching 345,000 in 1962 and even surpassing the circulation of the *New York Herald Tribune*. *Newsday* was by far the country's largest suburban daily, benefiting immensely from the tremendous postwar growth in the Long Island suburbs of New York City.[66] One reason for its success, Patterson said in 1959, was the paper's intense coverage of news in Long Island, a strength the metropolitan dailies in New York were hard-pressed to compete with.[67]

Many other suburban newspapers also saw tremendous growth in the postwar years, including established dailies, weeklies converted to dailies, and papers started from scratch. Between 1945 and 1963, for example, the *Waukegan* (IL) *News-Sun*, north of Chicago, gained 14,000 readers, almost doubling its circulation. The *Daily Tribune* in Royal Oak, Michigan, north of Detroit, increased from 16,000 to 50,000. And the *Beaver County Times*, northwest of Pittsburgh, jumped from 9,000 to 30,000. In suburban San Francisco, the *Palo Alto Times* increased from 8,000 to 37,000 in this period, while the *San Gabriel Valley Tribune*, founded outside Los Angeles in 1955, reached 55,000 by 1962.[68] "The new suburbia has opened up a new frontier in American journalism: the suburban newspaper," declared Charles Hayes, managing editor of the Paddock Publications in Chicago, in 1960.[69]

The Paddock Publications were indeed a success story all their own. A chain of weekly newspapers Stuart Paddock founded in the suburbs surrounding Chicago, by 1959 the chain had thirteen papers. They benefited from a tremendous growth in the suburbs they served, where population jumped from 32,000 in 1950 to 120,000 in 1959. "When folks move out from the city," Paddock said, "they want to put roots down. So they buy the local paper to keep up with the PTA meetings, the village council, and all the problems of the community." In the late 1950s, Paddock Publications was one of the fastest-growing suburban newspaper chains in the country. Its fat weeklies, sometimes containing up to eighty pages, served readers in such northwest Chicago suburbs as Prospect Heights, Elk Grove, Addison, Hoffman, Rolling Meadows, and Arlington Heights.[70] The circulation of the chain's newspapers jumped from 9,000 at the end of World War II to 34,000 in 1959, ensuring the Paddocks a healthy profit, a goal explicit in the newspapers' slogan: "Tell the truth, fear God, and make money."[71]

Suburban newspapers profited not only from population shifts but also from the spread of cheap offset printing. Offset presses—cheaper to buy and to operate than letterpress—enabled entrepreneurs in the growing suburbs to found newspapers with minimal investments. Publishers without the funds to buy offset presses could contract with other publishers to print their newspapers inexpensively.[72] "The drastic cost savings realized through new production techniques," as one scholar of the suburban press has observed, "made it possible for suburban newspapers with limited financial resources to stake out a narrowly defined, yet profitable, market niche by positioning themselves as their community's only local editorial voice."[73]

With readers moving to the suburbs and circulations shifting, both metropolitan and suburban journals struggled to keep up with the changes. The metropolitan papers, for their part, tried frantically to keep up with a changing readership, both in circulation and in news coverage. For them, chasing readers into the suburbs would prove to be an expensive proposition. More reporters were required to cover the suburban areas, and delivering newspapers to communities distant from the central city was expensive. "Cost of servicing subscribers in Suburbia is much greater than servicing them in the city of publication," lamented Ralph E. Heckman of the Fort Wayne, Indiana, newspapers in 1959.[74]

Metropolitan and larger newspapers responded to the exodus in various ways. In circulation, they initiated efforts to follow readers into the suburbs and to hire adults rather than children to deliver newspapers.[75]

The *New York Times*, for example, recognized the growing suburban trend in 1951 and sent salesmen canvassing new subdivisions selling subscriptions. "The whole trend of suburban living makes it imperative that we pursue suburban circulation," said William M. Pike, the *Times'* suburban circulation manager, in 1959. Home delivery subscriptions were crucial, according to Pike, because housewives did not have access to newsstands and because commuters could not read while driving. "We must get them back at home, where they have reading time," he declared.[76] The *Times* effort was successful. Its daily suburban circulation grew by 50 percent, to 157,000, through the 1950s.[77]

In 1957, the *Times* appointed a suburban editor, Kalman Seigel, to direct suburban coverage. His assignment was to coordinate news coverage of the suburban areas newly added to the *Times* circulation area. The news stories were concentrated on a "second front page" inside the newspaper, though other articles about suburbia were scattered throughout each day's issue. The suburban reporters concentrated on news stories of particular interest to the growing population—urban renewal, school and housing integration, population growth, medical care, business migration, education issues, and taxes.[78]

Like Seigel at the *Times*, other editors across the country tried numerous ways to keep their papers relevant to a growing suburban readership increasingly disengaged from news of the city. Many papers began hiring suburban reporters in the 1950s, and some set up special neighborhood editions, newspapers containing news targeted to a particular community and delivered only to that area. The *Cleveland Press*, for example, in 1956 employed a staff of eight full-time reporters, a photographer, and ten part-time "stringers," all to cover the suburbs.[79] The *Newark News* set up extensive zoned editions. "If some editors look a bit more tired than usual," *Detroit Free Press* managing editor Frank Angelo said in 1957, "pity the poor fellows. They're chasing their customers into Suburbia."[80]

The challenge of getting and keeping the new readers was considerable, Angelo said. Suburban subscribers, he said, often continued taking the city paper immediately after their move to the hinterlands but then steadily lost interest in central city news as their attention to local affairs grew. As they become ensconced in their new communities, suburbanites often switched from the metropolitan newspaper to the suburban daily or weekly. "The concentrated drive for suburban news by the metropolitan papers simply is providing more 'dope' for the reader to keep his wonderful habit of reading our papers going," Angelo said. Consequently, newspapers played up local news in the suburban editions, often at the expense of more important national news.[81]

The battle for circulation was often heated. In 1959, the *Cleveland Press* undertook a campaign to bolster circulation by printing suburban editions. Smaller community papers, led by editor Harry Volk of the

Shaker Heights News Press, fought the *Press'* encroachment onto their circulation areas. In editorial columns, the suburban editors portrayed their competition with the *Press* as a David vs. Goliath battle, dubbing *Press* editor Louis Seltzer "King Louie." The editors appealed successfully to advertisers and readers to remain loyal to their community newspapers. "We urge you to buy a less greedy newspaper," Volk urged readers. The *Press*, after losing the public relations battle and suffering other business setbacks, lost 4,000 readers in 1959 to the community newspapers.[82]

The suburban newspapers threatened larger newspapers for advertisers as well as readers. The far-flung shopping districts that sprang up around the new housing developments emptied some downtown areas of businesses and patrons, depriving some metropolitan newspapers of their largest customers, the department stores. This "downtown problem," as *Editor & Publisher's* Robert U. Brown described it, was a substantial worry for both retailers and newspaper executives. He wrote:

> The simple truth has been that if the nation's downtown areas lost out in the competitive battle with the shopping centers for customers then the newspapers would suffer along with the retailers, who up to now spend 75 percent of the retail advertising dollar.[83]

Some newspapers tried to help downtown businesses save themselves. In Memphis, Phoenix, San Jose, Tulsa, Pittsburgh, Buffalo, Milwaukee, Los Angeles, and other cities, newspapers coordinated advertising campaigns by downtown merchants to attract shoppers. They also undertook research with downtown merchants to explore ways to keep suburban customers shopping in their stores.[84] A few newspapers turned down advertising from suburban merchants to protect central city merchants, maintaining a policy to accept advertising only from within the city of publication.[85]

Some newspapers were slow to respond to the shift of businesses to the suburbs. As James Hoge, longtime publisher of the *Chicago Sun-Times*, recalled years later, "We watched Chicago rot away right up to our loading bays before we realized what the death of the central city meant to us."[86] The *Brooklyn Eagle* folded in 1955, having concentrated its circulation and advertising sales in Brooklyn at a time when its readers were leaving the borough in droves for Long Island and other suburbs. After an American Newspaper Guild strike shut down the newspaper on January 28, 1955, an arbitrator who examined the case found that the paper died not from union demands but because it had outlived its "economic usefulness" to the city it served. "The epitaph of the *Brooklyn Eagle*," the arbitrator wrote, "will have to be that it died not at the hands of the Newspaper Guild of New York, but rather because it had become an economic anachronism."[87]

A second long-term population trend also faced newspapers. After strong circulation growth in the 1940s, they continued to grow during the 1950s and early 1960s but not at a rate that matched the rapid growth in population in these years. "There is less tendency," researcher Jon G. Udell wrote in a study for the ANPA in 1965, "for a household to read more than one or two newspapers each day."[88] This decline in multiple readership, which dated to the end of World War II, was due to many factors: larger newspapers, growth of the suburban press, and competition from television chief among them. While the average US household had read 1.33 newspapers a day in 1946, it read only 1.07 in 1963. Daily nationwide newspaper circulation had continued to hit new records almost every year after World War II, but the number of households had grown at an even faster pace. Daily newspaper circulation increased by 16 percent from 1946 to 1963, when it reached 58,905,251. The number of households, meanwhile, had grown by 44 percent in the same period, reaching 55,189,000 in 1963.[89]

Publishers often discounted this trend, correctly pointing out that the Baby Boom generation would not reach young adulthood—newspaper reading age—until the 1960s. Still, they took notice of the population trend and took steps to entice young people into reading newspapers. Many papers began programs to encourage newspaper reading in elementary and secondary schools, arguing that it would build both better citizens and healthier newspapers.[90] Publishers were particularly eager for young readers to acquire the newspaper "habit" because of competition from television. They worried that children reaching maturity in the television era might be less inclined to turn to the printed word.

The ANPA inaugurated a Young Reading Program in the mid-1950s. The program, ANPA general manager Stanford Smith proclaimed in 1960, "has cut across blockades never before breached in journalistic history." He said both teachers and editors had quickly become sold on the program, which organized workshops across the country to train teachers in methods of incorporating newspapers into classroom work. Newspapers of all sizes were participating in the program, which had been founded by C.K. Jefferson of the Des Moines (IA) Register & Tribune in 1955 and had spread through the efforts of ANPA and the International Circulation Managers Association.[91]

Newspapers across the country either participated in the ANPA's program or started their own youth-readership initiatives. At the La Crosse (WI) Tribune, managers undertook a "concentrated effort to get our newspaper into as many schools in our area as possible," reported circulation manager Ed Keefe in 1955. The newspaper sent sample subscriptions to 900 area schools and wrote letters to teachers suggesting ways to use the newspaper in the classroom, resulting in 300 school subscriptions.[92] The *Miami Herald* assembled a two-week high school course outline on newspaper reading and provided it free of charge to Dade County schools. The *Herald* provided a text for the course called "How to Get the Most Out of Your Newspaper." The *New York Times, Milwaukee Journal, New York Herald Tribune*, and other newspapers organized similar programs. *Editor & Publisher* columnist T.S. Irvin noted the growth in such efforts in 1956 and recommended that all newspapers adopt them "unless we are to sit by and watch reading becoming a fading and secondary if not an altogether lost art."[93]

In population trends as in other long-term trends in printing technology and suburbanization, editors and publishers recognized the potential threat to newspapers and had begun to take steps to adjust. But there was little sense the long-term changes threatened newspapers' very existence. While many publishers and editors agreed that newspapers were indeed lagging behind in updating their technology, they also agreed that newspapers were otherwise confronting their problems head-on and with some success. While some newspapers had closed or merged in the largest cities through the 1950s, overall the newspaper industry seemed healthy at decade's end. This perception would not last long into the 1960s, however, when a host of these and other long-term trends would combine and push the newspaper industry into crisis.

Chapter 7

Kennedy and the Press, 1960–1963

For newspapers and for print journalists, the election of President John F. Kennedy signaled profound change. With a series of innovations, he strained a press-president relationship that had been growing steadily more fractious since World War II. In his facility with television, his attempts to court individual reporters and newspapers, and his overall press policies, Kennedy and his administration contributed to a greater distrust between the press and government even as he enjoyed warm relationships with many individual reporters. Many journalists believed that the innovations of the Kennedy years had made them more skeptical of government and of officials.

Chief among Kennedy's innovations was his decision to allow live television coverage of his news conferences, which substantially changed these regular meetings of the press and the president, increasing television's influence while diminishing newspapers' influence. In addition, Kennedy stepped up so-called news management techniques before and during the foreign policy crises in Cuba in 1961 and 1962. Reporters thus found that their access to some information was becoming more limited even as they enjoyed easier access to routine information. Kennedy's well-known close personal relationships with some reporters alienated those not favored with preferential treatment.

Kennedy's press policies added to press-government antagonisms that had been building throughout the administration of his predecessor, Dwight Eisenhower.

Under Eisenhower, the increasing government secrecy that had characterized the Truman administration had continued. Editors and publishers had been disappointed that Executive Order 10501—Eisenhower's 1953 directive revising President Truman's security classification system— while modifying the government's classification system nevertheless had kept it in place. Journalists often complained that government secrecy had become more entrenched as the Cold War wore on. James Reston, Washington bureau chief of the *New York Times*, told a national television audience in 1959 that increasing government secrecy and news management were keeping important news from the American people. "I know a great many of my colleagues are very worried about this," he said. "They think there is a great conspiracy in Washington to suppress the news."[1]

Journalists indeed lined up to protest what they perceived as increasing government secrecy. So many had complained of the withholding of information that Representative John E. Moss of California had begun hearings in 1955. "We are disturbed by the withholding of information in many areas of government—local, State, and Federal, legislative, executive, and judicial," J.R. Wiggins, executive editor of the *Washington Post & Times Herald*, told Moss' subcommittee at the opening session of the hearings, which stretched throughout the remainder of the decade. Wiggins and other editors agreed that while journalists were willing to withhold information for the protection of national security, they also worried that the government was increasingly withholding information on the pretense of safeguarding national security. He noted that during 1955 alone, the Army had refused to release a letter for fear it would be "misunderstood," that Defense Department officials had been instructed to release only "constructive" news, and that defense contractors were ordered to withhold any information of potential value to the enemy. The government's defense information policies, Wiggins said, amounted to "a scorched freedom policy."[2]

A few journalists also sounded warnings about Eisenhower's refusal to release some information to Congress under the doctrine of executive privilege. Clark R. Mollenhoff of the Washington bureau of the Cowles publications called the use of executive privilege "probably one of the greatest threats to freedom of information in our time." Since Eisenhower had first cited executive authority as justification to withhold information from Congress during the Army-McCarthy hearings, Mollenhoff told Moss' subcommittee in 1955, seventeen executive agencies had withheld documents by citing Eisenhower's precedent.[3] In his 1954 letter to Congress, Eisenhower had stated that he as president had the right to withhold executive information when "what was sought was confidential or its disclosure would be incompatible with the public interest or jeopardize the safety of the nation." This policy, he asserted, was necessary to protect secrecy in policy-making discussions and for the separation of powers.[4]

As the 1960s began, after two terms of tangling with Eisenhower's administration over access to news, it appeared that a change in administration would improve press-government relations. Kennedy gave every indication that his press relations would be far different from his predecessor's. Both he and his opponent in the 1960 presidential election, Vice President Richard M. Nixon, had pledged to the news media to place a high priority on making information available. After his election, Kennedy had reiterated his commitment to open information policies. In a January 1961 letter to Turner Catledge, executive editor of the *New York Times* and the president of the American Society of Newspaper Editors (ASNE), he wrote: "[W]ithin the rather narrow limits of national security the people of the United States are entitled to the fullest possible information about their government—and the president must see that they receive it."[5]

Kennedy not only promised a more open government, but he also promised a warmer relationship with reporters. Beginning in the 1960 campaign, national press corps reporters had expected that they would enjoy greater personal rapport with the young, vital Kennedy than they had with the aloof, patrician Eisenhower. Indeed, Kennedy's one-on-one relationships with reporters were totally at odds with anything veteran Washington reporters had ever witnessed. "Unlike his predecessor, who regarded reporters as visitors from another planet," observed *New York Post* correspondent Mary McGrory late in 1961, "Kennedy tends to think of them as fellow lodge members."[6] Kennedy had worked briefly as a reporter for the International News Service after World War II, covering, among other things, the formation of the United Nations and the postwar elections in Great Britain.[7]

While Eisenhower had avoided reporters, Kennedy unabashedly befriended them. Elected by a razor-thin margin, he courted journalists because he viewed the press as an important manipulator of opinion in the policy-making process. "I think the press was important to him because he knew a lot of people," recalled Kennedy's national security adviser, McGeorge Bundy. "He knew how they worked, and he knew that what the press said would have an effect on what people thought."[8] Roger Hilsman, an assistant secretary of state in the Kennedy years, said administration officials believed that the press was the most important interpreter of policy issues.[9] Kennedy's aide Arthur M. Schlesinger, Jr., said that Kennedy had genuine affection for his reporter friends, but he cultivated them for political as well as for personal reasons. "Kennedy," he recalled, "liked newspapermen; they liked him; and he recognized that they provided him with a potent means of appealing to readers over the heads of publishers."[10]

Accordingly, Kennedy sought out the company of reporters, editors, and publishers, both to award snippets of news and to mix with them socially. This was a radical violation of protocol for Washington reporters, who had traditionally opposed one-on-one interviews because they gave unfair advantage to favored correspondents. Kennedy began to flout this tradition from the earliest days of his presidency. After his inaugural ball, he and the presidential party dropped in for a quick visit with columnist Joseph Alsop. In subsequent days he stopped by to chat with Walter Lippmann at the columnist's home and to dine with reporter Rowland Evans, Jr., of the *New York Herald Tribune*. Some journalists, such as Kennedy's old friend Charles Bartlett of the *Chattanooga* (TN) *Times*, were even invited to the president's weekend retreat on the Massachusetts coast.[11] Once in office, Kennedy continued close friendships with Bartlett and other journalists such as Benjamin Bradlee of *Newsweek* magazine. "It's hard," Kennedy once joked to visitors to his office in late 1961, "not to get invited to the White House these days."[12] His friendly relations with journalists, especially columnists, were well-known and much publicized throughout his administration.

"In his dealings with the press," wrote *New York Times* columnist Reston in late 1961, "President Kennedy has broken every rule in the book and got away with it." Particularly revolutionary, he concluded, was Kennedy's personal relationships with individual reporters and his willingness to meet with them one-on-one. Reston pointed out that Kennedy's intimacy with reporters would not have been remarkable in the nineteenth century, but it was certainly new for the middle of the twentieth. "[Kennedy] has not only allowed columnists to see him privately," he wrote, "but has permitted them to publish his remarks. He has given television interviews on some networks and not on others. He has been the darling and collaborator of all budding biographers." The president's many innovations, in Reston's estimation, had proven extraordinarily successful at exploiting the news media. "[A]s a political instrument the new accessibility of the White House is undoubtedly effective," he concluded.[13]

Bill Lawrence of the *New York Times'* Washington bureau was one of Kennedy's closest confidants, and their relationship illustrates the degree to which the new president befriended individual journalists. "I never knew any President as well as I knew Jack Kennedy, who was a close friend in and out of the White House," recalled Lawrence, who was Kennedy's frequent golfing partner and often a beneficiary of his leaks and trial balloons. "I found with Kennedy that a round of golf could be much more fruitful in news terms than many formal presidential news conferences. John Kennedy thoroughly enjoyed 'leaking' a news story, and I was lucky enough to be the recipient of so many breaks on big stories."[14] Lawrence had grown close to Kennedy during the 1960 presidential campaign, when the candidate had carefully cultivated the reporters traveling with him.[15]

Reporters not as favored as Lawrence took notice of the preferential treatment accorded some journalists and resented it. A few veterans grumbled that many of their younger colleagues were getting far too close to their sources. "Kennedy worked hard to develop and maintain his ties with reporters and editors," remembered journalist Sarah McClendon, whose one-woman news service served dozens of smaller newspapers. Of Kennedy's relationship with the press, she recalled years afterward, "The public believed the press courted the Kennedys; it was actually the Kennedys who courted the press." The president created "media stars," she asserted, by feeding exclusive stories to favored reporters. "His pets—Charlie Bartlett, David Wise, Joe Kraft, Rowland Evans, Tom Ross, Ben Bradlee—mined Kennedy as if he were the mother lode," McClendon wrote. "They cultivated his favors and friendship socially and professionally."[16]

Kennedy courted not just reporters but also their employers. He held a succession of private, off-the-record dinners with publishers to discuss administration policies. Nicknamed "Operation Publisher," the Kennedy practice was to invite groups of publishers from a single state or geographic area to two- to three-hour meetings at the White House. Once inside, the publishers found a solicitous and inquiring president courting their support. "Everything is handled in such an informal manner you feel at ease," reported a Republican publisher after emerging from one of these meetings.[17] Charles Schneider, editor of the *Memphis* (TN) *Press-Scimitar*, had this assessment after meeting with Kennedy: "He charmed the birds out of the trees."[18]

Another significant innovation in presidential-press relations was Kennedy's decision to permit live broadcasting of his press conferences. The Eisenhower administration had allowed filming of the conferences but had also required White House approval of any film clips to be broadcast. Kennedy, who had proven his ability in front of the cameras during his televised debates with Nixon during the presidential campaign, proposed allowing live coverage of the conferences. He wanted live coverage, his press secretary Pierre Salinger recalled, in order to bypass the traditional news media to appeal directly to the public for support. "This is the right thing," Kennedy told Salinger during the discussions over the switch to live television. "We should be able to go around the newspapers if that becomes necessary."[19] Moreover, advances in electronic technology had made the live broadcasting of presidential press conferences inevitable, Salinger told the 1961 convention of the American Society of Newspaper Editors (ASNE). He maintained that print journalists' complaints about the new practice were rooted in nostalgia for the small, intimate presidential press conferences of the 1930s and 1940s.[20]

Still, most newspaper reporters were chagrined at the new practice. When Kennedy's aides unveiled the broadcasting plans before representatives of the White House Correspondents Association, print-press antagonisms nearly overwhelmed the meeting. "At one point," Salinger said, "I thought the meeting would be reduced to violence as the voices ran across the table."[21] Print reporters complained that the new practice interfered with the traditional close contact between newspaper reporters and the president. "By accommodating television," Robert J. Donovan of the *New York Herald Tribune* wrote in 1961, "Mr. Kennedy has robbed the presidential press conference of much of its best flavor. The intimacy between the President and the reporter has been diluted by distance." Donovan said he feared that live broadcasting of presidential press conferences would diminish the presidency, making it "commonplace."[22] Other newspaper reporters were equally unenthusiastic. *New York Post* Capitol correspondent William V. Shannon said live telecasting had killed all spontaneity in the press conference.[23] The *New York Times'* Reston pronounced live telecasting the "goofiest idea since the hula hoop."[24]

A few journalists, however, were enthusiastic about the innovation. "Televised Presidential press conferences would increase understanding of governmental problems and policies and that is all to the good," said Paul Veblen, executive editor of the *Santa Barbara* (CA) *News Press*.[25] Other editors said that live television was a worthy experiment in the presidential press conference, which was, after all, an evolving institution for which ground rules had been updated through the years. "The only way to see if it will work is to try it," said the *St. Louis Post-Dispatch's* Raymond P. Brandt.[26]

Ben Bagdikian, a correspondent for the *Providence* (RI) *Journal and Bulletin*, complained in early 1961 that Kennedy's innovations had affected print reporters and newspapers in many ways. For one thing, the conference was now much more formal, given that it had been moved from the small but intimate Indian Treaty Room in the old State Department Building to an imposing 800-seat auditorium in the department's new, modern headquarters. Print reporters had lost the initiative in the press conferences because of Kennedy's practice of beginning the meeting with a twenty-minute formal statement, which he often used to make announcements that would dominate the headlines and the evening news. Television had also hurt reporters' public image, Bagdikian said, because television viewers had complained about the "rudeness" of reporters jockeying for the president's attention during the press conferences. More importantly, according to Bagdikian, live coverage had reduced print journalists' accounts of the press conference to irrelevance. Because many of their readers had already witnessed the news conference firsthand, print reporters were left only to interpret the event, not report it.[27] After live telecasting of news conferences began, so few newspapers saw the need to print verbatim transcripts of the conferences that the

Associated Press (AP) ended its longtime practice of transmitting transcripts to member papers.[28]

"I think it is not only a mess as it is presently constituted," *Chicago Daily News* Washington bureau chief Peter Lisagor said in 1961, "but I think it is the nearest thing we have in this town to anarchy." Because of the televised press conference, he said, print reporters had been transformed at these events into mere props for the television cameras. More importantly, the press conference had lost much of its coherence because the mass of reporters in attendance asked questions on widely divergent topics. Lisagor also complained that reporters tended to be too deferential to Kennedy in the formal surroundings of the State Department auditorium.[29]

New York Herald Tribune television columnist John Crosby, echoing a common complaint among newspaper reporters, criticized the conferences because they gave the president so much control over meetings with the media. By skillfully avoiding the crux of reporters' questions, he could appear to the public to have answered a question when in fact he had failed to provide any new information. Of the press conferences, Crosby said, "They remind me of a Chinese dinner. You eat and eat of a dozen different dishes—but an hour later you find yourself hungry."[30]

But Kennedy's mastery of the televised press conference, beginning with the first live broadcast on January 25, 1961, made it clear that the innovation was a success, at least as far as the new president was concerned. "Live television has become the new arm of presidential communication with the public," wrote United Press International (UPI) correspondent Merriman Smith the day after Kennedy's inaugural press conference. Kennedy had handled himself "coolly and confidently," Smith wrote, thereby putting to rest any fears that he might embarrass himself or the country through a misstatement before the television cameras.[31] Both the *Washington Post* and the *New York Times* praised his performance. Other newspapers also lauded the innovation. "Mr. Kennedy's first Presidential Press conference last night," wrote an editorialist in the *Baltimore Sun*, "was a measured, confident performance, and an artful one."[32] Even *Editor & Publisher* was impressed. "The entire performance," the magazine's editors wrote, "could be called a crashing success for him from all angles—politically, diplomatically and dramatically."[33]

Live television at presidential press conferences would prove, by the mid-1960s, to be only one of several innovations in electronic journalism that would threaten newspapers. However, live news conferences affected newspapers in two ways. First, they increased the influence of television in the news media's relationship to the presidency. Television gained credibility as a news medium by offering, for the first time, live coverage of a routine newsmaking event. Newspapers' reports now seemed irrelevant to the process of reporting the news conference when readers could regularly witness the event themselves. While administration officials such as Salinger argued that television increased reader interest in press conferences, most White House correspondents believed that it caused readers to ignore their reports.[34] Second, Kennedy's mastery of the live conference was part of larger administration efforts to control the flow of news coming out of the administration. The broadcasts gave him a way to bypass traditional news media and speak to the public directly. Taken together with the president's skillful handling of the press in other areas, they increased his power to directly manipulate the news.

Print journalists believed officials were consistently trying to "manage the news," that is, to control the press by keeping tight reins on reporters and on the release of information. The debate about "news management" in the Kennedy administration was not new, of course. In fact, Washington reporters had expressed the same concerns during the Eisenhower administration. But they believed that the Kennedy administration was both more brazen and more skillful in its efforts to manage the news than previous administrations. "The Kennedy administration may try to manage the news a bit more than some of its predecessors," wrote the *St. Louis Post-Dispatch*'s Richard Dudman in 1963. "The big difference here is that the Kennedy administration admits it manages the news and tries to justify it."[35] Kennedy's emphasis on press relations and his administration's efforts to force all branches to speak with one voice vastly expanded journalists' concern about government control of news. "News management" moved to center stage not only in journalistic circles but also in the public eye, emerging as a bona fide news story in the administration's handling of several foreign policy crises. The conflict between press and government was reaching new heights.

Even the cornerstone of Kennedy's press relations, his personal relationships with individual reporters, was widely considered part of this effort to manage the press. Kennedy used friendships with reporters both to launch trial balloons and to attempt to control what reporters wrote about his administration. Veteran *New York Times* political columnist Arthur Krock wrote in 1963 that Kennedy's close relationships with reporters were a form of news management, a "social flattery of Washington reporters and columnists—many more than ever got this treatment in the past—by the President and his high level subordinates." Krock believed that Kennedy's handling of the press was "the most intensive indirect effort by any President of the United States to manage the news."[36]

CBS correspondent Charles Collingwood, surveying Kennedy's press relations in a 1961 broadcast, said he was skillfully manipulating the press through exclusive interviews, which heretofore had been "rarer than the whooping crane." Relatively few correspondents complained about the practice because so many benefited, and beneficiaries overlooked the manipulation inherent in the interviews. "In fact, your Washington correspondent is not nearly so fierce a dog as he likes to make out," Collingwood observed. "If he's given a few kind words and a bone now and then, he's apt to be quite content and won't steal the roast off the table."[37]

Kennedy also managed news with well-targeted criticisms of reporters' work. Krock and other correspondents charged that he displayed a "bristling sensitiveness to critical analysis [that] has not been exceeded by that of any previous occupant of the White House."[38] One Washington correspondent argued that the president, a prodigious and speedy reader, "reads every damn thing written" about him, while "his skin is as thin as cigarette paper."[39] Kennedy and administration officials were quick to criticize correspondents when a news article did not meet their satisfaction. Merriman Smith of UPI was among those who were amazed at the sensitivity of the president and his staff. "How they can spot an obscure paragraph in a paper of 3,000 circulation 2,000 miles away is beyond me," Smith marveled. "They must have a thousand little gnomes reading the papers for them."[40] Presidential aide Arthur M. Schlesinger, Jr., recalled that Kennedy "retained an inexhaustible capacity to become vastly, if briefly, annoyed by hostile articles or by stories based on leaks." Kennedy once grew so incensed at *New York Herald Tribune* editorials that he ordered the White House's subscription to the newspaper canceled. After tempers cooled, the White House renewed the subscription.[41]

More significant to Kennedy's news management efforts were his administration's efforts to control the flow of news out of federal offices. Press complaints about these efforts began almost immediately after Kennedy was elected. Barely a month after his inauguration, *Editor & Publisher* complained of a "disturbing trend" in government information policies. Its editors were upset because of several new actions and policies of the new administration. Secretary of State Dean Rusk had barred officials from releasing information about preliminary discussions of foreign problems. Congressional leaders were being discouraged from revealing to reporters the nature of their discussions with the president. And heads of executive agency departments were holding weekly meetings to coordinate their activities regarding the press. Moreover, the administration had pressured the *New York Herald Tribune* to withhold publication of a news story so that the story could be released at the president's news conference.[42]

A turning point in press-government relations was the administration's handling of the press during the invasion of Cuba at the Bay of Pigs in April 1961, the U.S.-backed attempt by Cuban exiles to overthrow

Cuban President Fidel Castro. Kennedy's news management in this and subsequent crises caused journalists to distrust his administration. They were angered at having caught officials in lies and resentful that Kennedy and his aides had placed some of the blame for the failed invasion at the feet of journalists. "The U.S. press is being made the scapegoat of the Cuban invasion debacle," complained *Editor & Publisher*. The press, the editors wrote, was being unfairly damned both for telling too much about invasion plans and for failing to tell the story soon enough and in adequate detail.[43]

The Kennedy administration not only tried to carefully manage the news of the Cuban invasion but also made numerous misstatements in the process of mounting it. The administration denied any official knowledge of an imminent invasion, deliberately handed out incomplete and inaccurate information about military preparations, pressured newspapers to alter or withhold news stories about Cuba, and chastised them afterward for being insufficiently cooperative in pursuing the country's Cold War goals.

New York Times' columnist Reston listed two of the government's lies during the crisis. After the troop landings began, officials told reporters in Miami that this was an "invasion" of 5,000 men, an exaggeration intended to impress Cubans and prompt them to rise up in support of the invaders. Then, once the landing force encountered stiff resistance, officials changed their story, saying that it was not an invasion at all, but merely a landing of several hundred men to deliver supplies to anti-Castro guerrillas. In fact, about 1,000 troops landed in Cuba, and officials had twice lied to reporters. "Both times," Reston wrote, "the press was debased for the government's purpose." Moreover, the Castro government and its Soviet advisers knew that the American government's statements were untrue. As a result, Reston said, "the American people were the only ones to be fooled."[44]

Moreover, Kennedy's credibility with reporters suffered because he and his subordinates had repeatedly denied American involvement in a possible invasion. Four days before the invasion, Kennedy was unequivocal about the matter in his regular news conference. "There will not be under any conditions an intervention in Cuba by the U.S. armed forces," Kennedy said.[45] The day the invasion began, Secretary of State Rusk had told reporters, "The American people are entitled to know whether we are intervening in Cuba or intend to do so in the future. The answer to that question is no."[46] Administration officials had, before the invasion, actively sought to prevent news outlets from writing about Cuba. Word of the invasion had spread in the news media, particularly in smaller publications, but the story was slow to catch on among larger newspapers and magazines. Before the invasion, recalled Schlesinger, the editor of *The New Republic* had sent the White House a detailed account of the

Central Intelligence Agency's plans to train Cuban exiles for the military operation, asking if the publication of the article would injure national security. At the president's request, the magazine had declined to print the article.[47] The *Miami Herald* had also refrained from publishing information about the invasion beforehand at the administration's request, even though the armed uprising by the Cuban rebels was well known among the large Cuban population in Miami. "Everyone in Miami knew about it," the *Herald*'s George Beebe told the Associated Press Managing Editors (APME) in 1961. "I had a five-part series in my desk for two months, but I didn't want to be the first S.O.B. to release the story." The large Cuban population of Miami was well aware of the invasion plans, and reporters had heard about it from multiple sources, Beebe said. The *Herald* had tried but failed to confirm the story with the CIA, the Federal Bureau of Investigation, and the State Department.[48]

The *New York Times* published an account of the invasion plans on April 7, 1961, but watered down the account for fear of compromising national security. It had written about the invasion preparations only once before, on January 10, 1961. The April 7 news story was in fact somewhat vague, omitting any direct mention of the CIA though it made clear that Americans were training the invasion force. Within the *Times*, editors had argued about whether to publish the article. Reston, concerned that it might endanger national security, believed the newspaper should not describe the timing of the invasion. Publisher Orvil Dryfoos and managing editor Turner Catledge were worried about the article's implications for national security, but Catledge wanted it published. The final version omitted any mention of the invasion as "imminent," as reporter Tad Szulc had originally described it, and discarded plans for a four-column headline in favor of a less prominent one-column heading. The story ran on Page 1. Some *Times* editors, such as managing editor Clifton Daniel and assistant managing editor Theodore Bernstein, had opposed any changes in Szulc's article because, they argued, as Daniel recalled in 1966, "never before had the front-page play in the *New York Times* been changed for reasons of policy."[49]

The Kennedy administration responded by citing the need to protect national security and by criticizing newspaper performance. The president's aides, and even Kennedy himself, offered two pointed but contradictory criticisms of the press' performance. On the one hand, Kennedy told reporters and publishers privately that the *Times* should have printed everything it had known about the invasion. "Maybe if you had printed more about the operation," Kennedy told Catledge a month after the invasion, "you would have saved us from a colossal mistake."[50] According to Daniel, Kennedy repeated essentially the same remark to Dryfoos in 1962.[51] On the other hand, he blamed the press for contributing to the Cuban fiasco and called for greater voluntary censorship. In a much-publicized speech before a meeting of the American Newspaper Publishers Association's Bureau of Advertising on April 27, 1961, he told publishers that they should consider the national security implications of news stories before publishing them. "Every newspaper now asks itself, with respect to every story: 'Is it news?'" Kennedy said. "All I suggest is that you add the question: 'Is it in the interest of national security?'"[52]

Journalists and publishers interpreted the president's remarks as a call for a meeting to discuss voluntary censorship. A meeting was held on May 9, 1961, but it accomplished little. For eighty minutes Kennedy conferred with officials from the American Newspaper Publishers Association (ANPA), the ASNE, AP, and United Press International (UPI). He told them that while the administration intended to continue free access to news, the press itself should show greater restraint. As evidence of press irresponsibility, he cited several news articles printed by the *Times* that he said had hurt national security. One was an article about Cuban invaders being trained in Guatemala, and the other detailed American tracking of Soviet missiles in Turkey. Catledge, who attended the meeting, told the president that the *Times* had gotten the runaround or half-truths in trying to confirm each of the two stories with the government. The *Times* would have withheld the articles, he said, if someone in the government had told the truth to Reston or to another high *Times* official in confidence.[53] The media representatives told Kennedy that any kind of censorship—voluntary or not—was unnecessary in peacetime and in any case would not work without adequate machinery to enforce it. ASNE President Felix R. McKnight of the *Dallas* (TX) *Times-Herald* told Kennedy that "only the declaration of a national emergency by the President of the United States would make imperative the imposition of news censorship."[54]

Reporters and publishers were aghast at having caught the administration in lies and half-truths. For journalists, it was one thing to withhold information in wartime or in a national emergency, but it was quite another for the government to lie to reporters outright in peacetime. The Freedom of Information (FOI) Committee of the Associated Press Managing Editors Association concluded that the events in Cuba had jolted editors. "The injustice of inferentially blaming the press for blunders that even tight wartime censorship could not have concealed brought indignant reaction," the committee members said.[55] The *New York Times* editorialized on May 10, 1961, that the danger posed by untruthful government officials "has raised a domestic question that is likely to come up again and again" until it is solved. When public officials in a democracy lie to the people, the *Times* wrote, the people lose confidence.[56]

For press critics, the problem had not been that the press had failed to cooperate with the government, but that the press had failed to adequately investigate an important news story vital to the interests of United States citizens. "As far as the public is concerned," complained CBS correspondent Charles Collingwood in an April 1961 broadcast, "last week's explosion in Cuba took place in a sort of vacuum of information and for this vacuum the press as the principal purveyor of information in this country must bear a large share of the responsibility." As Collingwood pointed out, U.S. involvement in preparations for the invasion had been made public as early as the winter of 1960. An academic journal had described invasion preparations in October 1960, and this account was discussed in the *Nation* of November 1960. On December 22, 1960, the *Los Angeles Mirror* had published an account of the Guatemalan training base from which the invasion was to be launched, and a much-shortened form of the *Mirror*'s account ran on the AP national wire. Yet most newspapers had given the invasion plans little notice until the *New York Times* ran its first article on the rebels' Guatemalan base on January 10, 1961, and even then few had explored the U.S. government's role in the invasion. Thanks to the nation's press, Collingwood reported, "we were left in the dark about Cuba."[57]

Publishers and journalists emerged from the Bay of Pigs fiasco angered that they had been lied to yet criticized both for reporting too much and for reporting too little. The experience served to increase distrust between the press and the government. It was, therefore, as *New York Times* managing editor Daniel put it, significant not only to the history of Latin America but "also important in the history of relations between the American press and the United States government." To Daniel, the incident underscored the principle that journalists have the duty to constantly question national leaders, who alone are responsible for national security. Journalists, he argued, should continue questioning leaders and their policies except in wartime or during a threat of war.[58] Reston espoused a similar principle in recalling, after his retirement, the lessons of these years. "My own experience was that governments usually got the voluntary cooperation of the media when secrecy was essential to national security," he wrote. "It was when governments were addicted to secrecy and used it to cover up their mistakes and protect their political and personal interests that representative government and a free press came into conflict."[59]

The Cuban missile crisis of 1962 added to the growing distrust between government and reporters. Over a period of several weeks, the Kennedy administration imposed tight controls over information provided to the news media. Officials sought to have the government "speak with one voice" to the Soviet Union following the disclosure that the Russians had installed offensive nuclear missiles in Cuba. Castro had approved Soviet Premier Nikita Khrushchev's request to install the missiles, partly in response to fears of another American invasion of Cuba. Until the

Russians agreed to remove the missiles after weeks of negotiations, the world stood at the brink of nuclear war. The American government tightly controlled what journalists could report and where they could go in covering the crisis. Reporters were angered both by the government's efforts to control the news and by officials' explanations immediately afterward that the government had been justified in doing so.

Newspaper groups contended that the government's "news management" had undermined American democracy. Gene Robb, publisher of the *Albany* (NY) *Times-Union* and vice president of the ANPA, told a Congressional committee examining the government's news policies in 1963 that, during the crisis, the press had caught officials lying on numerous occasions. "We have, as a result, we believe," Robb testified, "a really serious crisis in the credibility of Government pronouncements. A government can successfully lie no more than once to its people. Thereafter, everything it says and does becomes suspect."[60] He said that while reporters and publishers had long understood that any administration would always attempt to put the best face on government programs, the Kennedy administration's "news management" policies had violated a basic tenet of democracy—that a government should always tell the truth to its citizenry.[61]

In a report to newspapers compiled in late 1962, the ASNE and the ANPA compiled a laundry list of the government's "news management" activities during the crisis. "[T]he major press complaint was not that news was being censored or suppressed for security reasons, but that there was deliberate deception and manipulation of news," said the report, compiled by John H. Colburn of the *Richmond* (VA) *Times-Dispatch*. He cited the following incidents as evidence of government deception: The Defense Department had reported on October 19, 1962, that it had no information indicating the presence of offensive weapons in Cuba, yet Defense Secretary Robert McNamara later acknowledged that he had received intelligence reports confirming such weapons as early as October 15. American officials had claimed during the crisis to have imposed a strict naval blockade of Cuba, when in fact only a selective blockade was enforced. And President Kennedy had canceled a political tour to return to Washington, claiming he had a cold, when actually he was returning to deal with the Cuban crisis.[62] Reporters could hardly judge the truth of the administration's pronouncements, since they had been prohibited from traveling on the quarantine ships to the Caribbean.[63]

If reporters were upset at news controls during the missile crisis, they were enraged that controls continued as it wound down. Most upsetting to them were the controls imposed in the Defense and State Departments in late October 1962. Both Arthur Sylvester, the Defense Department spokesman, and Robert Manning, the State Department spokesman, had issued directives requiring more restrictive oversight of information given to reporters.[64] The Defense Department, for example, had required employees to report to superiors all conversations with reporters. Journalists believed that this policy, issued at the direction of the White House, would keep them from learning details of policy disputes. They viewed the rule as a "Gestapo tactic," said Washington correspondent Clark R. Mollenhoff of the Cowles publications. "The Cuban crisis has resulted in one of our most dramatic examples of the high-level handout."[65]

Journalists were angered not only at the Pentagon's news controls but also at Sylvester's admission, on October 30, 1962, that the government had indeed managed the news during the crisis. Sylvester said the government had spoken with "one voice" so as to clearly state its position to the Soviets. News, he said, "was part of the weaponry that a President has in the application of military force and related forces to the solution of political problems, or to the application of international political pressure."[66] Sylvester later said the government had, in his words, a right "to lie to save itself" when facing the threat of nuclear war.[67] His frankness prompted an immediate response from Lee Hills, executive editor of Knight Newspapers and ASNE president, who protested that the press "must not be used as an implement to mislead the public."[68]

The nation's newspapers were equally vehement. "There is no doubt," wrote the editors of the *New York Times*, "that 'management' or 'control' of the news is censorship described by a sweeter term. There is no doubt that it restricts the people's right to know."[69] Representatives of the National Editorial Association (NEA, the organization of weeklies and small dailies), the ANPA, and ASNE met December 13, 1962, and issued a joint statement condemning the Kennedy administration's policies. The statement expressed concern that news management would suppress information "as a means to some desired end" and thus exceed legitimate censorship of military information. "Security of the nation," the statement said, "can be maintained only by the full reporting of all the truth that is not harmful to the national military interest."[70]

Sylvester was initially unrepentant for his remarks, however, and insisted that they had been taken out of context. Kennedy instructed his aide Theodore C. Sorensen to draft a letter for Sylvester to sign explaining both the president's and Sylvester's abhorrence of censorship, but Sylvester did not want to appease his critics and refused to sign it. But in March 1963, he appeared before the House Subcommittee on Government Information and qualified his earlier statement. He said that the government had the right only "to lie to save itself when it's going up into a nuclear war" in moments of imminent attack. "The government does not have the right to lie to the American people."[71]

Kennedy and his aides maintained that the government had not lied, but instead had withheld news from the public so as to keep the information from the country's enemies. "We did not lie to the American people," Salinger told the Women's National Press Club in March 1963. "We did not deprive the American people of any information except that which, for the highest national security, had to be withheld from our adversaries." Kennedy was justified, the press secretary said, in withholding information about the crisis until the quarantine of Cuba was announced October 22, 1962. "This policy was an absolute necessity for the success of the president's quarantine plan—and I believe played an integral part of his success." He added that some newspapers, not the government, were managing the news by printing articles critical of the administration.[72]

Kennedy himself had defended the administration's news policies immediately after the Cuban crisis ended. In his press conference of November 20, 1962, he offered no apologies for keeping details of the incident in "the highest levels of government" and for controlling information that was released to the public and to the Russians. He said that if news about the Soviet buildup had leaked out before the US government was sure of its response, disaster could have resulted. Of the Sylvester and Manning directives, Kennedy said their purpose was to prevent highly sensitive information from leaking to the press. He said he did not believe that the directives had inhibited the flow of news out of the Pentagon and that he would revoke the orders if that were proven the case. The State Department's directive was withdrawn a week later.[73]

The increasing distrust between reporters and government officials in the Kennedy years expanded a rift that had been gradually widening since World War II. "Sylvester's candor touched off a furor in journalistic circles," recalled UPI correspondent Helen Thomas. "The debate was the forerunner of 'the credibility gap' that caused the downfall of two of Kennedy's successors."[74] Whether Kennedy's actions in Cuba were justified or not, the press was growing increasingly inclined to distrust government pronouncements during national crises. The distrust grew despite Kennedy's warm personal relationships with many correspondents and despite the national peril posed by the Cuban missile crisis. It would continue to grow through the mid-1960s during the administration of Kennedy's successor, a man far less skillful in dealing with the press and facing international crises of his own.

Chapter 8

An Industry in Crisis, 1960–1965

Familiar challenges that had confronted the nation's daily newspapers to varying degrees since the end of World War II intensified in the early and middle 1960s. The media marketplace was changing rapidly. Mergers and closings continued in the largest cities, where newspapers were most susceptible to the multiple pressures of steadily rising costs, shifting readership, and rapid technological change. Chain ownership grew exponentially. Meanwhile, newspapers' most aggressive competitor—television—competed with newspapers in both familiar and surprising ways. Television advertising continued to cut into newspaper profits, and television news earned newfound credibility following its blanket coverage of President Kennedy's assassination in 1963. All of these long-term trends had been building for years, even decades, but by 1965 they held center stage in a newspaper industry confronted by rapid change on multiple fronts. While the industry remained prosperous overall, the challenges and changes confronting daily newspapers—both as businesses and as journalistic institutions—threatened profits and clouded publishers' optimism about newspapers' future. The accelerating pace of change convinced many publishers and critics that newspapers had been far too slow to adapt as these trends were building in the years following World War II.

Despite these trends, newspapers—and the other largest media industries—appeared to have survived the tumultuous 1950s largely unscathed. Only the national magazines appeared to have been deeply wounded by television, and even they showed some increase in profits in the early 1960s.[1] By contrast, the rapid reemergence of radio as a lucrative, locally oriented medium was little short of phenomenal. Radio "is stalking the land like a zombie," *Newsweek* marveled in 1965, "long dead but somehow still alive." As *Newsweek*'s reporter put it, the medium had been "reborn as an entirely different creature" by appealing to a mobile, local audience—one that television often missed—with music and talk programs. A few critics, such as Newton N. Minow, former chairman of the Federal Communications Commission, lamented the degeneration of radio into a purely entertainment medium. "Too many stations have become publicly franchised jukeboxes," he complained in 1965. But radio's ubiquity in the 1960s—spurred by the postwar invention of the transistor—nonetheless was a remarkable turnaround from the moribund 1950s. "Everybody's tuned in," as *Newsweek* observed of the reborn radio industry. "It's what's happening, baby."[2]

Spokesmen for newspapers were no less enthusiastic. "The newspaper business in these United States today is growing, healthy and prosperous," proclaimed an *Editor & Publisher* editorial in 1965.[3] In the number of newspapers in operation, their circulation, and their advertising revenues, the newspaper industry appeared healthy and stable indeed. In 1965, according to the American Newspaper Publishers Association (ANPA), 1,751 daily newspapers were published in the United States, two more than had been published in 1945. Daily circulation reached 60,357,563 in 1965, an increase of 25 percent over 1945 and only slightly less than the all-time high circulation set in 1964.[4]

"In 1963, by all measurable standards, newspapers were doing better than ever," declared Lloyd Wendt, editor of the *Chicago American*. The vital statistics, he said, were a rebuff to critics who pointed to recent mergers and closures as evidence of an industry in trouble.[5] Robert U. Brown, publisher of *Editor & Publisher* and an outspoken and enthusiastic optimist on the subject of the industry's prospects, flatly dismissed what he called the "myth" of newspaper decline. "The No. 1 problem of journalism today," he said in a 1965 lecture to fellow journalists, "is the lack of information or the amount of misinformation about the newspaper business." The founding of new dailies had more than offset the closings of some newspapers, Brown said, and readership was up substantially since 1945.[6]

Government and trade association statistics, for the most part, substantiated this bright picture. By 1966, newsprint sales in the United States—always a good barometer of newspaper health—reached an all-time high of 9.12 million tons, more than twice the usage of 1945. Even more encouraging, in 1966 newspapers continued their long-standing lead over all other media in advertising expenditures, with $4.9 billion in revenues, a healthy 29.5 percent of every dollar spent on advertising. Newspapers also attracted 29 percent of all national advertising in 1963 and even increased their share to 29.3 percent in 1964 and 1965, the first increases since television had begun to siphon off lucrative national accounts in the late 1940s. Moreover, despite television's competition, newspapers were prosperous enough to pour more than $100 million annually into capital improvements and plant expansion from the late 1950s through the mid-1960s. Newspapers spent more than $130 million on plant improvements in 1966 alone.[7]

Newspapers' collective health was apparent in their physical size, which had continued to grow during this period. While the average daily of more than 100,000 circulation in 1945 had published twenty-two pages, by 1965 the average newspaper published fifty pages, an increase of 127 percent. Even though advertising content had increased at a faster pace than had editorial content, the latter nonetheless rose from an average of 12.3 pages in 1946 to 19.7 pages in 1965, an increase of 60 percent. Moreover, newsprint consumption for newspapers under 100,000 circulation indicated that total pages and editorial content had increased at an even higher rate than that of their big-city counterparts.[8]

But many inside and outside the industry regarded the same statistics not with hope but with alarm. "Spokesmen for the newspaper industry quote figures that appear to make newspapering a healthy, wealthy, and growing business," a writer for *Television Magazine* noted in 1962. "Other observers of the industry, not quite so close to the forest, see dry rot setting in." Optimistic publishers, the writer correctly observed, often preferred to overlook the industry's most pressing problems: circulation had failed to keep pace with population growth since 1945. Consolidations and mergers were killing dozens of newspapers each year. And rising costs, strikes, and suburbanization were challenging all newspapers, particularly large metropolitan journals.[9]

In fact, even the most optimistic publishers were mindful of these vast challenges facing the industry. Though most newspapers remained profitable, overall the industry was feeling the effects of rising competition and escalating costs. Meanwhile, the face of the industry was changing. Suburban newspapers prospered while dailies in large metropolitan cities—where costs were highest and competition stiffest—suffered. Dozens of metropolitan publishers went bankrupt each year at the same time suburban publishers were getting rich.[10] The only constant across the industry were the intense changes and challenges confronting all newspapers in a host of areas.

In circulation growth, newspapers had held their own since World War II but nothing more. While total daily circulation had steadily increased after the war, the growth was only enough to match increases in overall adult population and lagged far behind total population growth. Adult population (aged twenty-one to sixty-four) had increased 18.4 percent between 1946 and 1965 while total newspaper circulation had increased 18.5 percent. (Newspaper publishers had long argued that newspaper circulation should be measured against adult population, not total population, because the booming younger population was not yet old enough to read newspapers.[11]) While circulation had remained even with population growth, circulation per household had declined in the twenty years following World War II. About 1.29 newspapers were sold per household in 1945, compared to 1.05 in 1965.[12]

But while overall circulation growth had been listless, it was booming for suburban newspapers. Since World War II, suburbs had been growing much faster than large cities, and newspapers' circulation trends had reflected these population shifts.[13] Kenneth R. Byerly, a journalism professor at the University of North Carolina, studied circulation trends in the postwar years and concluded in 1965 that newspapers were not fading but instead were getting closer and closer to their readership. "The smaller the city of publication," Editor & Publisher concluded in reporting Byerly's study, "the faster the rate of circulation growth." Byerly found that between 1945 and 1964, the largest metropolitan dailies—those in cities of more than 1 million—had lost 14.4 percent in circulation while dailies in medium-sized cities (500,000–1 million in population) had remained virtually unchanged. But in cities of fewer than 250,000 population, circulation had increased 28.6 percent, and in towns of fewer than 50,000, circulation had increased by 32.1 percent. Suburban dailies had blossomed in the metropolitan areas surrounding the nation's ten largest cities, increasing their circulation by 80.5 percent, while the large dailies based in those cities had increased a minuscule 1.9 percent.[14]

The weakening metropolitan newspapers weighed heavily on publishers' minds. Large metros across the country were confronted with an acceleration of trends well underway since the late 1940s. Readers were moving to the suburbs, along with many of the large retailers that were the newspapers' largest advertisers. In their new communities, readers turned to any of the numerous weeklies and dailies that had sprung up in suburbia. To hold onto these readers, metropolitan newspapers launched expensive zoned editions and metropolitan sections, but often to no avail.[15] At the same time that the metros were losing their core readership and some of their best advertisers, they faced rising expenses, both in higher distribution costs required for a more widely dispersed readership and in higher wages. In addition, labor disputes intensified in the early 1960s as unions and management tangled over the introduction of new technologies. Nationally, the newspaper industry experienced just ten strikes in both 1960 and 1961, but strikes jumped to twenty-seven in 1962, twenty-five in 1963, twenty-four in 1964, and twelve in 1965.[16]

Confronted with rising costs, more than 400 newspapers merged or closed in the twenty years following World War II, although the total number of daily newspapers in the United States remained constant because of the founding of new, mostly suburban, dailies. The failing newspapers were often the least profitable daily journals in competitive metropolitan markets. However, among the most prominent casualties in the early 1960s were many large, well-established newspapers: the *Cleveland News*, the *Pittsburgh Sun-Telegraph*, and the *Detroit Times* all closed in 1960. The *Los Angeles Evening Mirror* folded and the *Los Angeles Examiner* was merged into a competitor in 1962. And the *Houston Press* closed in 1964, the largest newspaper loss of the year. In 1965, the two corporations owning the three San Francisco newspapers merged into one company and split the newspaper market between the two surviving dailies, which remained editorially independent.[17]

Many of the newspapers that closed had been established in the years after the war. Particularly vulnerable were those that had been established in competitive markets. The *Jackson State Times*, for example, had been founded in 1955 in Jackson, Mississippi, to compete against the *Jackson Clarion-Ledger* and *Jackson Daily News*, both owned by a prominent local family, the Hedermans. It lasted only until 1962, when rising costs and a shortage of operating capital forced its closure. "[T]he more trouble the paper seemed to have, the more pressure mounted to cut back, cut back, cut back," recalled Norman Bradley, the *State Times*' founding editor.[18] New dailies in competitive markets faced nearly insurmountable odds in cities both large and small. In Georgia, the *Atlanta Times* was founded in 1964 but closed after just fourteen months of operation; in Portland, Oregon, the *Reporter* began publication in 1961 but suspended in 1964; and in Phoenix, the *Arizona Journal* closed in 1963.

Most significant among the suspensions was the closure of a handful of the largest newspapers in Los Angeles in 1962 and in San Francisco in 1965. The mergers and closures in these two metropolitan areas symbolized the financial precariousness of the nation's largest newspapers and fueled public concern about increasing monopoly in the newspaper industry. In Los Angeles in early 1962, the Times-Mirror Company decided to suspend the *Evening Mirror* at virtually the same time that the Hearst newspaper group announced the closing of the morning *Examiner*. The *Mirror* and the *Examiner* had each suffered as readers had moved to the suburbs, where thirty dailies thrived in the towns and small cities surrounding Los Angeles. The closings left just two newspapers in the nation's second largest city, Times-Mirror's *Los Angeles Times* in the morning and Hearst's *Los Angeles Herald Examiner* in the afternoon.[19] Norman Chandler, publisher of the *Times* and the *Mirror*, testified before Congress in 1963 that the *Mirror* had lost $25.7 million between its founding in 1948 and its closing. Both papers, he said, had been hurt by rising competition from television stations, suburban and community newspapers, and radio stations. He and the Hearst interests had each closed their newspapers after receiving assurance of Justice Department clearance. But he said that while he had consulted with Hearst representatives before the closings, there were "no agreements restricting competition between the two companies."[20]

The joint operating agreement reached between the *San Francisco Chronicle* and the *San Francisco Examiner* in September 1965 was another milestone of metropolitan consolidations. Under the agreement, reached between the Chronicle Publishing Company and the Hearst chain, owners of the *Chronicle* and the *Examiner*, respectively, the two newspapers merged their business operations but maintained separate editorial staffs. The *Chronicle* was printed in the morning and the *Examiner and News Call Bulletin* in the afternoon in a single publishing plant, and the Sunday editions of the two newspapers were combined into the *Sunday Examiner & Chronicle*. The Hearst afternoon newspaper was created by the combination of the old morning *Examiner*, which had competed with the *Chronicle*, and the old *News Call Bulletin* in the afternoon. Charles Thieriot, editor and publisher of the *Chronicle*, wrote in 1969 that the merged operation was the natural result of increased competition and rising costs. "By 1964," he recalled, "it was a foregone conclusion that either Chronicle or Hearst would have to cease publication in San Francisco." The two companies notified the U.S. Justice Department of their negotiations, and the agreement was signed after department representatives said they would not pursue antitrust actions.[21]

Joint operating agreements had become more common after World War II as publishers sought ways to cut costs. In the agreements, as in San Francisco, publishers of two previously independent newspapers— usually a morning daily and an afternoon daily—combined the business operations but kept the editorial operations separate. In this way publishers could profit from the efficiency of combined printing plants while maintaining two distinct editorial voices. After World War II, such agreements were signed between newspapers in Madison, Wisconsin, in 1948; in Fort Wayne, Indiana, Bristol, Tennessee, Birmingham, Alabama, and Lincoln, Nebraska, in 1950; in Salt Lake City, Utah, and Shreveport, Louisiana, in 1953; in Franklin, Pennsylvania, in 1956; in Knoxville, Tennessee, in 1957; in Charleston, West Virginia, in 1958; in Columbus, Ohio, in 1959; in St. Louis, Missouri, in 1959; in Pittsburgh, Pennsylvania, in 1961; and in Honolulu, Hawaii, in 1962.[22] The proliferation of the agreements prompted a U.S. Justice Department investigation, which resulted in a lawsuit in 1965 challenging the practices as an infringement upon free trade. The Supreme Court ultimately agreed with the Justice Department and ruled that the agreements violated the Sherman Antitrust Act, prompting a drive among publishers to legalize the agreements. The drive finally bore fruit with congressional approval of the Newspaper Preservation Act in 1970.[23]

Newspaper executives maintained that the closings, consolidations, and joint operating agreements were part of a long-term trend. The economic realities of modern newspaper publishing, argued American Press Institute (API) director J. Montgomery Curtis in 1963, meant that most cities could support only one newspaper. "The sad fact is that high quality and even good management is no longer enough for newspaper survival," he wrote. "In many cities, even some large ones, the advertising and circulation income potential is sufficient to support only one newspaper."[24] Arthur B. Hanson, the ANPA general counsel, told Congress in 1969 that the weaker newspapers in competitive markets decline quickly once they fall behind.[25]

Indeed, the steady elimination of competition in city after city was part of a long-term trend dating back to the 1920s. As a result, by the mid- and late 1960s, only a handful of American cities had competing newspapers under separate ownership. "To be specific," Raymond B. Nixon, the industry's leading authority on consolidation, reported in 1969, "only forty-five of the 1,500 daily newspaper cities in the United States had two or more locally competing dailies at the beginning of 1968." That meant that only 3 percent of all cities with daily newspapers had true competition. By contrast, 117 cities—8.3 percent of all cities with dailies—had had competing newspapers in 1945. Mergers and closings had accelerated after World War II, Nixon said, as publishers sought economies of scale to fight rising costs and competition from suburban newspapers and television. Between 1945 and 1965, 421 daily newspapers merged or closed, while only 409 were founded.[26]

Congress was concerned enough about the pattern of newspaper closings to conduct hearings. Representative Emmanuel Celler, Democrat of New York and chairman of the House Judiciary Committee, announced in 1962 that his committee would gather facts about closings and investigate concentration of ownership within both the newspaper and broadcast industries. The newspaper consolidations in Los Angeles had prompted him to undertake the investigation. Hearings began in early 1963 and included lengthy testimony from ANPA representatives.[27]

Central to the ANPA's argument was that downsizing reflected long-term economic trends, not an effort by publishers to pursue monopoly. The ANPA also argued that the ownership of daily newspapers remained widely dispersed. Even in the face of consolidations and mergers, the ANPA maintained, the concurrent proliferation of television and radio stations had ensured a diversity of media voices. It quoted a study by Princeton University researcher Jesse Markham showing that in 1963 Americans had access to a plethora of media. "After allowances are made for joint and multiple ownership," Markham concluded, "the number of independent entities engaged in disseminating news over the air or through daily newspapers amounts to 4,993, comprising 1,211 daily newspapers, 2,957 standard broadcast (AM) radio stations, 485 FM radio stations, and 340 TV ownership interests."[28] Stanford Smith, the

ANPA's general manager, told Congress not to assume that the failures of some newspapers had caused a decline of competition or a decline in the diversity of media voices. "This broad base of ownership," he said, "hardly indicates cause for concern over any form of centralized control of the press in the United States." The ANPA opposed as unconstitutional any government action to curb newspaper mergers, to limit newspaper ownership of broadcast stations, or to restrict the growth of chains.[29]

The Celler hearings rattled newspaper executives but did not result in any proposals from the judiciary committee for government action. Stewart R. MacDonald, the manager of the ANPA's Newspaper Information Service, called the hearings "one of the most searching inquiries into the newspapers of America in the history of Congress." MacDonald's hyperbole reflected publishers' deep interest in the hearings and their desire to answer congressional and public concern about newspaper consolidations and closures. So many publishers requested summaries of the ANPA's arguments that it compiled the information in news story form and distributed it to member newspapers. After the hearings, it collected all association testimony into a 374-page book, *Newspapers 1963*, that it mailed to all member publishers.[30]

The Justice Department was concerned about the pattern of closings and consolidations and filed suit several times in the 1950s and 1960s to ensure that publishers, in their zeal to cut costs, were not using anticompetitive practices. In 1964, for example, the Justice Department sued the *Lima* (OH) *News* for acquiring a competing newspaper. The lawsuit ended with a consent decree. In 1965, the department sued to force the *Los Angeles Times* to sell the recently acquired *San Bernardino Sun* after finding that the acquisition had violated antitrust laws because of the *Time*'s and *Sun*'s overlapping circulation areas.[31] In 1964, the department also successfully sued to block the E.W. Scripps Company from acquiring the morning *Cincinnati Enquirer* because the company also owned the *Cincinnati Post and Times-Star*.[32]

As closings had accelerated during the 1950s and 1960s, so had chain ownership. While the overall number of daily newspapers had remained largely unchanged from 1945 to 1965, the number of papers owned by chains had doubled, from 368 in 1945—21 percent of all dailies—to 750 in 1965, or 43 percent. "Across the nation," the *Wall Street Journal* reported in December 1965, "newspaper chains—two or more dailies under common ownership in separate cities—couldn't be in finer fettle."[33] Most of the growth in chain ownership came in the late 1950s and early 1960s, a trend encouraged by the growing consolidation in the newspaper industry. Chains were attracted to monopoly markets, which were growing in number and which offered high profits without the risks of competition. "If you own a newspaper in a one-newspaper market, and if you give it competent management, little misfortune can befall you," observed Gardner Cowles, the chairman of the Cowles Communications newspaper chain, in 1965. "You can sleep well."[34]

Several factors encouraged the growth of chains, or "groups," the name preferred within the industry. For one thing, tax laws allowed publishing companies to avoid taxes on any accumulated earnings that were used to buy related businesses. Chains could therefore avoid some taxes by using their profits to buy other newspapers. For another, high personal income and inheritance taxes encouraged the matriarchs and patriarchs of newspaper families to sell to chains. As veteran newspaper publisher J. David Stern observed after his retirement, newspaper owners usually paid taxes twice—once on dividends and again in personal income taxes. By selling out to a chain or to the opposition, as Stern had done with his old *Philadelphia Record* back in 1947, a newspaper owner could avoid inheritance taxes altogether and pay only capital gains taxes on the sale. Sellers thus ensured a healthier income for themselves and a more substantial estate for their heirs. Sometimes heirs were forced to sell newspapers to chains to pay inheritance taxes.[35]

The largest chains, in terms of circulation, were the seven newspapers operated by the Chicago Tribune Company, with 26 million circulation; Hearst, with nine papers and 18 million; Newhouse, with eighteen papers and 18 million; Scripps-Howard, with seventeen papers and 17 million; Knight, with six papers and 9 million; and Gannett, with twenty-five papers and 7 million. *Editor & Publisher* recorded 930 sales of newspapers, many of them to chains, between 1945 and 1966.[36] These and smaller chains such as Thomson Newspapers (owned by Lord Thomson of Fleet) and Donrey Media Group would eventually dominate newspaper ownership. Two chains with typical growth were Knight Newspapers and Ridder Publications. Knight, the owner of the *Miami Herald* and *Akron* (OH) *Beacon-Journal*, bought the *Charlotte* (NC) *Observer* in 1955, the *Charlotte* (NC) *News* in 1959, and the *Tallahassee Democrat* in 1965. Ridder Publications purchased the *San Jose* (CA) *Mercury & News* and the *Long Beach* (CA) *Independent and Press-Telegram* in 1952, the *Pasadena* (CA) *Star-News* in 1956, and the *Gary* (IN) *Post-Tribune* in 1966.[37]

Publishers staunchly defended chain ownership, largely on the grounds that corporate owners often permitted their editors editorial freedom and that chains often improved a local paper after acquiring it. Paul Miller, president of Gannett, praised chains in 1965 as benefiting newspapers overall. "It is my firm conviction," he said, "that a newspaper group, properly motivated and managed, has all the advantages of single ownership, plus some that are beyond the scope of all but the most successful individual newspapers."[38] Al Neuharth, general manager of Gannett's *Rochester* (NY) *Times-Union*, said in 1963 that only "impractical theorists" and "prejudiced politicians" opposed chains. The growth in corporate ownership, he claimed, was due simply to economics and had improved more newspapers than not. "The era of a chain owner using his chain for selfish political or personal motives is gone," he declared. "Let's forget it. And we will not turn the clock back on this era of weak competitive newspapers giving way to strong monopolies. Let's welcome it."[39]

But many within the industry did not welcome the growth of chains. In 1957, John S. Knight, himself the owner of a group of newspapers, had deplored the growth of corporate ownership, a phenomenon he, like Stern, blamed on stiff inheritance taxes. Knight said he doubted whether newspapers could remain aggressive and individualistic under chain ownership. "The danger," he said, "is that newspapers under public ownership will be too conformist in their thinking, and their managements more attentive to the stockholders than to the public interest."[40]

At the same time that chain ownership was expanding, other national trends buffeting newspapers led to the most prolonged, costly newspaper strike of the postwar years, the New York City strike of 1962–1963. To publishers, the strike represented the convergence of the challenges facing newspapers: the financial ill health of many of the largest journals, the multiple complications of new technologies sweeping through the industry, and growing labor-management antagonisms in the face of industry change. The mammoth 114-day length of the strike—one of the nation's most prolonged and costliest newspaper strikes—served only to prove to publishers the extent to which the industry had few answers to meet these continuing and complex problems.

The genesis of the strike was the high wage demands of the International Typographical Union (ITU), which was seeking, in its negotiations with the New York publishers, to regain its leading role among the national newspaper unions.[41] For years, the American Newspaper Guild, the union of editorial employees, had set the standard for industrywide contracts in New York because its contracts had expired a few weeks earlier than those of the printers and typesetters, which were put in the position of following the Guild's lead in contract negotiations. In response, the ITU's New York local, known as the Big Six, and its outspoken leader, Bertram A. Powers, were determined to reinstate the ITU as the pre-eminent craft union while reclaiming for its members wage increases that Powers said had declined precipitously under Guild leadership. In ITU negotiations with the *New York Times*, the *New York Daily News*, the *New York Journal-American*, and the *New York World-Telegram & Sun*, the union had demanded $38 a week in increased pay and benefits, an amount four times higher than what the employers had offered.[42] "We have a lot to catch up," Powers said, noting that the union had fallen behind in wage settlements in recent years, "and the union is ready to do it now."[43] Publishers maintained that the union demands were far in excess of what their newspapers could afford and would threaten the very existence of several of the newspapers.

While a demand for substantially improved wages played a large part in the strike, equally significant was the growing concern within union ranks about automation. The publishers, facing rising costs and a combination of economic forces unique to metropolitan newspaper publishing, wanted the benefits of technological innovations to combat their multiple financial problems. Accordingly, publishers had sought the right to take advantage of advances in Teletypesetter technology to set all stock exchange and financial tables into type using the machines. In exchange, publishers offered the typesetters a guarantee that no workers would lose their jobs. But publishers balked at the union's demand that a portion of any savings should be used for a special fund to pay for retraining, retirement benefits, and unemployment payments for displaced workers. Other issues of contention were the union's demands for a shorter work week (from just over thirty-six hours to thirty-five hours) and for a common expiration date for all union contracts.

The strike began December 8, 1962, and dragged on for almost four months with little progress represented either in continued contract negotiations or in any of the third-party efforts to end the strike. In addition to the four newspapers initially involved in the contract dispute, four other newspapers—the New York Mirror, the New York Herald Tribune, the New York Post, and the Long Island Star Journal—closed down by agreement among the New York-area publishers, which negotiated jointly with the newspaper craft unions through their organization, the Publishers Association. By the time the strike ended on March 31, 1963, following mediation by New York Mayor Robert F. Wagner, the two sides had finally agreed on a contract that substantially scaled back the union's wage demands but granted concessions on automation issues. The final contract allowed $12.63 a week in wage increases and higher benefits over two years, reduced the work week to thirty-five hours, and allowed the use of Teletypesetters for stock tables. In return for their use of greater automation, publishers agreed not to lay off any employees and to pay for worker retraining.[44]

Observers agreed that the contract was significant because it finally allowed the use of automation already widely in use at other newspapers, but nonetheless it was devastating to the newspapers affected. During the work stoppage, the newspapers lost an estimated $108 million in advertising and circulation revenues. The 19,000 employees affected by the strike lost $50.4 million in wages and benefits. The newspapers missed publishing an estimated 5.7 million copies. The New York Times estimated the total economic cost of the strike, including losses to business, labor, and government, at between $190 million and $250 million.[45] For months after the strikers returned to work, the newspapers struggled to regain advertising and circulation, which for most of the dailies dipped dramatically from pre-strike levels. The seven major New York newspapers lost ten percent of their weekday circulation after the strike, or about 500,000 copies a day.[46]

The strike settlement further weakened New York journalism. The agreement prevented publishers from laying off any workers, minimizing the cost savings of switching to new technologies. Moreover, the wage increases, even scaled back from levels the union had demanded, burdened the newspapers, particularly the least profitable. None of the major dailies—except for the *New York Times* and the *New York Daily News*—consistently made money even before the strike, and most were supported by their publishers using revenues from other enterprises.[47] The 880,000-circulation *New York Mirror* closed October 16, 1963, and the Hearst Corporation, owner of the newspaper, blamed the strike for its demise.[48] Other closings and mergers in New York would follow later in the 1960s.

The devastating effects of the New York strike were typical of the other lengthy, expensive strikes that shook metropolitan journalism in the early 1960s, including the 117-day Minneapolis strike in 1962, the 129-day Cleveland strike of 1962–1963, and the 134-day Detroit strike in 1964. These strikes were important both individually and collectively. Individual strikes, as in New York, often provided the final crippling blow to the weakest journals in a city. And the strikes as a whole emphasized the declining state of metropolitan journalism, providing a symbol of both publishers' and unions' failure to come to grips with the vast change transforming the newspaper industry.

The strikes also highlighted the extent of union unrest about computer automation, which made its first inroads into the nation's daily newspapers in the early 1960s. Computers, like offset printing, had long promised benefits to newspaper publishing but did not gain wide acceptance until the early 1960s, adding to the upheaval within the industry. The push toward computer automation was accelerated, of course, by publishers' continuous desire to offset rising costs, particularly the labor-intensive costs of typesetting and printing. "The importance of that—to all of us—needs no underlining," observed Charles L. Bennett of the *Oklahoma City Oklahoman and Times* in 1964. "This way lies survival."[49] A panel of editors at the 1964 Associated Press Managing Editors (APME) meeting agreed that levels of automation were increasing all across the country. "Automation of newspaper production is here," said Ted Durein of the *Monterey* (CA) *Peninsula-Herald*, "and growing fast."[50]

For publishers, automation and computers showed promise in several areas. The new electronic technology was most immediately useful as a supplement to the Teletypesetting (TTS) operation. Computers were programmed to accept Teletypesetter tape and produce a new tape that would set "justified" type—to produce copy with flush margins on both sides. Computers were also used in photocomposition, which, when paired with the growing use of offset presses, could simplify production and eliminate the need for typesetting by typographers. Among the first newspapers to use computers were the *Los Angeles Times* and the *Palm Beach* (FL) *Post-Times*. Both began experiments with computerized typesetting in late 1962. The *Times*, the *Post-Times*, and other newspapers also used computers to aid in bookkeeping, to set classified advertisements into type, to lay out display advertisements, to automate mail rooms, and to keep records in the circulation department.[51]

Newspaper computer use grew quickly in the early and middle 1960s. In 1962, only a handful of dailies had used computers. But 38 were using them in typesetting in 1964, 89 in 1965, and 184 in 1966. The computer industry catered to publishers by manufacturing more machines and designing models specifically for newspapers. By the mid-1960s, IBM, RCA, National Cash Register, American Type Founders, and numerous other companies were making machines specifically for typesetting in newspapers.[52]

Computers promised, eventually at least, to revolutionize all phases of newspapering, not just the industry's production methods. "I have never seen an industry that is going to be more completely changed in the next decade as the result of automation, nor one which today realizes it less," management consultant John Diebold told the American Society of Newspaper Editors (ASNE) in 1963. He predicted that computers would transform all editorial operations within a decade.[53] Florida newspaperman John H. Perry Jr., publisher of the *Palm Beach Post-Times*, also predicted a production revolution. "I can visualize a composing room of the future," he said in 1963, "that will automatically compose a page in the newspaper starting from a typewritten page to a finished page without any human hands touching it until it is finished and ready for the press."[54]

In newspaper circles, talk of computers was ubiquitous. "Everywhere you go in the newspaper business today," remarked *Editor & Publisher's* Robert U. Brown in 1964, "someone is talking about computers and their possible application to or effect on the newspaper of the future." *Editor & Publisher, Quill*, and the other journalism trade journals were overrun in the mid-1960s with articles about computers. Many editors and publishers were smitten with computers' potential to transform the editorial operation, and interest in the new technologies ran high.[55] The ASNE convention of 1963 and the APME gathering of 1964 each devoted an entire session to the promise of computers in the newsroom and production room.[56] In 1965, more than 200 editors and publishers visited the *Orlando Sentinel-Star* and other south Florida newspapers to see how they were benefiting from automation. The *Sentinel-Star*, the *Miami Herald*, and the *West Palm Beach Post and Times* were each using computers to process Teletypesetter tape for justification. The *Sentinel-Star* was also using computers to sort advertisements, set them in type, and do circulation bookkeeping.[57]

In Orlando, New York, and elsewhere, labor relations were unsettled by the coming of automation. *Miami Herald* president James L. Knight said in 1965 that in "the unbelievably short time that computers have been around" they had shaken the newspaper industry to its foundations. "Management cannot grasp the implications of what this monster does, or of what it is capable of doing," Knight said. "Labor, on the other hand, is really distressed. The average man in the shop regards the thing with curiosity and perhaps with some suspicion, but his big union chief is getting apoplectic."[58]

Publishers and the craft unions strongly disagreed about automation. Publishers wanted to move faster, but unions wanted automation introduced only by degrees. The typographical unions did not oppose automation outright but instead sought to limit its use so as to minimize its effect upon union workers. "We are not opposed to automation in the composing room," Bertram A. Powers of the New York ITU said in 1964. "The question is how and when."[59] Elmer Brown, the ITU national president, opposed publishers' efforts to reduce the work force through attrition as automation increased, fearing that this would decimate the craft unions. "We feel that our many years of devoted service to the industry entitle us to continued employment in the industry we helped to build," he said in 1965.[60] Publishers, for their part, said that the unions' insistence on extra money for retraining and retirement programs negated automation's cost-savings. The ANPA Labor Relations Committee concluded in a 1965 report that unions were overreacting to automation, which remained in its earliest stages. "We have not had true automation as yet," the report said. "We have had a limited degree of improved mechanization."[61]

The coming of computers coincided with the growing use of offset presses in the early 1960s. Several developments, most notably the increased efficiency of web offset presses, accelerated the trend toward offset that had begun at weeklies and at small dailies in the 1950s. "Every time we make a survey of offset papers, our figures become outdated before we're through," commented Charles H. Tingley of the ANPA in 1963.[62] By 1967, more than one-third of all weekly newspapers and 290 daily newspapers were using offset. The steadily improving process had great potential to cut printing costs when paired with computers and other emerging technologies such as photocomposition.[63]

Editor & Publisher editorialized in 1965 that publishers were exhibiting "a tidal wave of enthusiasm" for the offset process. Demand for new offset presses was high, and manufacturers around the country stepped up their production. The newer offset presses were fast and efficient enough to print even larger weekly and daily newspapers. *Grit*, the national weekly rural newspaper with a circulation of 1 million, switched to offset production in 1963. The next year, the *Daytona Beach* (FL) *News-Journal*, a 60,000-circulation daily, switched to offset, the largest daily to make the switch up to that time.[64]

The new process offered several advantages over hot type. Offset presses could be operated by unskilled, non-union labor, a feature that appealed to cost-conscious publishers. As the *Wall Street Journal* observed in 1963, "Because offset lends itself to a typewriter-clip-and-paste preparation of newspaper pages by relatively unskilled labor, the offset publisher can greatly reduce or even eliminate his dependence on high-salaried printers and press plate casting operators."[65] Another advantage was that the process resulted in sharper, cleaner reproduction of type and pictures. When the *Ithaca* (NY) *Journal* switched to offset in late 1964, readers were pleased. "Reaction of readers was overwhelmingly favorable," said editor William J. Waters. "Most agreed the newspaper was sharper, pictures were reproduced with much greater clarity, and the type was more readable."[66]

Just as offset presses and computer technology gained wider acceptance in the early 1960s, so too did another challenge to newspapers—television news. The increasing credibility of television news in the 1960s stood in marked contrast to the 1950s, when publishers and editors had dismissed the electronic medium as posing little competition to the printed word, either for advertising or in newsgathering. While television had certainly been a threat to advertising revenues, its threat had been minimized because of the booming economy and the resultant boom in advertising spending. Similarly, television's threat to newspapers' long-standing supremacy in newsgathering had been minimal. Television's coverage of special events such as political conventions had, in fact, seemed to benefit newspaper circulation rather than to hurt it.[67]

But in the 1960s, television news began to mature. Local news came into its own. National news coverage expanded with the lengthening in 1963 of the national television network newscasts from fifteen to thirty minutes a day. And the special events coverage unique to the 1960s seemed to enhance television's reputation as a serious public affairs medium. Specifically, television's coverage of the 1960 presidential debates, of America's growing space program, and of the assassination of President Kennedy in 1963 all highlighted television's growing importance as a source of information.

The four presidential debates between Kennedy and Nixon, the first televised debates ever, proved pivotal in the former's razor-thin victory that November. Particularly in the first debate on September 26, 1960, in

Chicago, Kennedy appeared much more at ease than his rival in front of the cameras. He was rested and tanned, while a profusely sweating Nixon, recovering from a recent illness, appeared haggard and tired. Kennedy's credibility as a presidential candidate shot up sharply as a result. "That night," reporter Russell Baker recalled, "image replaced the printed word as the natural language of politics."[68]

Television's coverage of the Kennedy assassination in 1963 greatly enhanced television's credibility. "Never before in history had such momentous news traveled so far so fast," *Time* magazine noted of television's coverage in the days following the assassination.[69] The three major networks each turned over broadcast time to full-time coverage of the assassination's aftermath. Each network devoted from sixty to seventy hours to the events, including the presidential funeral and the shooting of Lee Harvey Oswald. Networks spent an estimated $32 million in direct expenses and lost advertising on the coverage. A.C. Nielsen Company estimated that virtually every home with a television set watched some of the assassination coverage. It was, *Broadcasting* magazine reported, "the most people, the most hours, the biggest losses and the most raw emotion that broadcasting had ever known."[70]

Even television's critics had to admit that the medium had been transformed into an even more powerful national force. Newton N. Minow, who as Federal Communications Commission chairman had derided television programming as a "vast wasteland" just two years earlier, now commended the medium. "Through calm, dignified, and steady devotion to the sad task at hand, television enabled the country to witness the example of a family of valor and the enduring strength of our democratic institutions," he wrote in a letter to *Time* magazine. "At a time of critical national transition, television grew up."[71]

Print journalists were mindful of television's impact. Most editors interviewed by the *ASNE Bulletin* after the assassination agreed that they had carefully taken television's coverage into account when planning their own. "We were all up against terrific competition from television," said Charles S. Gallagher of the *Lynn* (MA) *Daily Item* in December 1963. "How could anything we printed, for instance, carry the solar plexus impact of the video presentation of Oswald's murder?" Thomas Winship of the *Boston Globe* said that the newspapers' chronological accounts of each day's news "seemed almost superfluous to us in the light of the magnificent saturation TV coverage, which everybody watched." Newspaper editors were put in the position of monitoring television and reacting to and expanding upon its coverage.[72]

Even before the assassination, news coverage had taken on more importance for both the national broadcast networks and for local television stations. Two of the national networks—CBS and NBC—expanded their news broadcasts from fifteen minutes to thirty minutes a night in the fall of

1963. The networks also placed renewed emphasis on documentaries. Such programs as Edward R. Murrow's "Harvest of Shame," a CBS program profiling the hardships of migrant farm workers, and ABC's "Close-up" series, brought greater visibility to network news teams. At the same time, local stations began to emphasize news coverage for the first time, with many following the networks' lead by expanding local newscasts to thirty minutes.[73] But local television news still had much growing to do, commented television news director Murray Seeger of Cleveland, Ohio, in 1964. "The stations are just beginning to learn their way around and discover their abilities," he said.[74]

Taken together, the enhanced credibility of television and television news made the electronic medium a greater threat to newspapers. "We have reached a point," said Robert Roesler of the New Orleans (LA) Times-Picayune in 1962, "where the television personality, the actor who delivers the news, is suddenly looked upon as a peer." And while print journalists disagreed about whether television was partially to blame for newspapers' listless circulation growth, they nonetheless agreed that editors had been slow to update their editorial content in response to the electronic medium. "I do not think that editors as a whole are responding, in the fashion they should, to this competition," said Fletcher Knebel, Washington correspondent for the Cowles publications, in 1962. John Denson of the New York Herald Tribune complained the same year that many newspapers were writing news much the same way they had in 1915.[75]

A poll conducted by Elmo Roper and Associates in 1964 found that, for the first time, more respondents named television as their major source of news than named newspapers. Television executives trumpeted the results of the poll, a scientific survey of 1,500 adults. The poll had asked the question: "Where do you get most of your news about what's going on in the world today?" Of the respondents, who were allowed to give more than one answer to the question, 55 percent named television, and 53 percent named newspapers. Newspaper executives downplayed the results and dismissed television's lead in the poll as statistically insignificant. Editor & Publisher's editors, displaying little knowledge of scientific polling methods, even doubted whether a poll of such a small sample could be generalized to the entire population.[76]

By 1965, the mounting problems of television, rising costs, and new technologies convinced many publishers and editors that the newspaper industry had too long ignored these trends while they were building. Newspapers seemed to be changing much too slowly to meet these multiple challenges, although the industry as a whole remained profitable. "The most important fact about newspapers today," the Wall Street Journal's Bernard Kilgore said in 1963, "is that this industry is trying to adjust itself to a journalistic revolution."[77] This "revolution" was evident in the technological change, rising competition, and escalating costs facing newspapers. Economic pressures, the *New York Times'* Turner Catledge observed in 1965, "seem to be descending upon the newspaper business in a sort of increasing volume."[78] Worst of all, newspapers were losing their primacy as the most important news medium, believed long-time newspaper editor Harry Ashmore, formerly of the *Arkansas Gazette.* "Their economic base," he said in 1962, "is complicated by their own inability, I think, to roll with the punch, to improve their methods." Newspapers, he concluded, had displayed little imagination in adapting to changing conditions. "And now, I think, it's late in the day, and I think the bell is tolling."[79]

Chapter 9

Reflections on the Postwar Press

On the surface, the American newspaper industry appears to have changed little from 1945 to 1965, remaining both healthy and prosperous. The number of newspapers in 1965 was about the same as in 1945, while during the twenty-year period advertising revenues increased substantially despite new competition from television. Just as in 1945, the vast majority of newspapers went to press with improved but old-fashioned letterpress methods in 1965. And newspaper reporters still professed a strong, if now somewhat shaken, faith in the federal government at the end of the twenty years.

But the surface appearance of both stability and profitability obscured profound change. In the two decades after World War II, the business of newspaper publishing changed significantly in myriad ways. By 1965, editors and publishers had recognized the extent of these changes and were beginning to adjust. Each of the changes was significant of its own accord, and the range of challenges throughout the period combined to transform newspapers and the nation they served by 1965. This transformation was evident, to varying degrees, in newspapers' content; their production methods; their economic position within the overall media marketplace; and their relationship with government. Newspapers—some more than others—made strides to keep up with and overcome some of these challenges. But in each of these areas, newspapers as a group were slow to respond to the problems facing journalism.

In content, newspapers began a long, slow journey to update their methods of reporting. The most significant trend during the two decades was the movement toward interpretation of the news. Rooted in the 1930s, interpretation spread in the 1950s as a response to the sensational rise of Senator Joseph R. McCarthy. The trend's roots did not go deep, however, and in 1965 proponents such as Lester Markel of the *New York Times* were continuing to complain that newspapers remained far too wedded to nuts-and-bolts, objective reporting of the facts offered without elaboration or explanation. Newspapers' coverage of the civil rights movement was symptomatic of the industry's commitment to its old ways and its resistance to change. Reporters tended to cover the movement from crisis to crisis, ignoring the long-term trends the crises represented. The deep-seated social movement of blacks' struggle for equality and the trend's roots in social and demographic shifts were often ignored. Most newspapers' reaction to the movement, and to news in general, was centered on the occurrence of day-to-day events. While the largest, most successful newspapers—such as the *Los Angeles Times* and the *New York Times*—indeed stepped up their interpretation of the day's news, the vast majority did not. In content and appearance, most newspapers changed little in the two decades following World War II. As the *Columbia Journalism Review* noted in a comparison of newspapers in 1947 and 1962, "On the front pages at least, not many of the stories on the 1962 front pages would have looked out of place on the 1947 pages." Postwar changes in newspapers' editorial content, the magazine concluded, could "hardly be called revolutionary."[1]

In coming to terms with television, their most threatening rival of the postwar years, newspapers were equally slow to adapt. In the 1940s and 1950s, editors and publishers dismissed television as an entertainment medium of limited threat—either in advertising or in newsgathering. If anything, television seemed to increase newspapers' readership, editors believed. Newspapers made a few token efforts to keep up with this upstart medium by hiring television critics and by publishing television listings. But, overall, they did little as television, year by year, made further advances into their national advertising revenues and became more deeply ingrained as part of American life. By the 1960s, when television ventured further into newsgathering, publishers at last recognized their electronic rival as a threat. But in the 1960s as in the 1950s, there was little editors could do about it.

In the audience newspapers served, vast changes swept the industry in the 1940s, 1950s, and 1960s. Publishers could only watch helplessly as the demographics of the audience shifted in the postwar years. As suburbs grew, so did suburban newspapers. As the big cities stagnated, so did metropolitan journals. Meantime, the postwar baby boom generation grew up in front of the television, and newspaper sales per household declined while overall circulation grew but slowly. Television's increasing news coverage coincided with the growth and expanded news coverage of the suburban press. Together they weakened readers' attachment to metropolitan journals.

The changes in audience, competition, and content were part of a larger shift in the business environment that profoundly affected the financial viability of American newspapers. Costs of doing business rose, both in wages and materials. New production methods that would eventually offset these rising costs were introduced in the 1940s, spread in the 1950s, and took firm root in the 1960s. But conversion to the new methods was hindered by publishers' commitment to letterpress, which remained entrenched both by union commitments to the old ways and by the high capital costs of updating pressrooms. Publishers had invested heavily in new letterpress equipment after World War II and were reluctant to start over. The rising spiral of costs cut deepest into the metropolitan newspapers, already suffering because of suburbanization. By contrast, the suburban dailies, flush with profits and largely free of union ties, turned more quickly to new production methods and prospered further.

All of these business trends were tempered and partially concealed by a fortuitous characteristic of the postwar years—the booming economy. The prosperous national economy, and the accompanying growth in advertising revenues, minimized many of the threats to newspapers. Television's capture of national advertising revenues was obscured, as were the challenges of rising costs, suburbanization, and new technologies. An abundance of advertising revenues slowed newspapers' response to these challenges until the early 1960s, when the trends accelerated and threatened newspapers' very existence, particularly the metropolitan journals. Also obscuring many of these trends was the very real health of much of the newspaper industry, particularly the suburban dailies. It was this overall health, particularly in suburban and monopoly markets, that encouraged the growth of chains in this period.

Newspaper chains had so long been a feature on the journalistic landscape that their growth during the 1950s and 1960s was rarely viewed with alarm. Newspaper editors and publishers were unanimous in interpreting the growth of chains as inevitable, resulting from tax laws favoring corporate expansion, the cost effectiveness of shared costs among chain-owned dailies, and the attractiveness of monopoly markets. But it was equally clear that chain ownership was not entirely good for journalism. Chains served to further increase the distance between newspapers and their readers, changing the fundamentally local character of the American newspaper. Increasing corporate ownership also served to increase the already-growing emphasis on newspaper profitability at the expense of the journalistic product.

In their relationship with government, newspapers and journalists recognized in the 1950s and 1960s that their trust in officials was eroding significantly. The growing Cold War secrecy took its toll on the longstanding journalistic acceptance of the government's military aims.

In the 1950s, journalists believed that officials were using Cold War secrecy as an excuse to keep other, non-military matters confidential. This spread of secrecy from military matters to non-military affairs prompted a greater distrust of government at all levels and a more adversarial stance by reporters. Such a response was to be expected given the unprecedented nature of the peacetime secrecy journalists faced in the early Cold War years. Reporters had long resented any peacetime withholding of information; what was new in the postwar era was the mushrooming extent of secrecy—at both federal and state levels. Journalists' concern with government secrecy and federal information policies was further heightened by the news management techniques of the Kennedy administration. Kennedy's efforts to control the press were not unprecedented in Washington, of course, but his blatant efforts to court the press and to stage-manage the news struck reporters as both ominous and threatening. Journalists were especially chagrined at having caught government officials in lies during the Cuban Missile Crisis. Even worse, some officials had defended the government's right to mislead the public should the national interest seem to require it. Accordingly, the press-government relationship had deteriorated substantially by the time of the Vietnam War.

Of course, accurate generalizations about the newspaper industry are extremely difficult to make. The "newspaper industry" in 1965 actually consisted of 1,751 newspapers in disparate markets, each facing discrete economic and journalistic challenges. But as an industry, American daily newspapers were slow to adapt to the changes and challenges transforming them in the postwar years. In these years, as James Reston of the *New York Times* lamented in 1959, newspapers exhibited the same reluctance to change that had long been a characteristic of print journalism. "I don't suppose the press is in a very different position from that of almost any other institution in America today—the university, the Executive branch of the government, the Legislature," he said. "We are making progress, but the basic problem of the country is that we are in a kind of race with our own history, and its pace is so swift that we should be going faster, we should be quicker, we should be achieving more than we are achieving." The press was not keeping up with the pace of society, Reston said, but neither were most other American institutions. "Nobody is doing as well as he could in this particular generation," he concluded.[2] Tom Leathers, editor of the *Country Squire* in Kansas City, Missouri, summarized newspapers' postwar transformation more succinctly: "These are shifting days for our industry," he said in 1966, "and newspapers can't expect to be an exception."[3]

But why were publishers—and their newspapers—so slow to respond to such profound shifts in their environment? Their delay had its roots in publishers' perceptions of themselves in the postwar era. Predominantly, publishers saw themselves as businessmen after World War II. This was no new phenomenon, as newspaper publishing had been growing steadily more complex since the mid-nineteenth century. By 1945, the days of one-man newspapers—when a hardy printer could start a newspaper with a shirttail full of type—were long gone. Newspapers were phenomenally expensive both to establish and to operate. Both the equipment and the manpower required for even a small-town newspaper were extensive. Newspaper publishers—though certainly concerned with the public they served and committed to the journalistic ideals they followed—were primarily concerned with operating sound, healthy businesses. At most newspapers, journalistic endeavors were of secondary importance to profitability.

To the vast majority of publishers, then, the postwar advertising boom mitigated against a response to the changes descending upon newspapers. Most journals continued to reap healthy profits in the earliest postwar years. As most continued to make money, it was certainly no surprise that owners remained unalarmed about potential threats. In the case of television, to repeat one example noted earlier, the new medium's inroads into newspapers' national advertising was minimized by the heady profits most newspapers were making.

Publishers were complacent—almost defeatist—about the changes facing their industry. They assumed that there was little they could do about long-term problems, displaying a passivity that discouraged them from responding to the many challenges they confronted. For example, throughout the postwar years, publishers assumed that the trend toward consolidation and mergers in the newspaper industry—a long-term process that had been underway for decades–was a monolithic, natural process that was beyond their control. This thinking was typified in the editorials of *Editor & Publisher*—the leading trade journal of the daily newspaper industry—and in articles by the postwar era's leading analyst of newspaper industry trends, Raymond B. Nixon. Both *Editor & Publisher* editor Robert U. Brown and Nixon consistently espoused the idea that newspaper closings and mergers were naturally occurring events. They believed that the newspaper industry was steadily evolving so that each American city or town could support just one newspaper and no more. It was certainly understandable that Brown, Nixon, and most publishers blamed this economic trend for newspapers' problems. The number of daily newspapers had been declining so long (since 1919 to be exact) that to publishers the steady diminution seemed the natural procession of events. Moreover, these arguments were an effective response to critics' charges of monopolistic tendencies in the newspaper industry, and in this respect the arguments had some validity. But while there is little doubt that newspaper trends resulted from long-term economic factors—not publishers' greed—there is also little doubt that this assumption was a strong indicator—and also a cause—of the passivity that dominated newspaper publishing in the postwar years, particularly in the booming years of high profits in the late 1940s and early 1950s.

But publishers held fast to these assumptions in the prosperous postwar years, reinforcing their passivity at a time when striking developments were transforming their business environment, a time when more decisive action might have strengthened many newspapers. This passivity, as noted earlier, led newspapers to act far too slowly to take advantage of technological developments. Publishers turned to new printing methods only briefly in the late 1940s, and the newspaper industry as a whole continued to spend but meager amounts on research throughout the 1950s and into the 1960s. The newspapers that did pioneer in the development of new technology—the *Wall Street Journal*, with its multiple printing plants using Teletypesetting (TTS), for example—prospered. But most newspapers adopted only the technological developments that offered immediate benefits. Publishers, flush with profits in the earliest postwar years, did not invest in their future when the time was ripe. An exception was in the suburbs, where entrepreneurial publishers did invest early in the new technologies of newspaper publishing—particularly offset—and prospered from the late 1950s onward as Americans fled the cities. It was in the suburbs, where a community-oriented, locally-focused press usually avoided controversy and grew fat with advertising, where daily journalism's future seemed to lie.

By the 1960s, publishers realized that they had waited too long to confront the economic challenges facing them, but various factors nonetheless mitigated against large-scale changes in American journalism. Among metropolitan newspapers, the "crisis" in publishing was so acute that it was too late to save the weakest newspapers in competitive markets. With little or no profits, owners of failing journals could hardly take action to meet the crisis, to take risks. Meanwhile, at the newspapers in small- and medium-sized cities, where the trend toward monopoly was most evident, publishers were even less inclined to be risk-takers. For these monopoly newspapers, profits were assured whether owners took risks or not. There was little incentive to change.

At the same time that publishers were greatly concerned with profits, various factors were shaping how individual journalists were approaching their work. For one thing, the stories that reporters covered affected how they approached journalism itself. For example, the dominant continuing domestic news story of the postwar years—the civil rights movement—pitted non-violent civil rights activists against law-breaking, violent defenders of the status quo. Journalists in the North sided with the civil rights workers as vociferously as those in the South criticized them. This dichotomy in the response of "objective" journalists had three effects. One was to prompt a greater criticism of objectivity both North and South, laying the foundation for support of the "New Journalism" that would emerge in the 1960s. (Interpretation, slowly taking root in this period, had already weakened the belief in objectivity.) A second effect was to further validate the longstanding journalistic tradition of support for the underdog. A third effect was a greater journalistic distrust of officialdom, since the racial policies editors and reporters opposed (whether North or South) enjoyed state sanction. In this way journalists' distrust of state and federal officials, already on the rise because of government secrecy, grew further.

Another factor affecting individual reporters was the professionalization of journalism, which continued in the postwar years. This growing professionalization was part of a national trend toward greater cohesiveness among workers. It was evident in the spread of newspaper-related organizations and in the many efforts to improve journalism that prospered at the grassroots level. In the late 1940s, for example, these improvement efforts could be seen in the founding of the American Press Institute (API), the growing popularity of interpretation, and the accreditation of journalism education programs. These efforts were fueled by journalists' realization of the need for improved methods of newspaper writing and presentation. The complex demands of postwar life seemed to demand better newspapers, many journalists believed.

Ironically, working editors and journalists were becoming more concerned with professional issues at the same time that the newspaper industry as a whole was solidifying its position as a business enterprise. As a result, even as professionalization grew, its influence in improving newspapers was limited by publishers' business concerns. For example, at the same time that journalists were calling for more interpretation of the news, the proportion of news-editorial space in American newspapers was dropping: The ratio of editorial content to advertising decreased from about 60:40 at World War II's end to about 40:60 shortly thereafter. This decline in the proportion of editorial material was due to the need for increased advertising revenue to offset rising costs. Moreover, the suburbanization of the American newspaper industry—the growth of the suburban press and the decline of metropolitan journals—further pinched many metropolitan newspapers and increased their reluctance to spend money to advance their reporting methods.

The necessary advances in journalism practices to meet the challenges of a changing media environment were slowed, then, by publishers' caution. Publishers were too concerned about diminishing profits to divert money into editorial improvements. The essential irony of this position was that the publishers' caution was not only bad for journalism, it was also bad for business. Publishers' delay in responding to television, to suburbanization, and to the other postwar editorial challenges weakened newspapers' greatest asset—their relevance as a public affairs medium. In the meantime, television gained in influence and profits, and at newspapers' expense. Publishers' ultimate failure in the postwar years was, as some journalists of the period were quick to point out, that they looked only to economic answers—not to journalistic ones—to meet the challenges of rising costs, population shifts, and competition.

This failure could be measured in newspapers' readership. To editors and publishers, steadily rising circulation after World War II attested to newspapers' continued importance and to their popularity as a public affairs medium. But, in fact, total national newspaper circulation failed to keep pace with overall population growth in the 1950s and 1960s. Newspapers may have remained the dominant local advertising medium, but their declining circulation penetration underscored their declining importance to readers.

Facing changing conditions that demanded improvements in a stagnant industry, newspapers moved only half-heartedly toward the solutions that might have met some of the challenges. Publishers might have met the increasing costs by switching more quickly to new technologies, for example, but they did not. Editors might have met the challenge of television by further emphasizing interpretation, but they did not. The breadth of challenges required bolder action than most editors and publishers would take, though there was wide agreement among themselves as to how they might meet the challenges. For American daily newspapers, then, the postwar years were a period of missed opportunities for an industry in decline.

Bibliographic Essay

Scholars have studied many specialized topics of interest concerning the American newspaper industry following World War II. Categories of studies have included ownership trends, changes in technology, declining newspaper competition, the press and the Cold War, and press-government relations. While there is a wealth of material available about this era, the vast majority of scholarship is specialized, describing specific issues, individual journalists, or individual newspapers.

Moreover, the historiography of modern newspapers tends to reflect the ideological and contemporaneous concerns of historians. They have held particularly strong opinions about the effects of the changing economic structure of the newspaper industry on the freedom of the press. This is partially due to the fact that much of modern newspaper history has been written by journalists writing about their own profession.

Studies of newspaper history since 1945 can be divided into the following categories.

BUSINESS TRENDS

A number of writers have considered the vast changes in the economic structure of newspapers since 1945, considering particularly the stagnation of newspaper circulation, the decline in competition, and the increase of corporate ownership. Historians have differed as to whether business trends in newspapers were a cause for great alarm or were simply the result of long-term cultural and economic trends.

Ben Bagdikian's *The Information Machines: Their Impact on Men and the Media* described the rapid advances in newspaper production technology prior to its publication in 1971, considering both the burgeoning increase in offset printing along with advances in Teletypesetting (TTS).[1] By 1983, when he published *The Media Monopoly*, Bagdikian had come to see the increasing concentration of ownership in newspapers in the years following World War II as a threat to press freedom. More ominous, he concluded, was the control of the American media by fifty corporations beginning in the 1960s. And, unique for a historian of newspaper business trends, Bagdikian described how newspaper content had been changed by newspapers' increasing reliance upon advertising following World War II.[2]

Like Bagdikian, Bryce Rucker, in *The First Freedom* (1968), also viewed the growth of the news media into multinational, interconnected conglomerates as a threat to press freedom and to democracy.[3] Similarly, Carl E. Lindstrom in *The Fading American Newspaper* (1960) argued that newspapers' effectiveness was diminishing because they had become primarily businesses rather than journalistic institutions. Lindstrom believed newspapers were disappearing because they had failed to compete with television.[4] Like Bagdikian, Lindstrom was a veteran journalist, not a historian.

Historians have tended to view the concentration of media ownership in more neutral terms. Benjamin M. Compaine et al., in *Who Owns the Media? Concentration of Ownership in the Mass Communications Industry* (1982), believed the trend toward mergers in the communications industry resulted from media firms' increasing profitability, which made them attractive to investors. Also, inheritance laws prompted independent owners to sell out to chains. Compaine and his co-authors argue that while chain ownership had increased by the early 1980s, no one chain held as high a percentage of overall newspaper circulation as did William Randolph Hearst at the close of World War II.[5]

The historian Raymond B. Nixon, in a number of studies, argued that newspapers were complemented, rather than threatened, by the emergence of television. In studies published in 1954 and 1961, Nixon maintained that the expansion of media voices that accompanied the rise of television after World War II ensured that newspapers would not monopolize the media marketplace. Moreover, he argued that newspapers were continuing to prosper despite recent mergers and consolidations, and that overall circulation of newspapers was increasing in proportion to the adult population. Nixon saw the postwar decades as an era of stability in which the lengthy decline in the number of dailies was beginning to subside, with the establishment of new dailies offsetting mergers and closures.[6] Nixon, unlike Bagdikian, regarded consolidations and mergers in the newspaper industry without alarm. He argued that the vast changes in the newspaper industry since 1900 were due to economic forces, increasing homogeneity among newspapers due to journalists' standards of objectivity, rising competition from electronic media, and the rapid growth of the suburbs.[7]

Jon Udell has described American newspaper trends in the period under study in two books, *Economic Trends in the Daily Newspaper Business, 1946 to 1970* (1970) and *Economics of the American Newspaper* (1978).[8] Like Nixon, Udell blamed economic factors for the evolving business fortunes of the newspaper.

Historians agree that the emergence of television in the 1950s had a profound effect on the health of American newspapers. Television eventually attracted a substantial share of advertising revenues, particularly national advertising, that previously had gone to newspapers. One well-known study, Maxwell McCombs' monograph on "Mass Media in the Marketplace," concluded that the amount of money advertisers and the public spend on all media remains constant over time, and that the addition of another mass medium into the marketplace erodes advertising support for existing media.[9]

THE PRESS AND THE COLD WAR

A central historical event of the postwar era was the Cold War. Still, surprisingly little has been written about the relationship between the press and the Cold War. Much of the historiography maintains that the press was culpable for America's Cold War excesses, such as McCarthyism, because of newspapers' support for government policies and reporters' commitment to standards of objectivity.

James Aronson's *The Press and the Cold War* (1970) argued that the press unquestioningly accepted the government's aims in the Cold War and thereby promoted those aims. This naturally resulted, Aronson argued, from the fact that the news media were controlled by big business, which cooperated with and shared the interests of the government.[10] Similarly, Louis Liebovich maintains in *The Press and the Origins of the Cold War* (1988) that newspapers failed to support any accommodation with the Soviet Union in the early years of growing tensions following World War II.[11] *Exporting the First Amendment: The Press-Government Crusade of 1947–1952* (1986), by Margaret A. Blanchard, describes the American press' unsuccessful postwar campaign to persuade foreign countries to adopt American-style press freedoms.[12]

Edwin R. Bayley took a charitable view of press practices in the early Cold War period in *Joe McCarthy and the Press*, published in 1981. He maintained that while newspapers' commitment to objectivity and conservative politics helped McCarthy early on, by 1954 McCarthyism had forced newspapers to change for the better. Thanks to McCarthy in the early 1950s, Bayley argued, interpretive reporting and news analysis—which had their origins in the 1930s—became firmly established in American journalism.[13] Lawrence N. Strout's *Covering McCarthyism: How the Christian Science Monitor Handled Joseph R. McCarthy, 1950–1954*, is an excellent study of one national newspaper's coverage of the Wisconsin senator.[14]

A number of books examine press coverage of other issues related to the Cold War. John F. Neville's *The Press, the Rosenbergs, and the Cold War* (1995) examines how Cold War passions affected the media's portrayal of the case. *Condensing the Cold War: Reader's Digest and American Identity* (2000), by Joanne P. Sharp, considers the implications of the magazine's portrayal of Cold War imperatives. Craig Allen examines the media relations of the nation's thirty-fourth president in *Eisenhower and the Mass Media: Peace, Prosperity, & Prime-Time TV*. Allen argues that Eisenhower, not his successor, should be considered the nation's first "television president" because he was adept at using the medium. Edwin M. Yoder, Jr., considers the important career of a leading national columnist in *Joe Alsop's Cold War: A Study of Journalistic Influence and Intrigue* (1995).[15]

Several books have considered the implications of American press coverage of the Vietnam War. Clarence R. Wyatt's *Paper Soldiers: The American Press and the Vietnam War* (1995) argues that press coverage was not nearly so adversarial as critics have charged. Daniel C. Hallin's *The "Uncensored War": The Media and Vietnam* (1986) similarly maintains that reporters were largely uncritical until late in the war. And military historian William M. Hammond argues in *Reporting Vietnam: Media and Military at War* (1998) that the Kennedy and Johnson administrations tried in vain to manipulate the press and therefore lost reporters' trust.[16]

THE CIVIL RIGHTS MOVEMENT AND THE PRESS

Though blacks' long struggle for equal rights in the American civil rights movement has been well documented, there have been relatively few books written about the interaction of the American press and the movement.

John Kneebone summarized the evolution of southern liberal thought in *Southern Liberal Journalists and the Issue of Race* (1985), but Kneebone's book stopped at World War II. No comparable study exists for the years after 1945.[17] Richard Lentz wrote about the newsmagazines' treatment of Martin Luther King in *Symbols, the News Magazines, and Martin Luther King* (1990), but no similar overview has been written about newspapers' coverage of the civil rights leader.[18] However, Jon Meacham's *Voices in Our Blood: America's Best on the Civil Rights Movement* (2001) has compiled narratives of the civil rights movement by journalists, novelists, historians, and artists.[19]

Community studies abound, however. Hugh Davis Graham described the reaction of one state's newspapers to desegregation in *Crisis in Print: Desegregation and the Press in Tennessee* (1967).[20] Ann Waldron profiled Hodding Carter, Jr.'s lengthy career in *Hodding Carter: The Reconstruction of a Racist* (1993). Gary Huey explores the life of Petal, Mississippi's P.D. East in *Rebel With a Cause: P.D. East, Southern Liberalism and the Civil Rights Movement* (1985). Norfolk, Virginia's desegregation crisis is deftly profiled in Alexander Leidholdt's *Standing Before the Shouting Mob: Lenoir Chambers and Virginia's Massive Resistance to Public-School Integration* (1997). David R. Davies' anthology of Mississippi editors' on civil rights activism through 1965 is *The Press and Race: Mississippi Journalists Confront the Movement*, published in 2001. A number of biographies detail Ralph McGill's leadership in Atlanta. Two recent volumes are Barbara Barksdale Clowse's *Ralph McGill: A Biography*, published in 1999, and Leonard Ray Teel's *Ralph Emerson McGill: Voice of the Southern Conscience*, published in 2001.[21] Many journalists active in the civil rights movement have published their memoirs.[22]

INDIVIDUAL NEWSPAPER HISTORIES

Books abound about individual newspapers and journalists in this period. The strength of many of these works is that they cover in great detail their specialized topics. Richard Kluger's *The Paper: The Life and Death of the New York Herald Tribune* (about the *New York Herald Tribune* and its ancestors), Gay Talese's *The Kingdom and the Power* (about the *New York Times*), and David Halberstam's *The Powers That Be* (about CBS, Time Inc., the *New York Times* and the *Los Angeles Times*) are exhaustive in their detail about the organizations they profile.[23] The specialization of these works would count as a weakness to a reader searching for a broader overview of the period. Moreover, many of the works, particularly those written by former journalists, often delve deeply into press practices and press coverage of particular issues at the expense of exploring broader issues of press-society interaction.

THE PROFESSIONALIZATION OF JOURNALISTS

Newspapermen and women solidified their positions as professionals in the twenty years following World War II. Hallmarks of professionalization, such as college training, professional journals, and journalists' organizations, flourished in these years as journalists came to see themselves as a profession with a standard set of training and practices.

While many works have acknowledged or described this trend, few have placed it within the context of other changes also taking place within journalism in this period. However, two studies that examined the status of journalists in the 1970s and 1980s provide valuable insights. They are John W.C. Johnstone et al., *The News People: A Sociological Portrait of American Journalists and Their Work* (1976) and David H. Weaver and Cleveland Wilhoit's *The American Journalist: A Portrait of U.S. News People and Their Work* (1986).[24]

A history of journalism on higher education is William R. Lindley, *Journalism and Higher Education: The Search for Academic Purpose* (1975). Paul Alfred Pratte's history of the American Society of Newspaper Editors (ASNE), *Gods Within the Machine: A History of the American Society of Newspaper Editors, 1923–1993*, was published in 1995.[25] Again, what's lacking in works of this kind is any effort to tie in these trends toward professionalization with the larger context of newspaper history in this period.[26]

GOVERNMENT/PRESS RELATIONS

Undoubtedly, the relationship between newspapers (and all of the news media) and the government changed dramatically in the years following World War II. Newspapers and reporters, which had tended to be uncritical of the government in the years leading up to and during the war, became increasingly critical of government officials and institutions in the 1950s and 1960s. This was due partly to the increased secrecy demanded by the government as the Cold War escalated and to the growing professionalization of journalists, who increasingly viewed themselves as watchdogs of the government and of the public interest. By the mid-1960s, in the aftermath of the civil rights movement and in the opening days of the Vietnam War, journalists were much more likely to question the motives and intentions of their government than were their journalistic forebears producing newspapers twenty years previously.

Historians have recognized this trend, though they have failed to place it in the broader context of what was happening in American newspapers in this time period. Most often, historians, particularly those who were former journalists, simply assumed that the adversary role of journalists was the appropriate one for journalists to take. See, for example, Talese's *The Kingdom and the Power* and Halberstam's *The Powers That Be*, cited above.

Of course, there are some ideological historians, as named above, who instead see the press as supporting the status quo throughout this time period.

Notes

BUSINESS TRENDS IN THE POSTWAR PRESS, 1945–1949

1. "Radio, 25, Looks to the Future," *Business Week*, November 10, 1945, 32; "Too Many Magazines," *Time*, June 17, 1946, 48–49.

2. Quoted in George A. Brandenburg, "Daily Circulation Reaches New Peak With 6.4 Percent Gain," *Editor & Publisher*, December 29, 1945, 5.

3. *Editor & Publisher International Yearbook*, January 31, 1946, 6; "New Circulation High, More Newspapers in '45," *Editor & Publisher*, March 2, 1946, 42. Newspaper circulations had increased steadily since 1920 except in the Depression years of 1930–1933 and 1938.

4. *Editor & Publisher International Yearbook*, January 31, 1947, 19; January 30, 1948, 17; January 31, 1949, 17.

5. "Future of Newspapers," *Editor & Publisher*, August 17, 1946, 36; ANPA statistics, Newspaper Association of America, Reston, Virginia. Each year's annual daily newspaper circulation figures are Audit Bureau of Circulation figures compiled by ANPA for the year ending September 30.

6. "Gannett Reaffirms Faith in Newspapers," *Editor & Publisher*, October 27, 1945, 24; "National Ads in Dailies Up $16 Million in '45," *Editor & Publisher*, June 22, 1946, 49.

7. ANPA statistics, using figures from the U.S. Department of Labor, U.S. Department of Commerce, *Media Records*, and *Editor & Publisher* yearbooks, quoted in Jon G. Udell, "The Growth of the American Daily Newspaper: An Economic Analysis," *Wisconsin Project Reports* 3 (1965): 14–16.

8. U.S. Department of Commerce, *Historical Statistics of the United States, Colonial Times to 1970*, 2 vols (Washington, DC: U.S. Government Printing Office, 1975) 2: 856.

9. Statistics quoted in *Newsprint Supply and Distribution*, Interim Report of the Special Committee to Study Problems of American Small Business, United States

Senate, Eightieth Congress, First Session, April 21, 1947 (Washington, DC: U.S. Government Printing Office, 1947) 4, 22–24.

10. "50,000-Circulation Daily Costs and Revenue Analyzed," *Editor & Publisher*, February 23, 1946, 7; Robert U. Brown, "46 Operating Costs up 27 Percent on 50,000-Circulation Daily," ibid., May 10, 1947, 7.

11. Profit figures cited in Frank Hughes, *Prejudice and the Press* (New York: Devin-Adair Co., 1950) 555.

12. Raymond B. Nixon, "Trends in Daily Newspaper Ownership since 1945," *Journalism Quarterly* 31 (Winter 1954): 14.

13. "Mechanical Equipment of 2,326 U.S. and Canadian Newspapers," *Editor & Publisher*, November 3, 1945, 1; Oral history interview with Carl Walters, April 27, 1974, Mississippi Oral History Program, University of Southern Mississippi.

14. "Papers Modernize and Expand Shops," *New York Times*, June 6, 1948, 37; "Newsprint Needs to 1960 Projected," *New York Times*, September 21, 1948, 21.

15. Lester Markel, "The Newspapers," in *While You Were Gone: A Report on Wartime Life in the United States*, ed. Jack Goodman (New York: Simon and Schuster, 1946) 372.

16. Frank E. Gannett quoted in "Gannett Reaffirms Faith in Newspapers," *Editor & Publisher*, October 27, 1945, 24.

17. Edwin Emery, *ANPA—75th Anniversary, 1887–1962* (New York: American Newspaper Publishers Association, 1962) 9.

18. Merlin Hall Aylesworth quoted in "Television Parley Attended by 1,200," *New York Times*, October 11, 1946, 21.

19. "Requests Filed by Newspapers," *Editor & Publisher*, November 10, 1945, 18.

20. Oral history interview with Robert W. Brown, November 3, 1973, Mississippi Oral History Program, University of Southern Mississippi.

21. Quoted in Hughes, *Prejudice and the Press*, 474.

22. *Proceedings, American Society of Newspaper Editors*, 23rd annual convention (Washington, DC: American Society of Newspaper Editors, 1946) 108. Hereafter cited as *ASNE Proceedings*.

23. Lee Wood quoted in "New York Editors Sum up Postwar Tasks," *Editor & Publisher*, September 8, 1945, 28.

24. Harrison E. Salisbury, *A Time of Change: A Reporter's Tale of Our Time* (New York: Harper & Row, 1988) 9; Harold A. Williams, *The Baltimore Sun: 1837–1987* (Baltimore, MD: Johns Hopkins University Press, 1987) 251.

25. Stanley Frank and Paul Sann, "Paper Dolls," *Saturday Evening Post*, May 20, 1944, 20.

26. Robert N. Pierce, *A Sacred Trust: Nelson Poynter and the St. Petersburg Times* (Gainesville, FL: University Press of Florida, 1993) 136.

27. "Metropolitan City Desk Becomes Female Job," *Editor & Publisher*, August 25, 1945, 38; "City Editor," *Time*, June 30, 1947, 61–62.

28. Nan Robertson, *The Girls in the Balcony: Women, Men, and the New York Times* (New York: Random House, 1992) 100–101.

29. Frank Luther Mott, *Time Enough: Essays in Autobiography* (Chapel Hill, NC: University of North Carolina Press, 1962) 157.

30. "Thirty-Four AASDJ Schools Report 9,603 Students," *Journalism Quarterly* 23 (December 1946): 427; Walter C. Johnson and Arthur T. Robb, *The South and Its Newspapers, 1903–1953* (1954; reprint edn, Westport, CT: Greenwood Press, 1974) 278.

31. See "Texts of Print Paper Limitation Orders," *Editor & Publisher*, January 9, 1943, 5; and "Suspension Orders Go Out with L-240," *Editor & Publisher*, December 29, 1945, 9.

32. "Newspaper Prices Rise in Some Areas," *New York Times*, August 31, 1946, 20, 23; Lawrence Resner, "Publishers See Costs as Problem with Newsprint Shortage Eased," *New York Times*, April 27, 1949, 25.

33. Johnson and Robb, *South and Its Newspapers*, 275; "ANPA Takes Stand for Price Decontrol," *Editor & Publisher*, October 5, 1946, 8.

34. L. Ethan Ellis, *Newsprint: Producers, Publishers, Political Pressures* (New Brunswick, NJ: Rutgers University Press, 1960) 230; Clara H. Friedman, *Newsprint: Summary of a Report on Newsprint Supply and Distribution* (New York: American Newspaper Guild, 1948) 9.

35. "Way Out of the Woods," *Time*, June 10, 1946, 68.

36. Ibid.

37. James J. Butler, "Small Dailies' Case To Be Aired Two Days," *Editor & Publisher*, January 4, 1947, 34; *Problems of American Small Business: Hearings Before the Special Committee to Study Problems of American Small Business*, 2 vols (Washington, DC: U.S. Government Printing Office, 1947) 1:1–5; "Urges Co-ops Finance Alaskan Paper Mills," *New York Times*, January 24, 1948, 24.

38. *Final Report on Newsprint and Paper Supply*, Select Committee on Newsprint and Paper Supply, House Report 2471, Eightieth Congress, Second Session (Washington, DC: U.S. Government Printing Office, 1948) 1–7.

39. Johnson and Robb, *South and Its Newspapers*, 277, 281.

40. Robert U. Brown, "Dailies' Costs Outrun Revenue Rise," *Editor & Publisher*, October 4, 1947, 7.

41. U.S. Department of Commerce, *Historical Statistics of the United States*, 1: 171.

42. "Press Seen Faced by Critical Period," *New York Times*, September 28, 1948, 38.

43. James E. Pollard, "Spiraling Newspaper Costs Outrun Revenues, 1939–1949," *Journalism Quarterly* 26 (1949): 270–276.

44. Johnson and Robb, *South and Its Newspapers*, 276; "Newspaper Prices Rise in Some Areas," *New York Times*, August 31, 1946, 20.

45. *ANPA Convention Bulletin* No. 4, May 2, 1946, 104–105; *ANPA Convention Bulletin* No. 3, April 28, 1948, 54.

46. *ANPA Convention Bulletin* No. 4, May 6, 1949, 74; *ANPA Convention Bulletin* No. 3, April 28, 1948, 55.

47. Joseph A. Loftus, "I.T.U. Closed Shop Declared Illegal; N.L.R.B. Is Unanimous," *New York Times*, October 29, 1949, 1, 23.

48. John S. Knight, "Strike Spurs Advances in Newspaper Typography," *Chicago Daily News*, December 6, 1947, typescript in Eugene Mayer Papers, Box 92, Library of Congress, Washington, DC.

49. Quoted in Millard B. Grimes, *The Last Linotype: The Story of Georgia and Its Newspapers Since World War II* (Macon, GA: Mercer University Press and the Georgia Press Association, 1985) 40.

50. William Reed, "Offset Printing Technique and Problems Discussed," *Editor & Publisher*, January 12, 1946, 9.

51. Johnson and Robb, *South and Its Newspapers*, 277. This was a new use for photo-engraving, previously used only for illustrations. Photo-engraving, put simply, is the mechanical process in which printed materials are transferred to relief printing plates. Offset printing is a lithographic process in which an inked impression is transferred first to a rubber roller and then to paper.

52. "Dailies to Issue Again," *New York Times*, August 11, 1945, 15.

53. *ANPA Convention Bulletin* No. 4, May 6, 1949, 74.

54. *St. Petersburg Times*, November 21, 1945, 1, quoted in Pierce, *A Sacred Trust*, 175.

55. Ibid., 173, 175.

56. "Chicago Showdown," *Time*, December 1, 1947, 70; "New Look in Chicago," *Time*, December 8, 1947, 62.

57. "Revolution?" *Time*, December 22, 1947, 62.

58. Basil Walters quoted in ibid.

59. Quoted in ibid. The Chicago strike, which lasted twenty-two months, ended in September 1949.

60. John S. Knight, "Strike Spurs Advances in Newspaper Typography."

61. Carl R. Kesler, "Cold Type, Hot Feet and Gimmicks," *Quill*, December 1948, 8.

62. Quoted in George A. Brandenburg, "Teletype Found to Speed Composing Room Operation," *Editor & Publisher*, July 13, 1946, 10.

63. Alexander H. Washburn quoted in ibid.

64. W.W. Ward quoted in Jack Rutledge, "Teletypesetter Biggest News in Printing Trade," *Abilene* (Texas) *Reporter-News*, March 2, 1947, 9, clipping in Millard Cope papers, Texas Tech University, Lubbock, Texas.

65. "ITU Policies Held to Alter Printing," *New York Times*, October 21, 1948, 16.

66. Emery, *ANPA—75th Anniversary*, 13–14.

67. Quoted in Johnson and Robb, *South and Its Newspapers*, 283.

68. Quoted in ibid.; Campbell Watson, "'Million for Research' Hailed as 'Insurance'," *Editor & Publisher*, June 26, 1948, 7.

69. Frank Gannett quoted in "Gannett Hints of Revolution in Printing," *Editor & Publisher*, June 21, 1947, 36.

70. Quoted in "Plenty of Business for Iowa Papers if They Can Handle It," *Iowa Publisher*, June 1946, 30.

IMPROVEMENT AND CRITICISM, 1945–1949

1. Erwin D. Canham, quoted in "Canham Visions Trend to Daily News Magazines," *Editor & Publisher*, January 19, 1946, 63.

2. Erwin D. Canham speech to American Association of Schools and Departments of Journalism convention, quoted in Dwight Bentel, "Fact-Finding Boards On Press Advocated," *Editor & Publisher*, January 10, 1948, 58.

3. Lester Markel, "The Newspapers," in *While You Were Gone: A Report on Wartime Life in the United States*, ed. Jack Goodman (New York: Simon and Schuster, 1946) 373.

4. Grove Patterson, *I Like People: The Autobiography of Grove Patterson* (New York: Random House, 1954) 258.

5. John H. Biddle speech to Pennsylvania Press Conference, quoted in Charles W. Duke, "More Readable Papers Called Voters' Need," *Editor & Publisher*, May 22, 1948, 20.

6. *ASNE Proceedings*, 1946, 106.

7. Ibid., 160.

8. Ibid., 153; Roscoe Ellard, "Now U.P. Grades Its News Stories," *Editor & Publisher*, October 13, 1945, 64; "The Unreadable Press," *Time*, March 3, 1947, 71.

9. Robert Gunning quoted in "The Unreadable Press," *Time*, March 3, 1947, 71.

10. Robert Gunning, *The Technique of Clear Writing* (New York: McGraw-Hill, 1952) 183.

11. Ibid., 23, 183.

12. "AP Report Simplified by New Flesch Formula," *Editor & Publisher*, February 21, 1948, 8.

13. Ibid. For Flesch's formula, see Rudolph Flesch, *The Art of Readable Writing* (New York: Harper and Brothers, 1949) 213–216.

14. "AP Editors Open Chicago Meeting," *New York Times*, November 10, 1948, 26.

15. Lee Hills quoted in "AP Report Simplified By New Flesch Formula," *Editor & Publisher*, February 21, 1948, 8; "Flesch Study Improves AP Report, Editors Say," *Editor & Publisher*, May 15, 1948, 28.

16. Alan J. Gould, "Foreword," in Flesch, *The Art of Readable Writing* (New York: Harper and Brothers, 1949) ix.

17. Roland E. Wolseley, *Still in Print: Journey of a Writer, Teacher, Journalist* (Elgin, IL: David C. Cook Foundation, 1985) 64.

18. Stanley B. Barnett quoted in "AP Editors open Chicago Meeting," *New York Times*, November 10, 1948, 26.

19. Ibid.

20. George E. Stansfield quoted in George Turnbull, "Interpretive Reporting Debated among 50 Editors," *Editor & Publisher*, April 12, 1947, 11.

21. James Reston quoted in "Papers Must Excel in Explanatory Reporting," *Editor & Publisher*, November 20, 1948, 9.

22. Vincent S. Jones, speech to American Association of Schools and Departments of Journalism, "Bold Experimentation Needed to Improve Newspaper Content," *Journalism Quarterly* 25 (1948): 17.

23. "U.S. Press Advised to Lift its 'Sights,'" *New York Times*, October 1, 1946, 21.

24. Don E. Carter and Malcolm F. Mallette, *Seminar: The Story of the American Press Institute* (Reston, VA: American Press Institute, 1992) 8.

25. Sevellon Brown quoted in John M. McClelland, Jr., "Talent, Energy and Truth a Professional Challenge," *Quill*, November–December 1946, 14.

26. Sevellon Brown quoted in "Keynote: Don't Drive Readers into Mental Fog," *Editor & Publisher*, October 5, 1946, 9.

27. Carl W. Ackerman quoted in "U.S. Press Advised to Lift Its 'Sights,'" *New York Times*, October 1, 1946, 21.

28. "Editors Open American Press Institute," *Editor & Publisher*, October 5, 1946, 9, 58; Carter and Mallette, *Seminar*, 8–11; W.S. Kirkpatrick, "First Seminar of American Press Institute at Columbia Reviewed By a Participant," *Journalism Quarterly* 23 (1946): 425–426.

29. Grove Patterson, "Social Responsibilities of the American Newspaper," *Vital Speeches*, May 1, 1948, 437–438; "American Press Institute Seeks $850,000 Endowment," *Editor & Publisher*, June 28, 1947, 10.

30. Carl R. Kesler, "Education for Journalism," *Quill*, July–August 1946, 3.

31. *ASNE Proceedings*, 1948, 129; "Long Courtship Links Educators, Newsmen," *Editor & Publisher*, May 17, 1947, 38; "Employer Appraisal Part of School Rating," *Editor & Publisher*, May 24, 1947, 44; "No Idea of Licensing in School Credit Plan," *Editor & Publisher*, May 31, 1947, 42.

32. *ASNE Proceedings*, 1948, 133.

33. Ibid., 1946, 28–29.

34. Ibid., 1948, 129.

35. "34 Colleges Accredited By ACEJ," *Quill*, August 1948, 6, 10.

36. *ASNE Proceedings*, 1948, 148–149.

37. Curtis D. MacDougall, "What Newspaper Publishers Should Know about Professors of Journalism," *Journalism Quarterly* 24 (March 1947): 1.

38. V.M. Newton, Jr., quoted in Dwight Bentel, "'We'll Take Grads,' Reply Majority of Eds," *Editor & Publisher*, February 28, 1948, 46.

39. V.M. Newton, Jr., quoted in Dwight Bentel, "'We'll Take Grads,' Reply Majority of Eds," *Editor & Publisher*, February 28, 1948, 46.

40. "Heeding Criticism," *Editor & Publisher*, January 19, 1946, 40.

41. Edwin Emery, *History of the American Newspaper Publishers Association* (Minneapolis, MN: University of Minnesota Press, 1950) 244.

42. Ibid.

43. Wilbur Forrest, "Anti-Press Literature," *Editor & Publisher*, June 8, 1946, 34.

44. Commission on Freedom of the Press, *A Free and Responsible Press: A General Report on Mass Communication, Newspapers, Radio, Motion Pictures, Magazines, and Books* (Chicago, IL: University of Chicago Press, 1947) v, 1–2.

45. Ibid., 20.

46. Ibid., 90.

47. Louis M. Lyons, "The Press and Its Critics," *Atlantic Monthly*, July 1947, 115–116.

48. Robert U. Brown, "Shop Talk at Thirty," *Editor & Publisher*, July 19, 1947, 60.

49. Frank E. Gannett quoted in "Free-for-all: Freedom of the Press," *Fortune*, June 1947, 24.

50. Frank Hughes, "'A Free Press' (Hitler Style) Sought for U.S.," *Chicago Tribune*, 27 March 1947, 38B. Hughes later wrote a book-length critical examination of the Hutchins report, *Prejudice and the Press* (New York: Devin-Adair Co., 1950).

51. "A Free and Responsible Press," *Herald Tribune*, March 28, 1947, 24; Lewis Gannett, "Books and Things," *Herald Tribune*, March 27, 1947, 27.

52. *Editor & Publisher Yearbook*, January 30, 1948, 17.

53. Morris L. Ernst, "Freedom to Read, See, and Hear," *Harper's Magazine*, July 1945, 51.

54. Morris L. Ernst, *The First Freedom* (New York: Macmillan, 1946). See especially Chapter 4, "Press," pp. 57–124.

55. Ernst, "Freedom to Read," 52.

56. Raymond B. Nixon, "Implications of the Decreasing Numbers of Competitive Newspapers," in *Communications in Modern Society* (Urbana, IL: University of Illinois Press, 1948) 44–47.

57. U.S. Congress, Senate, Special Committee to Study Problems of American Small Business, *Survival of a Free Competitive Press: The Small Newspaper, Democracy's Grass Roots*, Senate Committee Print 17, Eightieth Congress, First Session, 1947, pp. 1–4; "Newspaper Survival," *Editor & Publisher*, January 4, 1947, 34.

58. G.V. Denny, Jr., "Is the American Press Really Free? Debate Presented on America's Town Meeting of the Air," *Reference Shelf* 20 (1947): 159–176; *Akron* (OH) *Beacon-Journal* editorial quoted in "Critics of Press Pack Akron Town Meeting," *Editor & Publisher*, October 26, 1946, 26.

59. Jerry Walker, "Editors Get Criticism Direct; 'No Debate,'" *Editor & Publisher*, October 2, 1948, 11.

60. A.J. Liebling quoted in Tom Wolfe, "Liebling and His Legend," *New York Herald Tribune*, December 29, 1963, 24. Liebling's press columns are collected in *The Wayward Pressman* (1947; reprint edn, Westport, CT: Greenwood Press, 1972b), *Mink and Red Herring* (1949; reprint edn, Westport, CT: Greenwood Press, 1972a), and *The Press* (New York: Ballantine, 1961).

61. Don Hollenbeck, "Who Is Right?" *Atlantic Monthly*, September 1948, 49–51; "CBS Station in New York Starts Criticism of Press," *Editor & Publisher*, June 7, 1947, 11, 95; "'CBS Views the Press' Wins Peabody Award," *Editor & Publisher*, April 17, 1948, 34.

62. George Seldes, *Witness to a Century; Encounters with the Noted, the Notorious, and the Three SOBs* (New York: Ballantine, 1987) 347–348, 381.

63. "Filling a Void," *Nieman Reports*, April 1947, 19. For the early history of *Nieman Reports*, see Louis M. Lyons, "Nieman Reports and the Nieman Fellowships," in Louis M. Lyons, ed., *Reporting the News: Selections from Nieman Reports* (Cambridge, MA: Belknap Press, 1965) 14–25.

64. Leon Svirsky, ed., *Your Newspaper: Blueprint for a Better Press* (New York: Macmillan, 1947) 8–30; Richard Watts, Jr., "Which Paper D'Ya Read?" *New Republic*, December 15, 1947, 27.

65. "Reading, Writing and Newspapers," special issue, *Nieman Reports*, April 1950; "Reading, Writing and Newspapers," *Nieman Reports*, July 1950, 20; Lyons, *Reporting the News*, 17.

66. Elizabeth Lamb, *The Inland: A Short History of the Growth and Development of the Services of America's Oldest and Largest Regional Daily Newspaper Association* (Chicago, IL: Inland Daily Press Association, 1950) 45; Ralph L. Crosman quoted in George A. Brandenburg, "Inland Publishers Debate Public Criticism of Press," *Editor & Publisher*, October 19, 1946, 11; Ralph L. Crosman, "The Case Against the Press As Stated by Ralph Crosman," *Editor & Publisher*, 10–11, 72.

67. Frank Tripp, "Leave Press to People, Tripp Tells Crosman," *Editor & Publisher*, November 2, 1946, 22.

68. Lamb, *The Inland*, 46.

69. *ASNE Proceedings*, 1948, 70.

70. Walter C. Johnson and Arthur T. Robb, *The South and Its Newspapers, 1903–1953* (1954; reprint edn, Westport, CT: Greenwood, 1974) 290.

71. Grove Patterson quoted in "Slanters 'Gangsters,' Says Grove Patterson," *Editor & Publisher*, October 4, 1947, 53.

72. *ASNE Proceedings*, 1947, 65–74; John S. Knight, "Sulzberger Challenged on Chain Ownership," *ASNE Bulletin*, June 1, 1947, 1–2.

73. Joseph Agor, "Editor Says Few Small City Papers Are Worth the Ink to Print Them," *ASNE Bulletin*, March 1, 1947, 3.

74. Hanson W. Baldwin, "The Press and Bikini," *New York Times*, August 3, 1946, 6; "Dirty Work at the Crossroads," *Time*, August 12, 1946, 65.

75. Richard B. Gehman, "Make Ours Hemlock," *Saturday Review of Literature*, August 7, 1948, 15.

76. Hobby's speech is reprinted in the *Congressional Record*, May 11, 1950, A3531–A3533.

GOVERNMENT, THE COLD WAR, AND NEWSPAPERS, 1950–1954

1. Quoted in Theodore F. Koop, "Censors Saved Lives," *Quill*, July–August 1945, 9.

2. Ibid.

3. Byron Price report to Harry S. Truman, quoted in James L. Butler, "Price Closes Book on War Censorship," *Editor & Publisher*, December 22, 1945, 72.

4. Quoted in "Kennedy of AP Scoops Whole World but Writers Call Him Double Crosser," *Newsweek*, May 14, 1945, 80.

5. Meyer Berger, *The Story of the New York Times, 1851–1951* (New York: Simon and Schuster, 1951), 514; S.J. Monchak, "Laurence Relates His Role on Atomic Bomb Project," *Editor & Publisher*, September 22, 1945, 9, 60.

6. See George Kennedy, "Advocates of Openness: The Freedom of Information Movement," Ph.D. Dissertation, University of Missouri, 1978, 16–62.

7. Quoted in "Notable Talks: Free Press Theme of Convention," *Quill*, November–December 1946, 5. See also Gilbert W. Stewart, Jr., "World Threat to Free Press," *Quill*, July 1951, 5–7, 20–21.

8. ASNE report to Truman, quoted in "The Well Traveled Skeptics," *Time*, June 25, 1945, 62.

9. Stewart, "World Threat to Free Press," 7.

10. "Report on Freedom of Information," *Quill*, January 1951, 12; Herbert Brucker, *Freedom of Information* (1949; reprint edn, Westport, CT: Greenwood Press, 1981) 210–211; *ASNE Proceedings*, 1951, 189.

11. James S. Pope, "Freedom of Information: A Ten-Year-Old Prodigy," *Speeches: First Annual Freedom of Information Conference*, December 11–12, 1958 (Columbia, MO: Freedom of Information Center, School of Journalism, University of Missouri, 1960) 1.

12. For journalists' assessment of the roots of the secrecy problem, see Hanson W. Baldwin, " 'Secrets' Arouse Foes of Censorship," *New York Times*, November 16, 1947, E4.

13. *Associated Press Managing Editors Red Book* (New York: Associated Press, 1952) 26. Hereafter cited as *APME Red Book*.

14. *ASNE Proceedings*, 1948, 191–196.

15. Ibid., 197.

16. Ibid., 296–297.

17. *ASNE Proceedings*, 1951, 174.

18. Quoted in undated letter from N.R. Howard, ASNE president, to Truman, in minutes of the American Society of Newspaper Editors board of directors, October 25–26, 1947, American Society of Newspaper Editors headquarters, Reston, Virginia. Hereafter cited as "ASNE minutes."

19. Quoted in "Gag Rule Protest By ASNE Board Widely Acclaimed," *Bulletin of the American Society of Newspaper Editors*, December 1, 1947, 4, which contains a roundup of negative press reaction to the order. Hereafter cited as *ASNE Bulletin*.

20. Both the ASNE board and Truman are quoted in ASNE minutes, October 25–26, 1947.

21. Walters letter to the World Freedom of Information Committee, quoted in "Walters Demands Publicity Spotlight on Public Servants," *ASNE Bulletin*, October 1, 1948, 1.

22. *ASNE Proceedings*, 1951, 12–13.

23. James S. Pope, "U.S. Press Is Free to Print the News But Too Often Is Not Free to Gather It," *Quill*, July 1951, 9.

24. Ibid., 9, 21. The FOI committees were successful in getting much of the information released in these cases. See Pope, "Freedom of Information," 2.

25. James S. Pope, "On the Domestic Front," in Alice Fox Pitts, *Read All About It! 50 Years of ASNE* (Reston, VA: American Society of Newspaper Editors, 1974) 186.

26. *ASNE Proceedings*, 1951, 181.

27. James S. Pope, "Harold L. Cross: Arch Foe of Secrecy," in *Speeches: Second Annual Freedom of Information Conference*, November 5–6, 1959 (Columbia, MO: Freedom of Information Center, School of Journalism, University of Missouri, 1960), 38–42; Harold L. Cross, *The People's Right to Know* (New York: Columbia University Press, 1953).

28. Quoted in Pope, "On the Domestic Front," 187. Emphasis in the original.

29. *ASNE Proceedings*, 1951, 174; Pope, "On the Domestic Front," 187.

30. Pope, "U.S. Press Is Free to Print the News," 9, 22.

31. *ASNE Proceedings*, 1951, 59.

32. Clark Mollenhoff, "Follow Through—That Is the Newspaper Answer to Secrecy in Government, Says a Crusading Correspondent," *Nieman Reports*, January 1954, 3.

33. *ASNE Proceedings*, 1950, 167.

34. Ibid., 183–185.

35. Jerry Walker, "Editors Would Rip Curtain That Shields New York Officials," *Editor & Publisher*, October 21, 1950, 5.

36. *ASNE Proceedings*, 1951, 68.

37. Erwin Knoll, "43 States Employ 700 to Publicize Governments," *Editor & Publisher*, April 7, 1951, 13.

38. "Report on Freedom of Information," *Quill*, January 1952, 18. The rapid growth in the number of government press agents had begun in the 1930s with the rise of the New Deal and was accompanied by rising press and Congressional concerns about news management. See Dick Fitzpatrick, "Measuring Government Publicity: Volume of Press Releases," *Journalism Quarterly* 26 (1949): 45–50.

39. "U.S. Adds Controls on Security Data," *New York Times*, September 26, 1951, 17; W.H. Lawrence, "President Accuses Press of Revealing Vital War Secrets," *New York Times*, October 5, 1951, 1, 12.

40. Truman memorandum to the secretary of defense, September 24, 1951, quoted in Herbert Lee Williams, *The Newspaperman's President: Harry S. Truman* (Chicago, IL: Nelson Hall, 1984) 113–114.

41. "Text of Truman Security Statement and Transcript of Discussion," *New York Times*, October 5, 1951, 12.

42. *APME Red Book*, 1951, 224–226, 231.

43. "Blackout," *Editor & Publisher*, September 29, 1951, 38.

44. Resolution passed by Sigma Delta Chi delegates, quoted in George A. Brandenburg, "Sigma Delta Chi Opposes Secrecy Rule," *Editor & Publisher*, November 24, 1951, 12.

45. "Classifying Information," *New York Times*, September 28, 1951, 30.

46. "Security Committee," *Editor & Publisher*, January 19, 1952, 34.

47. *APME Red Book*, 1953, 175–176.

48. J. Russell Wiggins, "No Compromise of Principle," *ASNE Bulletin*, February 1, 1954, 4.

49. Jameson G. Campaigne, "Milestone or Millstone," ibid., 3.

50. *ASNE Proceedings*, 1952, 96–100, 104.

51. David Halberstam, *The Fifties* (New York: Villard Books, 1993) 73.

52. For a concise overview of the war, see James L. Stokesbury, *A Short History of the Korean War* (New York: Morrow, 1988).

53. Quoted in Michael P. Roth, *Historical Dictionary of War Journalism* (Westport, CT: Greenwood Press, 1997) 171.

54. Ray Erwin, "Voluntary Censorship Asked in Korean War," *Editor & Publisher*, July 8, 1950, 7.

55. Ibid.

56. Ibid.

57. Ray Erwin, "New Censorship Rules Face Reporters on War Front," *Editor & Publisher*, July 29, 1950, 7.

58. See "Chronology of the Cold War," in Ernest R. May, ed., *American Cold War Strategy: Interpreting NSC 68* (New York: St. Martin's Press, 1993), 202–205.

59. See Richard Norton Smith, *The Colonel: The Life and Legend of Robert R. McCormick, 1880–1955* (Boston, MA: Houghton Mifflin, 1997) and Rodney P. Carlisle, *Hearst and the New Deal: The Progressive as Reactionary* (New York: Garland, 1979).

60. Jack Anderson and Ronald W. May, *McCarthy: The Man, the Senator, the "Ism"* (Boston, MA: Beacon Press, 1952) 266–267.

61. Alan Barth speech before Association for Education in Journalism, quoted in "Better Reporting Held Modern Need," *New York Times*, August 27, 1952, 21.

62. Secondary works on McCarthy and Cold War anticommunism abound. Two standard biographies of McCarthy are Thomas Reeves, *The Life and Times of Joe McCarthy* (New York: Stein and Day, 1982), and Richard H. Rovere, *Senator Joe McCarthy* (New York: Harcourt, Brace, Jovanovich, 1959). The only book-length work on McCarthy's relationship with newspapers is Edwin R. Bayley, *Joe McCarthy and the Press* (Madison, WI: University of Wisconsin Press, 1981). A useful chapter on McCarthy and the press is found in David M. Oshinsky's biography, *A Conspiracy So Immense: The World of Joe McCarthy* (New York: The Free Press, 1983), 179–190. See also Jean Franklin Deaver, "A Study of Senator Joseph R. McCarthy and 'McCarthyism' as Influences upon the News Media and the Evolution of Reportorial Method," Ph.D. dissertation, University of Texas at Austin, 1969; and Lloyd Chiasson, Jr., "McCarthy's Journalism," in *The Press in Times of Crisis*, ed. Lloyd Chiasson, Jr. (Westport, CT: Praeger, 1995) 153–167. Press coverage of the House Un-American Activities Committee in the postwar years is detailed in Frank J. Donner, *The Un-Americans* (New York: Ballantine Books, 1961) 147–162.

63. Quoted in Oshinsky, *A Conspiracy So Immense*, 118.

64. Anderson and May, *McCarthy*, 267.

65. Richard H. Rovere, "Letter from Washington," *New Yorker*, May 13, 1950, 96, 98.

66. Quoted in *APME Red Book*, 1953, 53.

67. Richard L. Strout, "Ordeal by Publicity: McCarthy Hearings Prove Once More the Distorting Effects of 'Straight Reporting,'" *Christian Science Monitor Magazine*, May 27, 1950, 5.

68. Quoted in Deaver, "A Study of Joseph R. McCarthy," 91.

69. Claremont (NH) *Daily Eagle*, April 5, 1951, cited in "Notice," *Nieman Reports*, July 1951, 34.

70. Quoted in Bayley, *Joe McCarthy and the Press*, 16–17.

71. Erwin D. Canham memorandum to Saville R. Davis, June 12, 1953; Saville R. Davis memorandum to American News Department, June 15, 1953, in personal and professional papers of Richard L. Strout, in possession of Alan Strout, Weston, Massachusetts. Strout was a longtime Washington correspondent of the *Christian Science Monitor*. His papers are held by his son, Alan Strout. Copies of these memoranda are in possession of the author.

72. Joseph Pulitzer II memorandum to Raymond L. Crowley, July 7, 1953, Papers of Joseph Pulitzer II, Library of Congress, Washington, DC Crowley was the *Post-Dispatch*'s managing editor.

73. See Daniel W. Pfaff, "The St. Louis *Post-Dispatch* Debate over Communism, 1940–1955," Paper presented to the Association for Education in Journalism and Mass Communication, August 10–13, 1989.

74. *APME Red Book*, 1953, 51, 53.

75. William H. Hornby, *Voice of Empire: A Centennial Sketch of the Denver Post* (Denver, CO: Colorado Historical Society, 1992) 64.

76. Arthur Hays Sulzberger speech to the Association for Education in Journalism, quoted in "Better Reporting Held Modern Need," *New York Times* August 27, 1952, 21.

77. Dozier C. Cade, "Witch-Hunting, 1952: The Role of the Press," *Journalism Quarterly* 29 (1952): 404–407.

78. Melvin Mencher, "McCarthy: Who Made Him?" *Nieman Reports*, January 1953, 47.

79. *Proceedings, Twentieth Annual Convention* (New York: American Newspaper Guild, 1953) 72.

80. Louis M. Lyons, *Newspaper Story: One Hundred Years of the Boston Globe* (Cambridge, MA: Belknap Press, 1971) 317–318.

81. Quoted in *APME Red Book*, 1950, 69–70.

82. Anderson and May, *McCarthy*, 269.

83. *APME Red Book*, 1950, 75–76.

84. Ibid. Hazen appealed to the APME membership to reopen the investigation but members refused. See ibid., 63–79.

85. Ibid., 109; *APME Red Book*, 1952, 170–171.

86. *APME Red Book*, 1952, 176–177, 227–228.

87. Bayley, *Joe McCarthy and the Press*, 126.

88. Will C. Conrad, Kathleen F. Wilson, and Dale Wilson, *The Milwaukee Journal: The First Eighty Years* (Madison, WI: University of Wisconsin Press, 1964) 165.

89. Anderson and May, *McCarthy*, 272.

90. Ibid., 280–284.

91. *State Department Information Program–Information Centers*, Hearings Before the Permanent Subcommittee on Investigations of the Committee on Government Operations, United States Senate, Eighty-third Congress, First Session, Parts 4 and 5, April 24, 1953, May 5, 1953, 253–281, 289–324.

92. John B. Oakes, "The Dangerous Obligations of a Newspaperman," *Nieman Reports*, October 1953, 6.

93. *Washington Post*, April 28, 1953, quoted in "Definition of Tyranny," *Nieman Reports*, July 1953, 22.

94. "Freedom and Fear," *New York Times*, May 9, 1953, 18.

95. The text of the committee report is reprinted in "The ASNE Report on the Wechsler Case," *Nieman Reports*, October 1953, 25–26. A minority on the committee dissented.

96. Arthur Krock, "In the Nation: A Professional Survey of Press Freedom," *New York Times*, May 19, 1953, 28.

97. Quoted in A.M. Sperber, *Murrow: His Life and Times* (New York: Freundlich Books, 1986) 443.

THE PRESS AND TELEVISION, 1948–1960

1. Frank Tripp column, September 12, 1948, reprinted in Frank Tripp, *On the Newspaper Front with Frank Tripp* (Rochester, NY: Gannett Newspapers, 1954) 55–56.

2. Richard W. Clarke, speech to the Silurian Society, November 1947, quoted in *Shoeleather and Printer's Ink* ed. George Britt (New York: Quadrangle, 1974) 326–327.

3. Paul W. White, "Spot News Is Better on Radio," *Broadcasting-Telecasting*, February 9, 1953, 84.

4. Sig Mickelson, "Growth of Television News, 1946–1957," *Journalism Quarterly* 34 (Summer 1957): 304.

5. Phillip O. Keirstead, "Network News," in *Encyclopedia of Television*, ed. Horace Newcomb (Chicago, IL: Fitzroy Dearborn, 1997) 1164–1167.

6. Erik Barnouw, *The Image Empire* (New York: Oxford University Press, 1970) 43. For press coverage of McCarthy, see Chapter 3.

7. Jerry Walker, "Tele News Coverage Dull Without Editing," *Editor &
Publisher,* February 16, 1946, 40. For background on the development of
television news in the early postwar years, see Kristine Brunovska Karnick,
"NBC and the Innovation of Television News, 1945–1953," *Journalism History*
26 (Spring 1988):26–34; Mickelson, "Growth of Television News," 304–310; Ted
Nielsen, "A History of Network Television News," in *American Broadcasting: A
Source Book on the History of Radio and Television,* ed. Lawrence W. Lichty and
Malachi C. Topping (New York: Hastings House, 1975), 421–428; and Barnouw,
Image Empire, 40–46.

8. *The First 50 Years of Broadcasting: The Running Story of the Fifth Estate,* by the
editors of *Broadcasting* magazine (Washington, DC: Broadcasting Publications,
1982) 88–89.

9. John Crosby column, June 23, 1948, in John Crosby, *Out of the Blue: A Book
About Radio and Television* (New York: Simon and Schuster, 1952) 240–242; Robert
E. Kennedy quoted in Robert U. Brown, "Shop Talk at Thirty," *Editor & Publisher*
July 24, 1948, 72.

10. FCC statistics, quoted in *Broadcasting Yearbook* 1966, A-158.

11. *Broadcasting Yearbook,* 1957–1958, 11; *Broadcasting Yearbook,* 1966, A-157.

12. FCC statistics, quoted in *Broadcasting Yearbook,* 1966, A-158; TV viewing
statistics compiled by *Telecasting* magazine, quoted in Wilbur Schramm, ed., *Mass
Communications* (Urbana: University of Illinois Press, 1960) 458.

13. McCann-Erickson statistics, quoted in J. Warren McClure, "To Them, All
Business Is Local," in *Advertising Today Yesterday Tomorrow: An Omnibus of
Advertising Prepared by Printer's Ink in its 75th Year of Publication* (New York:
McGraw Hill, 1963) 222.

14. McCann-Erickson statistics, quoted in Richard A.R. Pinkham, "The
Glamour Medium—and Some Men Who Made It," in ibid., 238.

15. American Newspaper Publishers Association (ANPA) statistics,
Newspaper Association of America, Reston, Virginia. The number of daily
newspapers fluctuated through the 1950s but was the same in 1960 as in
1946—1,763 newspapers.

16. McCann-Erickson statistics, quoted in Leo Bogart, *The Age of Television*
(New York: Frederick Ungar, 1958) 185.

17. Harold S. Barnes, "How TV Affects Newspapers," *Editor & Publisher,*
October 8, 1949, 6; "What's That You Say?" *Editor & Publisher,* May 24, 1958, 9.

18. Quoted in Will Fowler, *Reporters: Memoirs of a Young Newspaperman*
(Malibu, CA: Roundtable Publishing, 1991) 160–161.

19. Ibid., 163. Young Kathy died before she could be rescued.

20. Hooperatings (a ratings service) cited in *The First 50 Years of Broadcasting,*
106.

21. Quoted in ibid., 106.

22. Jack Gould, "The Crime Hearings: Television Provides Both a Lively
Show and a Notable Public Service," *New York Times,* March 18, 1951, Sec. 2,
p. 13.

23. John W. Bloomer, "The Impact of TV on the Press and Public," talk before
the Georgia Press Institute reprinted in *Advancing Journalism,* ed. John E. Drewry
(Athens GA: University of Georgia Press, 1953) 1–8.

24. "The MacArthur Show," *Newsweek,* April 30, 1951, 57; *The First 50 Years of
Broadcasting,* 104.

25. Quoted in "Mac on TV," *Time,* April 30, 1951, 91.

26. Ibid.

27. *ASNE Proceedings,* 1951, 158–159.

28. Quoted in "TV Increases Demand for Press Coverage," *Editor & Publisher* December 12, 1953, 49.

29. Quoted in "Proof," *Time,* June 15, 1953, 63. The exact effect of televised news events on newspaper street sales is, of course, difficult to determine—after all, big news usually increases circulation somewhat, even without television. But newspaper publishers were unanimous in crediting television for the phenomenon.

30. *APME Red Book,* 1951, 119.

31. Arthur Hays Sulzberger memo to Turner Catledge, March 26, 1951; Turner Catledge letter to E.C. Hoyt, March 23, 1951, in Turner Catledge papers, Mitchell Memorial Library, Mississippi State University, Starkville, Mississippi. Hereafter cited as Catledge papers.

32. Jack Gould, "What Is Television Doing to Us?" *New York Times Magazine,* June 12, 1949, 7.

33. NBC study results, quoted in "What TV Is Doing to America," *U.S. News & World Report,* September 2, 1955, 39.

34. Bogart, *The Age of Television,* 154.

35. *ASNE Proceedings,* 1951, 146, 153.

36. "Television Convention," *Newsweek,* July 14, 1952, 84–85; "Radio-TV is Intent of the Convention," *New York Times,* July 7, 1952, 9.

37. Thomas Sancton, New Orleans *Item,* July 20, 1952, quoted in "Video Will Change Coverage of News," *Nieman Reports,* January 1953, 14–15.

38. Alistair Cooke in the *Manchester Guardian,* quoted in O.J. Bue, "The Editor Has a Look at His Hole Card," *Quill,* December 1952, 7.

39. Jack Gould, "Reporting by Video: Coverage of the Republican Convention Shows Advantages and Limitations," *New York Times,* July 13, 1952, Sec. 2, p. 9.

40. Sig Mickelson, "Two National Political Conventions Have Proved Television's News Role," *Quill,* December 1956, 15–16.

41. Quoted in "Press v. Picture," *Time, August 27, 1956,* 54.

42. Walter Trohan, *Political Animals: Memoirs of a Sentimental Cynic* (Garden City, NY: Doubleday & Co., 1975) 399.

43. "Remarks to the National Association of Radio and Television Broadcasters," Dwight D. Eisenhower, *The Public Papers of the Presidents, 1955* (Washington, DC: United States Government Printing Office, 1959) 527–531.

44. "White House TV," *Editor & Publisher,* April 4, 1953, 36.

45. James Hagerty quoted in "First Photographed Press Conference," *Life,* January 31, 1955, 22–23.

46. James Reston and William S. White quoted in Robert U. Brown and George A. Brandenburg, "Reporters at Convention Ask TV 'Ground Rules,' " *Editor & Publisher,* July 12, 1952, 7, 69. See also T.S. Irvin, "TV Scoops Newspapers on Convention Boost," *Editor & Publisher,* July 12, 1952, 67; Burton W. Marvin, "What Will Television Do to Politics, Radio and Press–and to TV Itself," *Quill,* September 1952, 12–14; and Walter T. Ridder, "The Decline and Fall of the Press Conference," *Quill,* September 1952, 7, 14.

47. Quoted in "The News–and TV," *Newsweek,* April 29, 1957, 73; "Jab to the Nose," *Time,* May 6, 1957, 90–91.

48. Quoted in "Jab to the Nose," *Time,* May 6,1957, 91.

49. Leo Fischer, "TV's Challenge to Sports Writer: Story Behind Victory," *Quill,* April 1951, 7; "What TV is Doing to America," *U.S. News & World Report,* 44.

50. Associated Press survey quoted in *APME Red Book,* 1955, 205.

51. Robert E. Garst memo to Turner Catledge, June 19, 1956, Catledge papers.

52. Turner Catledge to John Paul Jones, June 19, 1956, ibid.

53. Harry C. Withers, "Slanting by Omission," *Editor & Publisher*, June 26, 1954, 81.

54. Herbert F. Corn, "Amateur Reporters," ibid.

55. Lester Markel, "Let Us Stick to News: TV Can't Compete," ibid., April 10, 1954, 12.

56. Robert U. Brown, "Shop Talk at Thirty," *Editor & Publisher*, September 13, 1958, 120; George Pieper, "Newspaper Color for Millions," in *Printing Progress: A Mid-Century Report* (Cincinnati, OH: International Association of Printing House Craftsmen, Inc., 1959) 419–430.

57. Arville Schalenben, "In a World of Color Most Newspapers Persist with Drab Black and White," *Quill*, June 1958, 15; Robert B. McIntyre, "E&P Presents: ROP Color as a Newspaper Achievement," *Editor & Publisher*, March 30, 1957, 9.

58. Oral history interview with Benjamin H. Reese, Oral History Research Office, Columbia University, New York; George Wise quoted in George A. Brandenburg, "Seltzer Hits 'Flabby' Investigative Sinews," *Editor & Publisher*, May 29, 1954, 9.

59. W.C. Todd, "Television: Do We Fight It or Capitalize on It?" *Circulation Management*, April 1955, 15–16.

60. *Variety* quoted in Robert U. Brown, "Shop Talk at Thirty," *Editor & Publisher*, December 10, 1955, 88.

61. Robert W. Sarnoff speech quoted in "Press-TV 'Conflict' Linked to Ad Dollar," *Editor & Publisher*, June 21, 1958, 82.

62. Robert U. Brown, "Shop Talk at Thirty," *Editor & Publisher*, July 19, 1958, 64.

63. "The Press v. Broadcasters," *Time*, February 8, 1954, 49; "Radio-TV Logs," *Editor & Publisher*, January 23, 1954, 34.

64. National Association of Radio and Television Broadcasters survey, cited in Sydney W. Head, *Broadcasting in America*, 2nd edn. (Boston, MA: Houghton Mifflin, 1972) 231.

65. *APME Red Book*, 1954, 62.

66. "The Changing Role of Radio," *Journal of Broadcasting* 8 (1964): 331–339; "Radio '65: Everybody's Tuned In," *Newsweek*, June 28, 1965, 80–82.

67. *U.S. Industrial Outlook 1966* (Washington, DC: U.S. Government Printing Office, 1965) 52–53.

68. Curtis Prendergast with Geoffrey Colvin, *The World of Time Inc.: The Intimate History of a Changing Enterprise, Volume 3: 1960–1980* (New York: Atheneum, 1986) 114.

69. McCann-Erickson statistics, cited in *Advertising Today Yesterday Tomorrow*, 218.

70. McCann-Erickson statistics, quoted in *The Mass Media: Aspen Institute Guide to Communication Industry Trends*, eds. Christopher H. Sterling and Timothy R. Haight (New York: Praeger, 1978) 124–131.

71. Gene Alleman, "TV Raids on Hometown Ads Worry Publishers," *National Publisher*, June 1957, 2. *National Publisher* was the publication of the National Editorial Association (NEA).

72. Interview with O.G. McDavid, 1980, Mississippi Oral History Program, University of Southern Mississippi, Hattiesburg, Mississippi.

73. "Newspaper Economics," *Editor & Publisher*, July 26, 1958, 6; Robert U. Brown, "Revenue Outpaces Expense," *Editor & Publisher*, April 16, 1960, 11.

74. "Comparison of 'Circulation'," February 18, 1956, 6.

75. *National Publisher*, October 1955, 15.

76. Alleman, "TV Raids on Hometown Ads Worry Publishers."

77. Richard Lloyd Jones, speech to NEA, reprinted in "The Road Ahead," *National Publisher*, April 1954, 23–24.

NEWSPAPERS AND THE CIVIL RIGHTS MOVEMENT, 1954–1957

1. "Dailies' Cooperation Asked in Solving Negro Problem," *Editor & Publisher*, August 4, 1945, 7; Robert B. Eleazer, "Churchman Sees Peril in 'Negro' Headlines," *Editor & Publisher*, December 27, 1947, 24. Pressure for the elimination of identification by race had also come from white churches.

2. "Race in the News," *New York Times*, August 11, 1946, 8E; "Answer," *Time*, 19 August 1946, 60.

3. Ben Bradlee, *A Good Life: Newspapering and Other Adventures* (New York: Simon and Schuster, 1995) 125.

4. Ira B. Harkey, Jr., "Jim Crow Days—The Way We Were" (speech given October 28, 1992 at Bennett Auditorium, University of Southern Mississippi, Hattiesburg, Mississippi). Harkey won the 1963 Pulitzer Prize for editorial writing for defending James Meredith's right to desegregate the University of Mississippi. His memoir is *The Smell of Burning Crosses: An Autobiography of a Mississippi Newspaperman* (Jacksonville, IL: Harris-Wolfe, 1967).

5. Harkey, *Smell of Burning Crosses*, 54–55, 60–61, 65.

6. Robert N. Pierce, *A Sacred Trust: Nelson Poynter and the St. Petersburg Times* (Gainesville, FL: University Press of Florida, 1993) 146.

7. Roger M. Williams, "A Regional Report: Newspapers of the South," *Columbia Journalism Review*, Summer 1967, 30.

8. "Negro Gets Press Card by Appeal to Senate," *Editor & Publisher*, March 22, 1947, 13; Gilbert W. Stewart, Jr., "He Erased the Color Line," *Nieman Reports*, October 1947, 12; *ASNE Proceedings*, 1955, 93.

9. Robert W. Wells, *The Milwaukee Journal: An Informal Chronicle of Its First 100 Years* (Milwaukee, WI: Milwaukee Journal, 1981) 377, 415.

10. Pierce, *A Sacred Trust*, 143.

11. Frank Angelo, *On Guard: A History of the Detroit Free Press* (Detroit, MI: Detroit Free Press, 1981) 195.

12. "How Integration Worked on One Newspaper Staff," *Nieman Reports*, October 1956, 39.

13. Armistead Scott Pride, "Low Man on the Totem Pole," *Nieman Reports*, April 1955, 21.

14. Pride, "Low Man on the Totem Pole," 21; John M. Harrison, *The Blade of Toledo* (Toledo, OH: Toledo Blade Co., 1985) 336.

15. Quoted in Bradlee, *A Good Life*, 280; Howard Bray, *The Pillars of the Post: The Making of a News Empire in Washington* (New York: Norton, 1980) 160–162.

16. *Brown v Board of Education of Topeka*, 347 U.S. 483 (1954); 349 U.S. 294 (1955); C.A. McKnight, "Text of Talk to N.C. Press Group," *Southern School News*, February 3, 1955, 11.

17. "High Court Bans School Segregation; Nine-to-Zero Decision Grants Time to Comply," *New York Times*, May 18, 1954, 1, 14–23; "Report on the South," *New York Times*, March 13, 1956, S1–S8; "Ten Reporters Traveled in South for Weeks on Integration Story," *New York Times*, March 13, 1956, S8; Arthur Hays Sulzberger, " 'The Word Negro Is Not to Appear Unless,': One Publisher's Attitude on Race," *Nieman Reports*, October 1957, 3–4.

18. Harrison E. Salisbury, *A Time of Change: A Reporter's Tale of Our Time* (New York: Harper & Row, 1988) 44.

19. John N. Popham to Turner Catledge, December 12, 1947, December 1, 1952, December 31, 1954; Turner Catledge to Arthur Ochs Sulzberger, April 7, 1953, Turner Catledge papers, Mitchell Memorial Library, Mississippi State University, Starkville, Mississippi. Hereafter cited as Catledge papers.

20. Turner Catledge to Lester Markel, May 14, 1958, Catledge papers.

21. "The Reporting Service . . . and How it Grew," *Southern School News,* May 4, 1955, 1; "SERS Reference Library Now Has 55,000 Items," *Southern School News,* March 1957, 1.

22. Hodding Carter, *Their Words Were Bullets: The Southern Press in War, Reconstruction, and Peace* (Athens, GA: University of Georgia Press, 1969) 64.

23. Interview with J. Oliver Emmerich, 1973, Mississippi Oral History Program, University of Southern Mississippi, Hattiesburg, Mississippi.

24. *The South Speaks Out for Law and Order: A Roundup of Southern Press Opinion* (National Council of the Churches of Christ in the United States of America et al., 1958) 4.

25. Don Shoemaker, ed., *With All Deliberate Speed* (New York: Harper, 1957) 31–34.

26. Reed Sarratt, *The Ordeal of Desegregation: The First Decade* (New York: Harper & Row, 1966) 248.

27. Harry Ashmore, *Civil Rights and Wrongs: A Memoir of Race and Politics* (New York: Pantheon Books, 1994) 63.

28. Ann Waldron, *Hodding Carter: The Reconstruction of a Racist* (Chapel Hill, NC: Algonquin Books, 1993) 251.

29. Andrew McDowd Secrest, "In Black and White: Press Opinion and Race Relations in South Carolina, 1945–1964," Ph.D. dissertation, Duke University, 1971, xiii.

30. Benjamin Muse, *Virginia's Massive Resistance* (Bloomington, IN: Indiana University Press, 1961) 94.

31. Lenoir Chambers to Harry Ashmore, February 6, 1958, quoted in William Howard Turpin, "Editorial Leadership in a Time of Crisis: Virginia's Massive Resistance, 1954–1959," Ph.D. dissertation, University of North Carolina, Chapel Hill, 1976, 138.

32. Carl E. Lindstrom, *The Fading American Newspaper* (1960; reprint edn, Glouchester, MA: Peter Smith, 1964) 32.

33. *ASNE Proceedings,* 1955, 81–86.

34. Ibid.

35. McKnight, "Text of Talk to N.C. Press Group," 11.

36. Shoemaker, *With All Deliberate Speed,* 31.

37. Walter Spearman and Sylvan Meyer, *Racial Crisis and the Press* (Atlanta, GA: Southern Regional Council, 1960) 27.

38. See, for example, Roy E. Carter, Jr., "Segregation and the News: A Regional Content Study," *Journalism Quarterly* 34 (Winter 1957): 3–18; and Warren Breed, "South's Newspapers Hew to Objectivity," *Editor & Publisher,* September 28, 1957, 40.

39. *APME Red Book,* 1957, 79.

40. T.R. Waring and Ralph McGill quoted in "Invasion of the South," *Newsweek,* April 2, 1956, 86.

41. Ibid.

42. David Halberstam, *The Fifties* (New York: Villard Books, 1993) 437.

43. Quoted in ibid., 438.

44. "Latest News on Till Trial," (Charleston) *Mississippi Sun*, September 22, 1955, 1.

45. "Mississippi: The Place, the Acquittal," *Newsweek*, October 3, 1955, 24, 29–30; Halberstam, *The Fifties*, 438.

46. Simeon Booker, "A Negro Reporter at the Till Trial," *Nieman Reports*, January 1956, 13–15.

47. James Hicks and Dan Wakefield quoted in Stephen J. Whitfield, *A Death in the Delta: The Story of Emmett Till* (New York: Free Press, 1989) 36–37.

48. John Chancellor, "Radio and Television Had Their Own Problems in Little Rock Coverage," *Quill*, December 1957, 9.

49. Ibid., 10, 21; Ray Moseley, "Northern Newsmen Withstood Mob's Abuse to Report Little Rock Story," *Quill*, December 1957, 8, 18.

50. Quoted in "Preston Raps Press Antics at Little Rock," *Editor & Publisher*, November 2, 1957, 66.

51. Benjamin Fine, "Guardsmen Curb Newsmen's Work," *New York Times*, September 6, 1957, 8.

52. Benjamin Fine to Hal Faber, September 5, 1957; Fine to Orval Dryfoos, November 18, 1957, in Catledge papers.

53. Philip N. Schuyler, "Panelists Agree: Journalistic Code Violated at Little Rock," *Editor & Publisher*, November 2, 1957, 11.

54. Ibid., 66.

55. See, for example, "Interviews with Southern Newspaper Editors," *U.S. News & World Report*, February 24, 1956, 44–50, 134–144.

56. Robert U. Brown, "Shop Talk at Thirty," *Editor & Publisher*, November 12, 1955, 80.

57. *ASNE Proceedings*, 1956, 72–98.

58. Thomas R. Waring, "The Southern Case Against Desegregation," *Harper's*, January 1956, 39.

59. Hall's invitation to Wechsler is reprinted in "Is Race Friction in North Being Fully Reported?" *U.S. News and World Report*, March 23, 1956, 48–50.

60. "Say Race Problems Sure to Increase," *Jackson* (MS) *Clarion-Ledger and Daily News*, October 14, 1956, 1; "Twenty New England Editors View Mississippi Race Relations on Tour," *Southern School News*, November 1956, 3.

61. Laura R. Walton, "Segregationist Spin: The Use of Propaganda by the Mississippi State Sovereignty Commission and the White Citizens' Council, 1954–1973," Ph.D. dissertation, University of Southern Mississippi, Hattiesburg, 106–107.

62. "Southerner Studies North for the U.P.," *Editor & Publisher*, March 1, 1958, 59.

63. *APME Red Book*, 1956, 87.

64. Harry Reasoner, *Before the Colors Fade* (New York: Knopf, 1981) 58–59.

65. Wallace Westfeldt cited in Halberstam, *The Fifties*, 681.

66. Peter J. Boyer, *Who Killed CBS?* (New York: Random House, 1988) 229–230. Emphasis in the original.

67. Harry S. Ashmore, "The Story Behind Little Rock," *Nieman Reports*, April 1958, 3–7.

68. *Newsweek*, August 26, 1963, 50–51.

69. Quoted in *The Black Press: Soldiers without Swords*, prod. and dir. Stanley Nelson, 90 minutes, Chicago Production Center, 1999, videocassette.

70. *Newsweek*, August 26, 1963, 50–51.

71. Review of Roland E. Eolseley, *Black Press U.S.A. Journalism Quarterly* 48 (Winter 1971) 788; L.F. Palmer, Jr., "Black Press in Transition," *Columbia Journalism Review*, Spring 1970, 31–36.

72. *New York Times v Sullivan*, 376 U.S. 254.

73. *Ibid.*, 279–283.

74. "Libel? You'll Have to Prove It," *Columbia Journalism Review*, November–December 2001, 57.

75. Barry Bingham, "Newspapers in Crisis," *Nieman Reports* October 1959, 17–18.

THE SEEDS OF LONG-TERM CHANGE, 1950–1963

1. Robert U. Brown, "Revenue Outpaces Expense," *Editor & Publisher*, April 16, 1960, 11.

2. Robert U. Brown, "Small Gain in Revenue Makes Profit Margin Tight Squeeze," *Editor & Publisher*, April 5, 1958, 9, 10.

3. Robert U. Brown, "50,000-Daily's Profit Was Lowest Since 1945," *Editor & Publisher*, April 19, 1958, 24.

4. Richard W. Slocum quoted in "The High Cost of Publishing," *Time*, June 21, 1954, 79–80.

5. "Why Newspapers are in Trouble," *U.S. News & World Report*, January 16, 1959, 75.

6. Soaring newsprint prices cannot be overstated as a root cause of newspapers' financial difficulties in the booming 1950s. Publishers had long relied, as *Fortune* magazine put it in 1951, upon a "formula" of cheap newsprint and circulation rate increases to remain profitable. In the postwar years, due to soaring paper prices and competition from television, the formula no longer worked. See "Newspaper Business: The Death of a Formula," *Fortune*, September 1951, 118–119, and L. Ethan Ellis, *Newsprint: Producers, Publishers, Political Pressures* (New Brunswick, NJ: Rutgers University Press, 1960).

7. "The High Cost of Publishing," 79–80.

8. *Media Records* statistics quoted in "Average Paper in 1952 Had 59 Percent Ad Content," *Editor & Publisher*, April 18, 1953, 128.

9. See Chapter 1.

10. James S. Pope, "A Managing Editor Discusses Need for Higher Standards," *Journalism Quarterly* 24 (March 1947): 30.

11. Charles V. Kinter, "Economic Problems in Private Ownership of Communications," in *Communications in Modern Society*, ed. Wilbur Schramm (Urbana: University of Illinois Press, 1948) 24–25.

12. Millard B. Grimes, *The Last Linotype: The Story of Georgia and its Newspapers Since World War II* (Macon, GA: Mercer University Press and the Georgia Press Association, 1985) 3.

13. Robert U. Brown, "Shop Talk at Thirty," *Editor & Publisher*, July 9, 1955, 76.

14. "It's Not Enough," *Editor & Publisher*, May 2, 1959, 6.

15. Warren Chappell, *A Short History of the Printed Word* (New York: Knopf, 1970) 224.

16. Harry Loose, "Watch New Printing Devices But Don't Let Them Worry You," *Iowa Publisher*, February 1946, 3.

17. John R. Thistlethwaite, "Louisiana Daily Has Been Offset Paper 17 Years," *National Publisher*, March 1956, 35.

18. Ibid.

19. Robert L. Norberg, "'Nothing But Advantages in Switching to Offset Method,' Weekly Publisher States," *American Press*, February 1958, 15, 24.

20. Allan Woods, *Modern Newspaper Production* (New York: Harper & Row, 1963) 181.

21. Jack Fidler quoted in Fred Troutman, "From Letterpress to Offset," *Missouri Press News*, April 1960, 8–9, 19.

22. Editorial, November 22, 1955, *Gainesville* (GA) *Morning News*, quoted in Grimes, *Last Linotype* 45.

23. Charles L. Hardy, Sr., column, *Morning News* July 31, 1956, quoted in Grimes, *Last Linotype*, 46.

24. Grimes, *Last Linotype*, 65.

25. "Thayer Named to Head New Committee on Offset Printing," *National Publisher*, January 1956, 29; *National Publisher*, December 1957, 28.

26. "Equipment Buying Spree Foreseen for Weeklies and Small Dailies," *American Press*, October 1960, 9.

27. Woods, *Modern Newspaper Production*, 181.

28. R. Randolph Karch and Edward J. Buber, *Graphic Arts Procedures: The Offset Processes* (Chicago, IL: American Technical Society, 1967) 5.

29. "Offset Printing: The Door to Your Future," *University of Missouri Bulletin* 65:31, Journalism Series No. 159, November 6, 1964.

30. Prescott Low quoted in Robert U. Brown, "More Daily Papers?" *Editor & Publisher*, October 1, 1960, 68.

31. John Tebbel, "The Quiet Offset Revolution," *Saturday Review*, December 9, 1961, 60–61.

32. Woods, *Modern Newspaper Production*, 178–179.

33. Ibid., 179–180.

34. Linofilm advertisement, *Editor & Publisher*, April 17, 1954, 58–59; "Printing Revolution," *Editor & Publisher*, 78.

35. "Survey Tells Editors' View of Cold Type," *Editor & Publisher*, May 31, 1958, 61; R.D. Allen, "New Typographical Techniques," *Nieman Reports*, July 1958, 19.

36. Martin M. Reed, "Cold Type at the Crossroads after Ten Years, $8,000,000," *Editor & Publisher*, January 18, 1958, 11.

37. Allen, "New Typographical Techniques," 20.

38. Roy N. Walden, "Hot Metal vs. Cold Type—A Cost Comparison," *Publication Management*, September 1959, 11.

39. Frederick H. Trantow, "Photon Machines—Their Use in the 'Cold Type' Process," *Publication Management*, February 1960, 20–21.

40. *APME Red Book*, 1952, 104.

41. Clifton E. Wilson, "Impact of Teletypesetter on Publishing Media," *Journalism Quarterly* 30 (1953): 372–73.

42. George A. Brandenburg, "TTS Advantages Told Inland News Editors," *Editor & Publisher*, April 19, 1952, 104.

43. "Teletypesetter Committee Report," *APME Red Book*, 1952, 111–114.

44. Ibid., 111.

45. Wilson, "Impact of Teletypesetter," 373.

46. Ray Erwin, "New AP Style Book Changes Newspaper Copy Very Soon," *Editor & Publisher*, June 6, 1953, 9.

47. Ibid.

48. "Walters Warns Tape Can Be Frankenstein," *Editor & Publisher*, February 2, 1952, 20.

49. "Timely Warning," ibid., 28.

50. George K. Moriarty, "Story Structure and the News Desk," *American Editor*, April 1957, 23.

51. Carl Lindstrom, *The Fading American Newspaper* (1960; reprint edn, Glouchester, MA: Peter Smith, 1964) 112–113.

52. "New High Speed TTS System Sends 600 Words a Minute," *Editor & Publisher*, July 24, 1954, 9.

53. Quoted in Robert U. Brown, "Shop Talk at Thirty," *Editor & Publisher*, October 30, 1954, 72.

54. Ibid.

55. "Automation Boom Spreads TTS Operation in Papers," ibid., June 18, 1960, 9, 66; "UP and INS Merge to Form United Press International," ibid., May 31, 1958, 9–10.

56. "Higher Quality, Lower Costs," *American Editor*, January 1960, 40.

57. U.S. Department of Commerce statistics, quoted in Jon G. Udell, "Economic Trends in the Daily Newspaper Business, 1946 to 1970," *Wisconsin Projects Reports* 4:6 (December 1970b): 10.

58. Poynter McEvoy, "Right Now the Battle of Production Costs," *American Editor*, July 1960, 40–45.

59. Quoted in "Editor Calls for Greater Production," ibid., November 29, 1958, 52.

60. Woods, *Modern Newspaper Production*, 184.

61. J. Russell Wiggins, "Journalism Faces Challenges," *Quill*, November 1959, 12–13.

62. James Homer Buckley, "Suburban Evangel: Trade Associations and the Emergence of the Suburban Newspaper Industry, 1945–1970," Ph.D. dissertation, University of Washington, 1986, 58–79.

63. Circulation figures using N.W. Ayer and Sons statistics, excluding the religious, racial, and trade press, compiled in Kenneth R. Byerly, "Supplementary (Final) Report on Community Newspapers (Daily and Weekly) and Metropolitan Dailies in the Nation's Ten Most Populous Metropolitan Areas," July 30, 1963, photocopy in Newspaper Association of America files.

64. Ibid.

65. "Newspapers: Lagging Downtown, New Life in Suburbs," *Business Week*, February 5, 1955, 134.

66. "Suburb and City," *Columbia Journalism Review*, Summer 1963, 13–14.

67. *ASNE Proceedings*, 1959, 2.

68. "Suburb and City," 15–21.

69. Charles Hayes, "The Exploding Suburban Press," *Grassroots Editor*, July 1960, 7.

70. Stuart Paddock quoted in "The Need to Holler," *Newsweek*, June 22, 1959, 88–89.

71. Jerrold Lee Werthimer, "The Community Press of Suburbia: A Case Study of Paddock Newspapers," Ph.D. dissertation, Northwestern University, 1960, 81, 96, 112.

72. David R. Bowers, "The Impact of Centralized Printing on the Community Press," *Journalism Quarterly* 46 (1969): 43–46, 52; Rick Friedman, "Starting a Weekly," *Editor & Publisher*, December 15, 1962, 46–47.

73. Buckley, "Suburban Evangel," 69.

74. Ralph E. Heckman, "Where Is This Place Called Suburbia?" *Publication Management*, September 1959, 13.

75. Ibid.

76. William M. Pike quoted in "Suburbia's Challenge Seized by N.Y. Times," *Editor & Publisher*, March 7, 1959, 52, 54.

77. Ibid.

78. Turner Catledge to Arthur Ochs Sulzberger, September 9, 1957; Kalman Seigel to Turner Catledge, October 11, 1962, Turner Catledge papers, Mitchell Memorial Library, Mississippi State University.

79. "Cleveland Press," *ASNE Bulletin*, January 1, 1957, 7. See also "Flight to the Suburbs: What Major Newspapers Are Doing about It," *ASNE Bulletin*, 7–11.

80. "Newark News," ibid., 9; "Detroit Free Press," ibid., 8.

81. Ibid.

82. Werthimer, "Community Press of Suburbia," 365–367.

83. Robert U. Brown, "Shop Talk at Thirty," *Editor & Publisher*, May 25, 1957, 100.

84. "Downtown vs. Suburban Areas: Effect of Decentralization on Newspapers," February 2, 1955, American Newspaper Publishers Association (ANPA), photocopied report in Newspaper Association of America files.

85. Campbell Watson, "Shopping Centers Forcing Broadened Linage Areas," *Editor & Publisher*, June 13, 1953, 9.

86. James Hoge quoted in Anthony Smith, *Goodbye Gutenburg: The Newspaper Revolution in the 1980s* (New York: Oxford University Press, 1980) 71–72.

87. Quoted in Raymond A. Schroth, *The Eagle and Brooklyn: A Community Newspaper, 1841–1955* (Westport, CT: Greenwood Press, 1974) 249–250.

88. Jon G. Udell, "The Growth of the American Daily Newspaper: An Economic Analysis," *Wisconsin Project Reports* 3 (1965): 4.

89. Bureau of the Census population statistics, *Editor & Publisher Yearbook* circulation figures, quoted in ibid., 15.

90. "What Newspapers Are Doing to Develop Young Readers," November 1955, photocopied report in Newspaper Association of America files.

91. Stanford Smith, "Teaching Johnny How to Read Newspapers in the Classroom," *Quill*, August 1960, 15–16; "Newspapers in the Classroom: A Report on Results of University Workshops," *ASNE Bulletin*, February 1, 1960, 1–2.

92. Ed Keefe, "How to Insure Future Readers With Promotion to Young People," *Circulation Management*, April 1955, 12.

93. T.S. Irvin, "Miami Herald Sparks Reading in High School," *Editor & Publisher*, March 10, 1956, 48; C.R. Conlee, "Newspapers Go to School," *Circulation Management*, March 1954, 16.

KENNEDY AND THE PRESS, 1960–1963

1. Transcript of "The Press and the People," reprinted in *Washington and the Press* (New York: Fund for the Republic, 1959) 5.

2. *Availability of Information from Federal Departments and Agencies*, Hearings Before a Subcommittee of the Committee of Government Operations, House of Representatives, Eighty-fourth Congress, First Session, November 7, 1955 (Washington, DC: U.S. Government Printing Office, 1956) 7–9.

3. *Availability of Information from Federal Departments and Agencies*, 32.

4. Eisenhower letter to Secretary of Defense Charles E. Wilson, May 17, 1954, reprinted in "Texts of Eisenhower Letter and Brownell Memorandum on Testimony in Senate Inquiry," *New York Times*, May 18, 1954, 24.

5. John F. Kennedy to Turner Catledge, January 3, 1961, photocopy in files of Freedom of Information Center, University of Missouri at Columbia. Hereafter cited as FOI Center files.

6. Mary McGrory, "Kennedy and the Press," *Publisher's Auxiliary*, December 23, 1961, 2.

7. James E. Pollard, *The Presidents and the Press: Truman to Johnson* (Washington, DC: Public Affairs Press, 1964) 96.

8. Quoted in Montague Kern, Patricia W. Levering, and Ralph B. Levering, *The Kennedy Crises: The Press, the Presidency, and Foreign Policy* (Chapel Hill, NC: University of North Carolina Press, 1983) 5.

9. Roger Hilsman, *The Politics of Policy Making in Defense and Foreign Affairs* (New York: Harper and Row, 1971) 114.

10. Arthur M. Schlesinger, Jr., *A Thousand Days: John F. Kennedy in the White House* (Boston, MA: Houghton Mifflin, 1965) 716.

11. James Reston, "How to Break the Rules without Getting Caught," *New York Times*, November 29, 1961, 40.

12. Quoted in ibid.

13. Ibid.

14. Bill Lawrence, *Six Presidents, Too Many Wars* (New York: Saturday Review Press, 1972) 4, 6.

15. Ibid., 239.

16. Sarah McClendon, *My Eight Presidents* (New York: Wyden Books, 1978) 50.

17. Quoted in William L. Rivers, *The Opinionmakers* (Boston, MA: Beacon Press, 1965) 164; Esther Featherer, "Kennedy and the Press," Freedom of Information Center Publication No. 120, April 1964, in FOI Center files.

18. Quoted in Kern et al., *The Kennedy Crises*, 5.

19. Quoted in Pierre Salinger, *With Kennedy* (New York: Doubleday, 1966) 56.

20. *ASNE Proceedings*, 1961, 32.

21. Ibid.

22. Quoted in "J.F.K. and the Conference," *Time*, March 24, 1961, 44.

23. Quoted in ibid.

24. Quoted in Jo Ranson, "Pressmen Growl at JFK's Plan," *Radio-TV Daily*, January 17, 1961, 1.

25. Quoted in "'Live' Press Conferences Stir Pro and Con Views," *Editor & Publisher*, January 7, 1961, 9.

26. Quoted in ibid., 10.

27. Quoted in *ASNE Proceedings*, 1961, 23–25.

28. Ibid., 22.

29. Ibid., 28.

30. John Crosby, "The Press Conference Makes Skimpy Repasts," *Washington Post*, May 1, 1961, 14B.

31. Merriman Smith, "Newsmen Miss Repartee in TV Press Conference," *Columbia Missourian*, January 26, 1961, 2.

32. "Debut," *Washington Post*, January 27, 1961, 12A; "Press Conference on Live TV," *New York Times*, January 27, 1961, 22. The *Baltimore Sun* editorial is quoted in "Opinion of the Week: President Evaluated," *New York Times*, January 29, 1961, E11, which is a roundup of nationwide press reaction to Kennedy's first conference.

33. "TV Press Conference," *Editor & Publisher*, January 28, 1961, 6.

34. *ASNE Proceedings*, 1961, 4.

35. Richard Dudman, "P.I.O.: Natural Enemy," *Nieman Reports*, March 1963, 5. Dudman's brief article is part of a *Nieman Reports* symposium called "The News Management Issue," 3–15.

36. Arthur Krock, "Mr. Kennedy's Management of the News," *Fortune*, March 1963, 82, 199, 202.

37. Transcript of "CBS Views the Press" broadcast of December 3, 1961, reprinted in Charles Collingwood, "Presidential Pressmanship," *Nieman Reports*, January 1962, 8–9.

38. Krock, "Mr. Kennedy's Management of the News," 82.

39. Quoted in Pollard, *Presidents and the Press*, 103.

40. Quoted in Rivers, *The Opinionmakers*, 160.

41. Schlesinger, *A Thousand Days*, 718.

42. "Disturbing Trend," *Editor & Publisher*, February 4, 1961, 6.

43. "News of Cuban Invasion," ibid., April 29, 1961, 6.

44. James Reston, "False 'News' from Officials in Cuban Crisis," *Kansas City Times*, May 10, 1961, clipping in FOI Center files.

45. "The President's News Conference of April 12, 1961," John F. Kennedy, *The Public Papers of the Presidents, 1961* (Washington, DC: United States Government Printing Office, 1962) 259.

46. "Text of Secretary Rusk's News Conference, Including Observations on Cuba," *New York Times*, 18 April 1961, 18.

47. Schlesinger, *A Thousand Days*, 261.

48. *APME Red Book*, 1961, 140.

49. Turner Catledge, *My Life and the Times* (New York: Harper & Row, 1971) 259–265; James Reston, *Deadline: A Memoir* (New York: Random House, 1991) 324–327; Tad Szulc, "Anti-Castro Units Trained to Fight at Florida Bases," *New York Times*, April 7, 1963, 1; Clifton Daniel, "National Security and the Bay of Pigs Invasion," in *Killing the Messenger*, ed. Tom Goldstein (New York: Columbia University Press, 1989) 107–118.

50. Catledge, *My Life and the Times*, 264.

51. Daniel, "National Security and the Bay of Pigs," 115.

52. "Address 'The President and the Press' Before the American Newspaper Publishers Association, New York City," April 27, 1961, John F. Kennedy, *Public Papers of the Presidents, 1961* (Washington, DC: United States Government Printing Office, 1962) 337.

53. "Notes on Conversation with Felix McKnight," memorandum in FOI Center files, May 12, 1961.

54. Felix R. McKnight, "President McKnight Reports to the ASNE Membership on White House Conference," *ASNE Bulletin*, June 1, 1961, 1; "Censorship Plan Avoided in Talk with President," *Editor & Publisher*, May 13, 1961, 11, 80.

55. *APME Red Book*, 1961, 156.

56. "The Right Not To Be Lied To," *New York Times*, May 10, 1961, 44.

57. Transcript of Charles Collingwood, "WCBS-TV Views the Press," April 23, 1961, in Turner Catledge papers; "Are We Training Cuban Guerrillas?" *Nation*, November 19, 1960, 378–379; Paul P. Kennedy, "U.S. Helps Train an Anti-Castro Force At Secret Guatemalan Air-Ground Base," *New York Times*, January 10, 1961, 1.

58. Daniel, "National Security and the Bay of Pigs Invasion," 112, 118.

59. Reston, *Deadline*, 473–474.

60. *Government Information Plans and Policies*, Hearings Before a Subcommittee of the Committee of Government Operations, House of Representatives, Eighty-eighth Congress, First Session (Washington, DC: U.S. Government Printing Office, 1963) 6–7.

61. Ibid., 7.

62. "Summary of News Management and Control by Federal Government," report prepared for ASNE and ANPA by John H. Colburn, *Richmond (VA) Times-Dispatch*, quoted in *Government Information Plans and Policies*, 9–16.

63. "Classic Conflict: The President and the Press," *Time*, December 14, 1962, 45.

64. Ibid.

65. Clark R. Mollenhoff, "Managing the News," *Nieman Reports*, December 1962, 3–6.

66. " 'Managed News'—A New 'Weapon' in U.S. Arsenal," *U.S. News & World Report*, November 12, 1962, 48.

67. Quoted in "Classic Conflict: the President and the Press," 45.

68. Quoted in " 'Managed News,' " 48.

69. "Managing the News," *New York Times*, October 31, 1962, 36.

70. "Where the National Interest Lies," joint statement of ASNE, ANPA, and NEA, *ASNE Bulletin*, January 1, 1963, 5.

71. Quoted in "Government Must be Honest in News, Sylvester Agrees," *Editor & Publisher*, March 30, 1963, 15; *Government Information Plans and Policies*, 146–147.

72. "Salinger Attacks 'News Managers,' " *Editor & Publisher*, March 30, 1963, 133.

73. "The President's News Conference of November 20, 1962," John F. Kennedy, *The Public Papers of the Presidents, 1962* (Washington, DC: United States Government Printing Office, 1963) 834, 836–837; *Government Information Plans and Policies*, 16.

74. Helen Thomas, *Dateline: White House* (New York: Macmillan, 1975) 31.

AN INDUSTRY IN CRISIS, 1960–1965

1. *U.S. Industrial Outlook 1966* (Washington, DC: United States Government Printing Office, 1965) 53.

2. "Radio '65: Everybody's Tuned In," *Newsweek*, June 28, 1965, 80–82.

3. "Newspaper Failures, Successes," *Editor & Publisher*, September 18, 1965, 6.

4. American Newspaper Publishers Association (ANPA) statistics, in Newspaper Association of America files, Reston, Virginia. Hereafter cited as NAA files.

5. Lloyd Wendt, "What's Right with the Newspaper Business," *Quill*, April 1964, 12.

6. "Cites Growth in Daily Press," *Kansas City Times*, December 11, 1965, clipping in FOI Center files.

7. *World Newsprint Supply-Demand: Outlook through 1969*, Report of the Committee on Interstate and Foreign Commerce, House Report 970, Ninetieth Congress, First Session (Washington, DC: United States Government Printing Office, 1967) 13–19.

8. *World Newsprint Supply-Demand: Outlook through 1968*, Report of the Committee on Interstate and Foreign Commerce, House Report 2196, Eighty-ninth Congress, Second Session (Washington, DC: United States Government Printing Office, 1966) 8; *Daily Newspapers in 1966—Highlights of a Record Year*, ANPA pamphlet, April 1967.

9. Morris J. Gelman, "Newspapers," *Television Magazine*, November 1962, 56–59.

10. Many newspapers were, in fact, doing quite well. *Editor & Publisher* reported in 1966 that an anonymous "average" daily newspaper of 50,000 circulation made a net profit of 11.3 percent of income in the previous year. (Robert U. Brown, "Net of $453,400 Is 11.3 Percent of Income," *Editor & Publisher*, April 16, 1966, 11, 47.)

11. *Daily Newspapers in 1966*; See also "Circulation vs. Population," *Editor & Publisher*, December 15, 1962, 6; Harold Riesz, "Why Newspaper Circulations Have Not Kept Pace with U.S. Population Growth," *Editor & Publisher*, February 6, 1960, 16.

12. Bureau of the Census and ANPA statistics, quoted in Benjamin M. Compaine, *Papers and Profits: A Special Report on the Newspaper Business* (New York: Knowledge Industry Publications, 1973) 9.

13. See Chapter 6 for a detailed discussion of the growth of suburbia and its effects upon newspapers after World War II.

14. Byerly's study is quoted at length in "Big Gains Recorded for Smaller Dailies," *Editor & Publisher*, March 13, 1965, 40.

15. See Chapter 6.

16. *World Newsprint Supply-Demand: Outlook through 1969*, 15; Sylvia Porter, "Soaring Costs a Cloud on Newspapers' Future," *Kansas City Star*, October 8, 1962, clipping in FOI Center files.

17. "U.S. Dailies Suspended, Merged, Or Gone Weekly," listing compiled from ANPA and *Editor & Publisher* statistics, reprinted in *Newspaper Preservation Act: Hearings before Antitrust Subcommittee*, Ninety-first Congress, First Session, September 10, 24, 25, and October 1, 1969 (Washington, DC: United States Government Printing Office, 1969) 215.

18. Oral history interview with Norman Bradley, June 2, 1976, Mississippi Oral History Program, University of Southern Mississippi.

19. Bruce Bliven, "Two Newspapers in Search of a City," *Reporter*, April 26, 1962, 22–23.

20. Quoted in "Probers Hear Los Angeles Times Chief," March 16, 1963, newspaper clipping reprinted in *Newspaper Preservation Act*, 327–328; "Chandler Defends Suspension of Two Los Angeles Newspapers," *New York Times*, March 16, 1963, 4.

21. Charles Thieriot to Emanuel Celler, September 8, 1969, reprinted in *Newspaper Preservation Act*, 178–179.

22. *Newspaper Preservation Act*, 81.

23. "17 Antitrust Cases Filed Against Papers Since 1890," *Washington Post*, August 2, 1977, D7, D10; *Citizen Publishing Company v United States*, 394 U.S. 131 (1969).

24. J. Montgomery Curtis to Turner Catledge, February 21, 1963, in Catledge papers.

25. "Statement of Arthur B. Hanson," in *Newspaper Preservation Act*, 141.

26. "Statement of Raymond B. Nixon," in ibid., 118–129.

27. Emanuel Celler, "The Concentration of Ownership and the Decline of Competition in the News Media," *Antitrust Bulletin* 8 (March–April 1963): 175–185.

28. Quoted in photocopied summary of ANPA presentation before Congress, April 1, 1963, in NAA files.

29. Ibid.

30. "Remarks of Stewart R. MacDonald on Celler Hearings Before National Newspaper Promotion Association Convention, May 5–8, 1963," photocopied report in NAA files; *Newspapers 1963: A Presentation by the American Newspaper Publishers Association Before the Antitrust Subcommittee of the House Judiciary Committee, 1963* (New York: American Newspaper Publishers Association) 1963.

31. "17 Antitrust Cases Filed Against Papers Since 1890," *Washington Post*, August 2, 1977, D7, D10. The *Times* had acquired the *Sun* in 1964.

32. "New Worry in Government: Not Enough Newspapers?" *U.S. News & World Report*, June 15, 1964, 111–112.

33. A. Kent MacDougall, "Newspaper Chains Buy More Dailies, Prosper in Monopoly Situations," *Wall Street Journal*, December 15, 1965, 1, 8.

34. Ibid., 1.

35. J. David Stern, *Memoirs of a Maverick Publisher* (New York: Simon and Schuster, 1962) 12–13.

36. Jerome H. Walker, "Weekly Circulation Totals Show How the Groups Stand," *Editor & Publisher*, April 9, 1966, 9–10.

37. *Knight-Ridder Factbook* (Miami: Knight-Ridder Newspapers, 1974) 2–3. The Knight and Ridder chains merged in 1974.

38. "Miller Sees Strength in Press 'Chain,'" *Editor & Publisher*, May 1, 1965, 39.

39. Al Neuharth, "I Belong to a Chain Gang and I'm Proud of It," *ASNE Bulletin*, July 1, 1963, 3–4.

40. Robert U. Brown, "Newspapers Are Threatened by Increased Costs—Knight," *Editor & Publisher*, November 16, 1957, 9.

41. Much of the material for this section is taken from the definitive account of the New York City newspaper strike, A.H. Raskin's "The Strike: A Step-by-Step Account," *New York Times*, April 1, 1963, 1, 22–24. A useful account of the strike is Nancy Baker, "New York Newspaper Strike," *Freedom of Information Publication No. 104*, July 1963, in FOI Center files.

42. Raskin, "The Strike," 1, 22.

43. Quoted in Baker, "New York Newspaper Strike," 1–8.

44. Raskin, "The Strike," 24; "After a Three-Month Shutdown—What Striking Printers Got," *U.S. News & World Report*, March 18, 1963, 98.

45. Sheldon Binn, "114-Day Newspaper Strike Ends as Engravers Ratify Contract; Loss in Excess of $190,000,000," *New York Times*, April 1, 1963, 1, 20.

46. Peter Kihss, "Papers Have Suffered Heavy Losses Since End of Blackout," *New York Times*, October 16, 1963, 31; "The Road Back," *Time*, September 13, 1963, 58.

47. T.A. Wise, "The Crisis on New York's Newspaper Row," *Fortune*, October 1964, 110–113, 228–236.

48. George Barrett, "The *Mirror* Is Closed by Hearst Corporation; Some of Assets Are Sold to The News," *New York Times*, October 16, 1963, 1, 30.

49. *APME Red Book*, 1964, 42.

50. Ibid., 37.

51. Roy R. Wimmer, "Aspects of Computer Automation in the Newspaper Industry," M.A. thesis, University of North Carolina at Chapel Hill, 1967, 13–15, 26–31; "Printing a Dream," *Time*, January 18, 1963, 68, 70; "All the News That's Fit to Automate,"*Time*, July 5, 1963, 52.

52. The computer statistics are taken from studies by Computer Information Services of Los Angeles, cited in "CIS Finds Nearly 300 Using Computing for Typesetting," *Publishers Weekly*, January 2, 1967, 103; Wimmer, "Aspects of Computer Automation," 2, 13.

53. *ASNE Proceedings*, 1963, 141–142.

54. "Computers Will be a Major Factor in Tomorrow's Typesetting," *Inland Printer/American Lithographer* 151 (1963): 66–67.

55. Robert U. Brown, "Computerized Future," *Editor & Publisher*, October 17, 1964, 88. See, for example, Richard E. Lewis, "The Newspaper and the Computer—Where We Are, Where We're Going," *Editor & Publisher*, September 18, 1963, 14, 62–65; Richard L. Tobin, "Newspapers of Tomorrow: The Man with the Pencil of Light," *Saturday Review*, August 29, 1964, 138–139, 194; Charles L. Bennett,

"Automation and the Journalist," *Quill*, November 1965, 18–24; and Edmund C. Arnold, "We've Never Done It This Way Before," *Quill*, 26–29.

56. *ASNE Proceedings*, 1963, 140–150; *APME Red Book*, 1964, 37–43.

57. Jerome H. Walker, "Over 200 Head to Florida to See Computers at Work," *Editor & Publisher*, February 15, 1964, 13, 65; Martin Andersen quoted in "Versatile Computer Service Displayed," *Editor & Publisher*, March 14, 1964, 64–65.

58. "Knight Warns: Production Processes Must Be Changed," *Editor & Publisher*, June 26, 1965, 12, 74.

59. Quoted in "Signs of the Future?" *Newsweek*, November 9, 1964, 88.

60. Quoted in "ITU's Brown and Publishers Differ on Helping Industry," *Editor & Publisher*, April 24, 1965, 114.

61. ANPA Labor Relations Committee report reprinted in "Automation 'Pain' Often Overstated," *Editor & Publisher*, April 24, 1965, 23.

62. Quoted in Theodore C. Turpin, "Smaller Newspapers Shifting to Offset Press for Printing to Help Cut Production Cost," *Wall Street Journal*, August 15, 1963, 12.

63. *World Newsprint Supply-Demand: Outlook Through 1969*, 19–20; James Neil Woodruff, "An Economic Analysis of Letterpress and Offset Printing Techniques in Daily Newspapers in the Mid-South," Ph.D. dissertation, University of Mississippi, 1971, 211. By 1975, more than 90 percent of all ANPA member newspapers used photocomposition; more than half printed by offset. (William H. Jones and Laird Anderson, "Newspapers Moving into a New Era," *Washington Post*, August 4, 1977, D1, D2.)

64. Turpin, "Smaller Newspapers Shifting to Offset Press," 12; "167 Dailies With 1,327,881 Circulation Move to Offset," *Editor & Publisher*, February 6, 1965, 9; "60,000-Daily Plans Conversion to Offset," *Editor & Publisher*, April 4, 1964, 14.

65. Turpin, "Smaller Newspapers Shifting to Offset Press," 12.

66. William J. Waters, "How the *Ithaca Journal* Converted to Offset," *Gannetteer*, January 1965, 4–6.

67. See Chapter 4 for an exploration of publishers' reaction to television in the 1950s.

68. Russell Baker, "Exchange is Calm," *New York Times*, September 27, 1960, 1; Claude Sitton, "Senator's 'Control' of TV Debate Is Cited," *New York Times*, September 28, 1960; Baker quoted in David Halberstam, *The Fifties* (New York: Villard Books, 1993) 732.

69. "Covering the Tragedy," *Time*, November 29, 1963, 84.

70. "A World Listened and Watched," *Broadcasting*, December 2, 1963, 36.

71. Newton N. Minow letter to *Time* magazine, *Time*, December 6, 1963, 17; Val Adams, "New FCC Chief Brands TV a Vast Wasteland," *Atlanta Constitution*, May 10, 1961, 28.

72. Gallagher and Winship quoted in "Editors Comment on the News Coverage of the Assassination," *ASNE Bulletin*, January 1, 1964, 3–5.

73. "CBS and NBC: Walter vs. Chet and Dave," *Newsweek*, September 23, 1963, 62–65; "TV News Gets into the Money," *Business Week*, June 9, 1962, 50–54.

74. Murray Seeger, "Local TV Tries More News," *Nieman Reports*, June 1964, 13–15.

75. *ASNE Proceedings*, 1962, 81, 90, 130.

76. "Television News," *Editor & Publisher*, February 1, 1964, 6; "Dr. Bogart Replies to TV News Claim," *Editor & Publisher*, 13.

77. Kilgore, "Journalism—The New Look," 7.

78. Transcript of "Open End" television program.

79. Quoted in Gelman, "Newspapers," 96.

REFLECTIONS ON THE POSTWAR PRESS

1. "1947 v. 1962: Two Days in the Press," *Columbia Journalism Review*, Summer 1962, 18–28.
2. Transcript of "The Press and the People," reprinted in *Washington and the Press* (New York: Fund for the Republic, 1959) 12–13.
3. Tom Leathers, "The Newspaper's Biggest Story," *Grassroots Editor*, July 1966, 29–30.

BIBLIOGRAPHIC ESSAY

1. Ben H. Bagdikian, *The Information Machines: Their Impact on Men and the Media* (New York: Harper and Row, 1971).
2. Ben H. Bagdikian, *The Media Monopoly* (Boston, MA: Beacon Press, 1983).
3. Bryce Rucker, *The First Freedom* (Carbondale, IL: Southern Illinois University Press, 1968).
4. Carl E. Lindstrom, *The Fading American Newspaper* (1960; reprint edn, Gloucester, MA: P. Smith, 1964).
5. Benjamin M. Compaine, Christopher H. Sterling, Thomas Gruback, and J. Kendrick Noble, Jr., *Who Owns the Media? Concentration of Ownership in the Mass Communications Industry*, 2nd edn (White Plains, NY: Knowledge Industry Publications, 1982).
6. Raymond B. Nixon, "Trends in Daily Newspaper Ownership Since 1945," *Journalism Quarterly* 31 (1954): 3–14; Raymond B. Nixon and Jean Ward, "Trends in Newspaper Ownership and Inter-Media Competition," *Journalism Quarterly* 38 (1961): 3–14. See also Raymond B. Nixon, "Concentration and Absenteeism in Daily Newspaper Ownership," *Journalism Quarterly* 22 (1945): 97–114, and Raymond B. Nixon, "Implications of the Decreasing Numbers of Competitive Papers," in *Communications in Modern Society*, ed. Wilbur Schramm (Champagne, IL: University of Illinois Press, 1948).
7. Nixon, "Trends in Newspaper Ownership," 3–14.
8. Jon G. Udell, *Economic Trends in the Daily Newspaper Business, 1946 to 1970* (Madison, WI: American Newspaper Publishers Association, 1970b); Jon G. Udell, *Economics of the American Newspaper* (New York: Hastings House Communication Arts Books, 1978).
9. Maxwell McCombs, "Mass Media in the Marketplace," *Journalism Monographs* 24: 55–56. A quantitative analysis of intermedia competition and its effect on newspapers is David Pearce Demers, "Structural Pluralism, Intermedia Competition, and the Growth of the Corporate Newspaper in the United States," *Journalism Monographs* 145: 1–43.
10. James Aronson, *The Press and the Cold War* (Indianapolis, IN: Bobbs-Merrill, 1970).
11. Louis Liebovich, *The Press and the Origins of the Cold War, 1944–1947* (Westport, CT: Praeger, 1988).
12. Margaret A. Blanchard, *Exporting the First Amendment: The Press-Government Crusade of 1945–1952* (New York: Longman, 1986).
13. Edwin R. Bayley, *Joe McCarthy and the Press* (Madison, WI: University of Wisconsin Press, 1981).
14. Lawrence N. Strout, *Covering McCarthyism: How the Christian Science Monitor Handled Joseph R. McCarthy, 1950–1954* (Westport, CT: Greenwood Press, 1999).
15. John F. Neville, *The Press, the Rosenbergs, and the Cold War* (New York: Praeger, 1995); Joanne P. Sharp, *Condensing the Cold War: Reader's Digest and American Identity* (Minneapolis, MN: University of Minnesota Press, 2000);

Craig Allen, *Eisenhower and the Mass Media: Peace, Prosperity, & Prime-Time TV* (Chapel Hill, NC: University of North Carolina Press, 1993); Edwin M. Yoder, Jr., *Joe Alsop's Cold War: A Study in Journalistic Influence and Intrigue* (Chapel Hill, NC: University of North Carolina Press, 1995).

16. Clarence R. Wyatt, *Paper Soldiers: The American Press and the Vietnam War* (Chicago, IL: University of Chicago Press, 1995); Daniel C. Hallin, *The "Uncensored War": The Media and Vietnam* (New York: Oxford University Press, 1986); William M. Hammond, *Reporting Vietnam: Media and Military at War* (Lawrence, KS: University Press of Kansas, 1998).

17. John T. Kneebone, *Southern Liberal Journalists and the Issue of Race* (Chapel Hill, NC: University of North Carolina Press, 1985).

18. Richard Lentz, *Symbols, the News Magazines, and Martin Luther King* (Baton Rouge, LA: Louisiana State University Press, 1990).

19. Jon Meacham, *Voices in Our Blood: America's Best on the Civil Rights Movement* (New York: Random House, 2001).

20. Hugh Davis Graham, *Crisis in Print: Desegregation and the Press in Tennessee* (Nashville, TN: Vanderbilt University Press, 1967).

21. Ann Waldron, *Hodding Carter: The Reconstruction of a Racist* (Chapel Hill, NC: Algonquin Books, 1993); Gary Huey, *Rebel with a Cause: P.D. East, Southern Liberalism and the Civil Rights Movement, 1953–1971* (Wilmington, DE: Scholarly Resources Inc., 1985); Alexander Leidholdt, *Standing Before the Shouting Mob: Lenoir Chambers and Virginia's Massive Resistance to Public-School Integration* (Tuscaloosa, AL: University of Alabama Press, 1997); David R. Davies, ed., *The Press and Race: Mississippi Journalists Confront the Movement* (Jackson, MS: University Press of Mississippi, 2001); Barbara Barksdale Clowse, *Ralph McGill: A Biography* (Macon, GA : Mercer University Press, 1998); Leonard Ray Teel, *Ralph Emerson McGill: Voice of the Southern Conscience* (Knoxville, TN: University of Tennessee Press, 2001).

22. Crusading Southern journalists, in particular, have published their autobiographies or have been the subject of book-length works. See J. Oliver Emmerich, *Two Faces of Janus: The Saga of Deep South Change* (Jackson, MS: University and College Press of Mississippi, 1973); Ira B. Harkey, Jr., *The Smell of Burning Crosses: An Autobiography of a Mississippi Newspaperman* (Jacksonville, IL: Harris-Wolfe, 1967); Gary Huey, *Rebel with a Cause*; and P.D. East, *The Magnolia Jungle: The Life, Times and Education of a Southern Editor* (New York: Simon and Schuster, 1960).

23. Richard Kluger, *The Paper: The Life and Death of the New York Herald Tribune* (New York: Knopf, 1986); Gay Talese, *The Kingdom and the Power* (New York: World, 1969); *David Halberstam, The Powers That Be* (New York: Knopf, 1979).

24. John W.C. Johnstone, Edward J. Slawski, and William W. Bowman, *The News People: A Sociological Portrait of American Journalists and Their Work* (Urbana, IL: University of Illinois Press, 1976); David H. Weaver and G. Cleveland Wilhoit, *The American Journalist: A Portrait of U.S. News People and Their Work* (Bloomington, IN: Indiana University Press, 1986). The similarity between the titles of the two books is intentional, as the latter study updates the former.

25. William R. Lindley, *Journalism and Higher Education: The Search for Academic Purpose* (Stillwater, OK: Journalistic Services, 1975); Paul Alfred Pratte, *Gods Within the Machine: A History of the American Society of Newspaper Editors, 1923–1993* (Westport, CT: Praeger Publishers, 1995).

26. A brief but useful account of the history of journalism education is included in Wm. David Sloan, *Makers of the Media Mind: Journalism Educators and their Ideas* (Hillsdale, NJ: Lawrence Erlbaum, 1990) 1–22.

References

UNPUBLISHED PAPERS AND DOCUMENTS

American Newspaper Publishers Associations files, Resource Center, Newspaper Association of America, Reston, VA.

American Society of Newspaper Editors files, American Society of Newspaper Editors headquarters, Reston, VA.

Turner Catledge Papers, Mitchell Memorial Library, Mississippi State University, Starkville, MS.

Millard Cope Papers, Texas Tech University, Lubbock, TX.

Robert H. Fleming Papers, State Historical Society of Wisconsin, Madison, WI.

Freedom of Information Center collection, University of Missouri at Columbia, Columbia, MO.

Eugene Meyer Papers, Library of Congress, Washington, DC.

Mississippi Oral History Program, University of Southern Mississippi, Hattiesburg, MS (Interviews with Norman Bradley, Robert W. Brown, J. Oliver Emmerich, Eleanor Jordan, O.G. McDavid, and Carl Walters).

Joseph Pulitzer II Papers, Library of Congress, Washington, DC.

Richard L. Strout Papers, in possession of Alan Strout, Weston, MA.

PUBLISHED PAPERS, DIARIES, AND DOCUMENTS

Agee, Warren K., (ed.) *The Press and the Public Interest: The William Allen White Lectures.* Washington, DC: Public Affairs Press, 1968.

American Society of Newspaper Editors. *Problems of Journalism: Proceedings of the ... Convention, American Society of Newspaper Editors.* Washington, DC: The Society, 1945–1965.

Associated Press Managing Editors Association. *Associated Press Managing Editors Red Book*. New York: Associated Press, 1947–1965.

Britt, George. (ed.) *Shoeleather and Printer's Ink*. New York: Quadrangle, 1974.

Brown v Board of Education of Topeka, 347 U.S. 483 (1954); 349 U.S. 294 (1955).

Citizen Publishing Company v United States, 394 U.S. 131 (1969).

Congressional Record, 1945–1965.

Newspapers 1963: A Presentation by the American Newspaper Publishers Association Before the Antitrust Subcommittee of the House Judiciary Committee. New York: American Newspaper Publishers Association, 1963.

Pitts, Alice Fox. *Read All About It! 50 Years of ASNE*. Reston, VA: American Society of Newspaper Editors, 1974.

Public Papers of the Presidents for Presidents Harry S Truman, Dwight D. Eisenhower, John F. Kennedy, and Lyndon B. Johnson. Washington, DC: United States Government Printing Office, 1945–1965.

U.S. Congress. House. *Final Report on Newsprint and Paper Supply*. Select Committee on Newsprint and Paper Supply. House Report 2471. Eightieth Congress, Second Session. Washington, DC: United States Government Printing Office, 1948.

——*Availability of Information From Federal Departments and Agencies*. Hearings Before a Subcommittee of the Committee of Government Operations. Eighty-fourth Congress, First Session. Washington, DC: United States Government Printing Office, 1956.

—— *Government Information Plans and Policies*. Hearings Before a Subcommittee of the Committee of Government Operations. Eighty-eighth Congress, First Session. Washington, DC: United States Government Printing Office, 1963.

——*World Newsprint Supply-Demand: Outlook Through 1968*. Report of the Committee on Interstate and Foreign Commerce. House Report 2196. Eighty-ninth Congress, Second Session. Washington, DC: United States Government Printing Office, 1966.

——*World Newsprint Supply-Demand: Outlook Through 1969*. Report of the Committee on Interstate and Foreign Commerce. House Report 970. Ninetieth Congress, First Session. Washington, DC: United States Government Printing Office, 1967.

—— *Newspaper Preservation Act: Hearings Before Antitrust Subcommittee*. Ninety-first Congress, First Session. Washington, DC: United States Government Printing Office, 1969.

U.S. Congress. Senate. *Newsprint Supply and Distribution*. Special Committee to Study Problems of American Small Business. Eightieth Congress, First Session. Washington, DC: United States Government Printing Office, 1947a.

——*Problems of American Small Business: Hearings Before the Special Committee to Study Problems of American Small Business*. 2 vols. Washington, DC: United States Government Printing Office, 1947b.

——*Survival of a Free Competitive Press: The Small Newspaper, Democracy's Grass Roots*. Special Committee to Study Problems of American Small Business. Senate Committee Print 17. Eightieth Congress, First Session. Washington, DC: United States Government Printing Office, 1947c.

——*State Department Information Program—Information Centers*. Hearings Before the Permanent Subcommittee on Investigations of the Committee on Government Operations. Eighty-third Congress, First Session. Washington, DC: United States Government Printing Office, 1953.

U.S. Department of Commerce. *Historical Statistics of the United States, Colonial Times to 1970.* 2 vols. Washington, DC: United States Government Printing Office, 1975.

CONTEMPORARY NEWSPAPERS, PAMPHLETS, AND OTHER PUBLICATIONS (FOR 1945–1965)

Newspapers

Atlanta Constitution, Chicago Defender, Chicago Tribune, Christian Science Monitor, Columbia Missourian, Greenville (MS) *Delta Democrat Times, Jackson* (MS) *Clarion-Ledger, New Orleans Times-Picayune, New York Herald-Tribune, New York Post, New York Times, New York Times Book Review, Wall Street Journal, Washington Post.*

Magazines

Atlantic Monthly, Aviation Week and Space Technology, Barron's, Business Week, Forbes, Fortune, Harper's Magazine, Life, Nation, New Republic, Newsweek, New Yorker, Reference Shelf, Reporter, Saturday Evening Post, Saturday Review of Literature, Southern School News, Television Magazine, Time, United Nations World, U.S. News & World Report, Vital Speeches.

Trade journals

American Editor, American Press, ANPA Bulletin, ASNE Bulletin, Broadcasting Telecasting, Broadcasting Yearbook, Circulation Management, Columbia Journalism Review, Editor & Publisher, Editor & Publisher International Year Book, Grassroots Editor, Iowa Publisher, Journalism Quarterly, Media Records, Missouri Press News, National Publisher, Nieman Reports, Publication Management, Publisher's Auxiliary, Quill, Radio-TV Daily.

Selected secondary sources

Advertising Today Yesterday Tomorrow: An Omnibus of Advertising Prepared by Printer's Ink in Its 75th Year of Publication. New York: McGraw Hill, 1963.

Allen, Craig. *Eisenhower and the Mass Media: Peace, Prosperity, & Prime-Time TV.* Chapel Hill, NC: University of North Carolina Press, 1993.

Anderson, Jack, and Ronald W. May. *McCarthy: The Man, the Senator, the "Ism".* Boston, MA: Beacon Press, 1952.

Angelo, Frank. *On Guard: A History of the Detroit Free Press.* Detroit, MI: Detroit Free Press, 1981.

Aronson, James. *The Press and the Cold War.* Indianapolis, IN: Bobbs-Merrill, 1970.

Ashmore, Harry. *Civil Rights and Wrongs: A Memoir of Race and Politics.* New York: Pantheon Books, 1994.

Bagdikian, Ben H. *The Information Machines: Their Impact on Men and the Media.* New York: Harper and Row, 1971.

Bagdikian, Ben H. *The Media Monopoly*. Boston, MA: Beacon Press, 1983.

Barnouw, Erik. *A History of Broadcasting in the United States*. Vol. 3, *The Image Empire*. New York: Oxford University Press, 1970.

Barth, Alan. *The Loyalty of Free Men*. New York: Viking Press, 1952.

———. *Government by Investigation*. New York: Viking Press, 1955.

Bayley, Edwin R. *Joe McCarthy and the Press*. Madison, WI: University of Wisconsin Press, 1981.

Berger, Meyer. *The Story of the New York Times, 1851–1951*. New York: Simon and Schuster, 1951.

Blanchard, Margaret A. "The Hutchins Commission, The Press and the Responsibility Concept." *Journalism Monographs* 49 (May 1977): 1–59.

———. *Exporting the First Amendment: The Press-Government Crusade of 1947–1952*. New York: Longman, 1986.

———. "The Business of a Free Press." *Gannett Center Journal* 4 (Fall 1990): 17–29.

Bogart, Leo. *The Age of Television*. New York: Frederick Ungar, 1958.

Boyer, Peter J. *Who Killed CBS?* New York: Random House, 1988.

Bradlee, Ben. *A Good Life: Newspapering and Other Adventures*. New York: Simon and Schuster, 1995.

Bray, Howard. *The Pillars of the Post: The Making of a News Empire in Washington*. New York: Norton, 1980.

Brown, Lee. *The Reluctant Reformation: On Criticizing the Press in America*. New York: David McKay Co., 1947.

Brown, Pamela A. "George Seldes and the Winter Soldier Brigade: The Press Criticism of *In Fact*, 1940–1950." *American Journalism* 6 (1989): 85–102.

Brucker, Herbert. *Freedom of Information*. 1949. Reprint, Westport, CT: Greenwood Press, 1981.

Buckley, James Homer. "Suburban Evangel: Trade Associations and the Emergence of the Suburban Newspaper Industry, 1945–1970." Ph.D. dissertation, University of Washington, Seattle, 1986.

Carter, Don E., and Malcolm F. Mallette. *Seminar: The Story of the American Press Institute*. Reston, VA: American Press Institute, 1992.

Carter, Hodding. *Their Words Were Bullets: The Southern Press in War, Reconstruction, and Peace*. Athens, GA: University of Georgia Press, 1969.

Catledge, Turner. *My Life and the Times*. New York: Harper & Row, 1971.

Celler, Emanuel. "The Concentration of Ownership and the Decline of Competition in the News Media." *Antitrust Bulletin* 8 (March–April 1963): 175–185.

Chappell, Warren. *A Short History of the Printed Word*. New York: Knopf, 1970.

Chiasson, Lloyd, Jr. (ed.) *The Press in Times of Crisis*. Westport, CT: Praeger, 1995.

Clowse, Barbara Barksdale. *Ralph McGill: A Biography*. Macon, GA: Mercer University Press, 1998.

Commission on Freedom of the Press. *A Free and Responsible Press: A General Report on Mass Communication, Newspapers, Radio, Motion Pictures, Magazines, and Books*. Chicago, IL: University of Chicago Press, 1947.

Compaine, Benjamin M. *Papers and Profits: A Special Report on the Newspaper Business*. New York: Knowledge Industry Publications, 1973.

Compaine, Benjamin M. "The Daily Newspaper Industry in the United States (1977): An Analysis of Trends in Production, Technology, Competition and Ownership, Economic Structure, Circulation, Advertising, Newsprint, and Labor." Ph.D. dissertation, Temple University, Philadelphia, 1977.

Compaine, Benjamin M., Christopher H. Sterling, Thomas Gruback, and J. Kendrick Noble, Jr. *Who Owns the Media? Concentration of Ownership in the Mass Communications Industry.* 2nd edn White Plains, NY: Knowledge Industry Publications, 1982.

"Computers Will Be a Major Factor in Tomorrow's Typesetting." *Inland Printer/ American Lithographer* 151 (1963): 66–67.

Conrad, Will C., Kathleen F. Wilson, and Dale Wilson. *The Milwaukee Journal: The First Eighty Years.* Madison, WI: University of Wisconsin Press, 1964.

Crosby, John. *Out of the Blue: A Book about Radio and Television.* New York: Simon and Schuster, 1952.

Cross, Harold L. *The People's Right to Know.* New York: Columbia University Press, 1953.

Curtis, J. Montgomery. *API: A Personal Remembrance.* Reston, VA: American Press Institute, 1980.

Daily Newspapers in 1966—Highlights of a Record Year. New York: American Newspaper Publishers Association, 1967.

Daniels, Jonathan. "Freedom of Public Expression." *Yale Review* 35 (1946): 726–727.

Davies, David R. (ed.) *The Press and Race: Mississippi Journalists Confront the Movement.* Jackson, MS: University Press of Mississippi, 2001.

Deaver, Jean Franklin. "A Study of Senator Joseph R. McCarthy and 'McCarthyism' as Influences upon the News Media and the Evolution of Reportorial Method." Ph.D. dissertation, University of Texas, Austin, 1969.

Demers, David Pearce. "Structural Pluralism, Intermedia Competition, and the Growth of the Corporate Newspaper in the United States." *Journalism Monographs* 145 (June 1994): 1–43.

Donner, Frank J. *The Un-Americans.* New York: Ballantine Books, 1961.

Drewry, John E. *Advancing Journalism.* Athens, GA: University of Georgia Press, 1953.

East, P.D. *The Magnolia Jungle: The Life, Times and Education of a Southern Editor.* New York: Simon and Schuster, 1960.

Ellis, L. Ethan. *Newsprint: Producers, Publishers, Political Pressures.* New Brunswick, NJ: Rutgers University Press, 1960.

Emery, Edwin. *History of the American Newspaper Publishers Association.* Minneapolis, MN: University of Minnesota Press, 1950.

———. *ANPA—75th Anniversary, 1887–1962.* New York: American Newspaper Publishers Association, 1962.

Emery, Edwin, and Joseph P. McKerns, "AEJMC: 75 Years in the Making," *Journalism Monographs* 104 (November 1987): 1–91.

Emmerich, J. Oliver. *Two Faces of Janus: The Saga of Deep South Change.* Jackson, MS: University and College Press of Mississippi, 1973.

Ernst, Morris L. *The First Freedom.* New York: Macmillan, 1946.

The First 50 Years of Broadcasting: The Running Story of the Fifth Estate. By the editors of *Broadcasting* magazine. Washington, DC: Broadcasting Publications, 1982.

Flesch, Rudolph. *The Art of Readable Writing*. New York: Harper and Brothers, 1949.

Fowler, Will. *Reporters: Memoirs of a Young Newspaperman*. Malibu, CA: Roundtable Publishing, 1991.

Friedman, Clara H. *Newsprint: Summary of a Report on Newsprint Supply and Distribution*. New York: American Newspaper Guild, 1948.

Goldstein, Tom. (ed.) *Killing the Messenger*. New York: Columbia University Press, 1989.

Goodman, Jack. *While You Were Gone: A Report on Wartime Life in the United States*. New York: Simon and Schuster, 1946.

Graham, Hugh Davis. *Crisis in Print: Desegregation and the Press in Tennessee*. Nashville, TN: Vanderbilt University Press, 1967.

Grimes, Millard B. *The Last Linotype: The Story of Georgia and Its Newspapers Since World War II*. Macon, GA: Mercer University Press and the Georgia Press Association, 1985.

Gunning, Robert. *The Technique of Clear Writing*. New York: McGraw-Hill, 1952.

Halberstam, David. *The Powers That Be*. New York: Knopf, 1979.

———. *The Fifties*. New York: Villard Books, 1993.

Hallin, Daniel C. *The "Uncensored War": The Media and Vietnam*. New York: Oxford University Press, 1986.

Hammond, William M. *Reporting Vietnam: Media and Military at War*. Lawrence, KS: University Press of Kansas, 1998.

Harkey, Ira B., Jr. *The Smell of Burning Crosses: An Autobiography of a Mississippi Newspaperman*. Jacksonville, IL: Harris-Wolfe, 1967.

Harrison, John M. *The Blade of Toledo*. Toledo, OH: Toledo Blade Co., 1985.

Head, Sydney W. *Broadcasting in America*. 2nd edn, Boston, MA: Houghton Mifflin, 1972.

Hilsman, Roger. *The Politics of Policy Making in Defense and Foreign Affairs*. New York: Harper and Row, 1971.

Hornby, William H. *Voice of Empire: A Centennial Sketch of the Denver Post*. Denver, CO: Colorado Historical Society, 1992.

Huey, Gary. *Rebel with a Cause: P.D. East, Southern Liberalism and the Civil Rights Movement*. Wilmington, DE: Scholarly Resources, 1985.

Hughes, Frank. *Prejudice and the Press*. New York: Devin-Adair Co., 1950.

Jackson, Hartley E. *Printing: A Practical Introduction to the Graphic Arts*. New York: McGraw-Hill, 1957.

Johnson, Walter C., and Arthur T. Robb. *The South and Its Newspapers, 1903–1953*. 1954. Reprint, Westport, CT: Greenwood Press, 1974.

Johnstone, John W.C., Edward J. Slawski, and William W. Bowman, *The News People: A Sociological Portrait of American Journalists and Their Work*. Urbana, IL: University of Illinois Press, 1976.

Karch, Randolph R., and Edward J. Buber. *Graphic Arts Procedures: The Offset Processes*. Chicago, IL: American Technical Society, 1967.

Karnick, Kristine Brunovska. "NBC and the Innovation of Television News, 1945–1953." *Journalism History* 26 (Spring 1988): 26–34.

Kelber, Harry, and Carl Schlesinger. *Union Printers and Controlled Automation.* New York: The Free Press, 1967.

Kennedy, George. "Advocates of Openness: The Freedom of Information Movement." Ph.D. dissertation, University of Missouri, 1978.

Kern, Montague, Patricia W. Levering, and Ralph B. Levering. *The Kennedy Crises: The Press, the Presidency, and Foreign Policy.* Chapel Hill, NC: University of North Carolina Press, 1983.

Kluger, Richard. *The Paper: The Life and Death of the New York Herald Tribune.* New York: Knopf, 1986.

Kneebone, John T. *Southern Liberal Journalists and the Issue of Race.* Chapel Hill, NC: University of North Carolina Press, 1985.

Knight-Ridder Factbook. Miami, FL: Knight-Ridder Newspapers, 1974.

Koop, Theodore F. *Weapon of Silence.* Chicago, IL: University of Chicago Press, 1946.

Lamb, Elizabeth. *The Inland.* Chicago, IL: Inland Daily Press Association, 1950.

Lawrence, Bill. *Six Presidents, Too Many Wars.* New York: Saturday Review Press, 1972.

Leidholdt, Alexander. *Standing before the Shouting Mob: Lenoir Chambers and Virginia's Massive Resistance to Public-School Integration.* Tuscaloosa, AL: University of Alabama Press, 1997.

Lentz, Richard. *Symbols, the News Magazines, and Martin Luther King.* Baton Rouge, LA: Louisiana State University Press, 1990.

Lichty, Lawrence W., and Malachi C. Topping. (eds.) *American Broadcasting: A Source Book on the History of Radio and Television.* New York: Hastings House, 1975.

Liebling, A.J. *The Press.* New York: Ballantine, 1961.

———. *Mink and Red Herring.* 1949. Reprint, Westport, CT: Greenwood Press, 1972a.

———. *The Wayward Pressman.* 1947. Reprint, Westport, CT: Greenwood Press, 1972b.

Liebovich, Louis William. "The Press and the Origins of the Cold War, 1944–1947." Ph.D. dissertation, University of Wisconsin, Madison, 1986.

Lindley, William R. *Journalism and Higher Education: The Search for Academic Purpose.* Stillwater, OK: Journalistic Services, 1975.

Lindstrom, Carl E. *The Fading American Newspaper.* 1960. Reprint, Gloucester, MA: P. Smith, 1964.

Lyons, Louis M. (ed.) *Reporting the News: Selections from Nieman Reports.* Cambridge, MA: Belknap Press, 1965.

———. *Newspaper Story: One Hundred Years of the Boston Globe.* Cambridge, MA: Belknap Press, 1971.

McCarthy, Joseph R. *McCarthyism, the Fight for America; Documented Answers to Questions Asked by Friend and Foe.* New York: Devin-Adair, 1952.

McClendon, Sarah. *My Eight Presidents.* New York: Wyden Books, 1978.

McCombs, Maxwell. "Mass Media in the Marketplace." *Journalism Monographs* 24 (August 1972): 1–104.

Meacham, Jon. *Voices in Our Blood: America's Best on the Civil Rights Movement.* New York: Random House, 2001.

Midura, Edmund M. "A.J. Liebling: The Wayward Pressman as Critic," *Journalism Monographs* 33 (April 1974): 1–46.

Mott, Frank Luther. *Time Enough: Essays in Autobiography.* Chapel Hill, NC: University of North Carolina Press, 1962.

Muse, Benjamin. *Virginia's Massive Resistance.* Bloomington: Indiana University Press, 1961.

Neville, John F. *The Press, the Rosenbergs, and the Cold War.* Westport, CT: Praeger, 1995.

Oshinsky, David M. *A Conspiracy So Immense: The World of Joe McCarthy.* New York: The Free Press, 1983.

Patterson, Grove. *I Like People: The Autobiography of Grove Patterson.* New York: Random House, 1954.

Pierce, Robert N. *A Sacred Trust: Nelson Poynter and the St. Petersburg Times.* Gainesville, FL: University Press of Florida, 1993.

Pollard, James E. *The Presidents and the Press: Truman to Johnson.* Washington, DC: Public Affairs Press, 1964.

Pratte, Paul Alfred. *Gods within the Machine: A History of the American Society of Newspaper Editors, 1923–1993.* Westport, CT: Praeger Publishers, 1995.

Printing Progress: A Mid-Century Report. Cincinnati, OH: International Association of Printing House Craftsmen, Inc., 1959.

Rafferty, Keen. "Editor and Publisher." *New Mexico Quarterly Review* 15 (Autumn 1945): 344.

Reasoner, Harry. *Before the Colors Fade.* New York: Knopf, 1981.

Reeves, Thomas. *The Life and Times of Joe McCarthy.* New York: Stein and Day, 1982.

Reston, James. *Deadline: A Memoir.* New York: Random House, 1991.

Rivers, William L. *The Opinionmakers.* Boston: Beacon Press, 1965.

Robertson, Nan. *The Girls in the Balcony: Women, Men, and the New York Times.* New York: Random House, 1992.

Rovere, Richard H. *Senator Joe McCarthy.* New York: Harcourt, Brace, Jovanovich, 1959.

Rucker, Bryce. *The First Freedom.* Carbondale, IL: Southern Illinois University Press, 1968.

Salinger, Pierre. *With Kennedy.* New York: Doubleday, 1966.

Salisbury, Harrison E. *A Time of Change: A Reporter's Tale of Our Time.* New York: Harper & Row, 1988.

Sarratt, Reed. *The Ordeal of Desegregation: The First Decade.* New York: Harper & Row, 1966.

Schlesinger, Arthur M., Jr. *A Thousand Days: John F. Kennedy in the White House.* Boston, MA: Houghton Mifflin, 1965.

Schramm, Wilbur. (ed.) *Communications in Modern Society.* Champagne, IL: University of Illinois Press, 1948.

———. *Mass Communications.* Urbana, IL: University of Illinois Press, 1960.

Schroth, Raymond A. *The Eagle and Brooklyn: A Community Newspaper, 1841–1955.* Westport, CT: Greenwood Press, 1974.

Secrest, Andrew McDowd. "In Black and White: Press Opinion and Race Relations in South Carolina, 1945–1964." Ph.D. dissertation, Duke University, Durham, NC, 1971.

Seldes, George. *Witness to a Century; Encounters with the Noted, the Notorious, and the Three SOBs.* New York: Ballantine, 1987.

Sharp, Joanne P. *Condensing the Cold War: Reader's Digest and American Identity.* Minneapolis, MN: University of Minnesota Press, 2000.

Shoemaker, Don. (ed.) *With All Deliberate Speed.* New York: Harper, 1957.

Smith, Anthony. *Goodbye Gutenburg: The Newspaper Revolution in the 1980s.* New York: Oxford University Press, 1980.

Southern Regional Council. *Race in the News: Usage in Southern Newspapers.* Atlanta, GA: Southern Regional Council, 1949.

South Speaks Out for Law and Order: A Roundup of Southern Press Opinion, National Council of the Churches of Christ in the United States of America et al., 1958.

Spackman, Peter, and Lee Ambrose. *The Columbia University Forum Anthology.* New York: Atheneum, 1968.

Spearman, Walter, and Sylvan Meyer. *Racial Crisis and the Press.* Atlanta, GA: Southern Regional Council, 1960.

Stein, M.L. *When Presidents Meet the Press.* New York: Julian Messner, 1969.

Stern, J. David. *Memoirs of a Maverick Publisher.* New York: Simon and Schuster, 1962.

Strout, Lawrence N. *Covering McCarthyism: How the Christian Science Monitor Handled Joseph R. McCarthy, 1950–1954.* Westport, CT: Greenwood Press, 1999.

Svirsky, Leon. (ed.) *Your Newspaper: Blueprint for a Better Press.* New York: Macmillan, 1947.

Talese, Gay. *The Kingdom and the Power.* New York: World, 1969.

Teel, Leonard Ray. *Ralph Emerson McGill: Voice of the Southern Conscience.* Knoxville, TN: University of Tennessee Press, 2001.

Thomas, Helen. *Dateline: White House.* New York: Macmillan, 1975.

Tripp, Frank. *On the Newspaper Front with Frank Tripp.* Rochester, NY: Gannett Newspapers, 1954.

Trohan, Walter. *Political Animals: Memoirs of a Sentimental Cynic.* Garden City, NY: Doubleday & Co., 1975.

Turpin, William Howard. "Editorial Leadership in a Time of Crisis: Virginia's Massive Resistance, 1954–1959." Ph.D. dissertation, University of North Carolina, Chapel Hill, 1976.

Udell, Jon G. "The Growth of the American Daily Newspaper: An Economic Analysis." *Wisconsin Project Reports* 3 (1965): 1–17.

———. *Economic Trends in the Daily Newspaper Business, 1946 to 1970.* Madison, WI: American Newspaper Publishers Association, 1970a.

———. "Economic Trends in the Daily Newspaper Business, 1946 to 1970." *Wisconsin Project Reports* 4:6 (December 1970b): 119.

———. *Economics of the American Newspaper.* New York: Hastings House Communication Arts Books, 1978.

Waldron, Ann. *Hodding Carter: The Reconstruction of a Racist*. Chapel Hill, NC: University of North Carolina Press, 1993.

Walton, Laura R. "Segregationist Spin: The Use of Propaganda by the Mississippi State Sovereignty Commission and the White Citizens' Council, 1954–1973." Ph.D. dissertation, University of Southern Mississippi, Hattiesburg, 2005.

Washington and the Press. New York: Fund for the Republic, 1959.

Weaver, David H., and G. Cleveland Wilhoit. *The American Journalist: A Portrait of U.S. News People and Their Work*. Bloomington, IN: Indiana University Press, 1986.

Wechsler, James A. *The Age of Suspicion*. New York: Random House, 1953.

Wells, Robert W. *The Milwaukee Journal: An Informal Chronicle of Its First 100 Years*. Milwaukee, WI: Milwaukee Journal, 1981.

Werthimer, Jerrold Lee. "The Community Press of Suburbia: A Case Study of Paddock Newspapers." Ph.D. dissertation, Northwestern University, Evanston, IL, 1960.

White, Walter. *How Far the Promised Land*. New York: Viking, 1955.

Whitfield, Stephen J. *A Death in the Delta: The Story of Emmett Till*. New York: Free Press, 1989.

Williams, Harold A. *The Baltimore Sun: 1837–1987*. Baltimore, MD: Johns Hopkins University Press, 1987.

Williams, Herbert Lee. *The Newspaperman's President: Harry S. Truman*. Chicago, IL: Nelson Hall, 1984.

Wimmer, Roy R. "Aspects of Computer Automation in the Newspaper Industry." M.A. thesis, University of North Carolina at Chapel Hill, 1967.

Wolseley, Roland E. *Still in Print: Journey of a Writer, Teacher, Journalist*. Elgin, IL: David C. Cook Foundation, 1985.

Woodruff, James Neil. "An Economic Analysis of Letterpress and Offset Printing Techniques in Daily Newspapers in the Mid-South." Ph.D. Dissertation, University of Mississippi, Oxford, 1971.

Woods, Allan. *Modern Newspaper Production*. New York: Harper & Row, 1963.

Wyatt, Clarence R. *Paper Soldiers: The American Press and the Vietnam War*. Chicago, IL: University of Chicago Press, 1995.

Yoder, Edwin M., Jr. *Joe Alsop's Cold War: A Study in Journalistic Influence and Intrigue*. Chapel Hill, NC: University of North Carolina Press, 1995.

Index

About the Author

DAVID R. DAVIES is Associate Professor of Journalism and Associate Director at the School of Mass Communication and Journalism at the University of Southern Mississippi. A former reporter for the *Arkansas Gazette* in Little Rock, he has written extensively about the newspaper industry and its coverage of the civil rights movement.